How America Eats

How America Eats

A Social History of U.S. Food and Culture

Jennifer Jensen Wallach

The American Ways Series

ROWMAN & LITTLEFIELD PUBLISHERS, INC.
Lanham • Boulder • New York • Toronto • Plymouth, UK

Published by Rowman & Littlefield Publishers, Inc.
A wholly owned subsidary of The Rowman & Littlefield Publishing Group, Inc.
4501 Forbes Boulevard, Suite 200, Lanham, Maryland 20706
www.rowman.com

10 Thornbury Road, Plymouth PL6 7PP, United Kingdom

British Library Cataloguing in Publication Information Available

Library of Congress Cataloging-in-Publication Data
Wallach, Jennifer Jensen, 1974–
  How America eats : a social history of U.S. food and culture / Jennifer Jensen
Wallach.
      p. cm.
  Includes bibliographical references and index.
  ISBN 978-1-4422-0874-2 (cloth : alk. paper) — ISBN 978-1-4422-0875-9
(electronic)
  1. Food habits—United States.   2. Food preferences—United States.
3. United States—Social life and customs.   I. Title.
  GT2853.U5W35 2013
  394.1'2—dc23
                                                                2012032388

Printed in the United States of America

For my mother, Carolyn S. Briggs

Contents

Acknowledgments

The centrality of the importance of food and its meaning to our daily lives was affirmed to me again and again as I worked on this project as people from various segments of my life shared personal stories, scholarly expertise, and reading materials about the subject. I am grateful to Lindsey Swindall, F. Todd Smith, H. Sophie Burton, Marianne Bueno, Guy Chet, Erica Charters, Elizabeth Hayes Turner, Rita Reynolds, D. Harland Hagler, John A. Kirk, Kelly Wisecup, Liana Krissoff, Natalie J. Ring, and Neilesh Bose for lending valuable scholarly expertise and reading suggestions. I received important training on how to interpret cookbooks as historical source material from Barbara Ketchum Wheaton at her 2011 seminar, "Reading Historic Cookbooks: A Structured Approach," held at the Schlesinger Library at the Radcliffe Institute for Advanced Study at Harvard University. I also gained inspiration from the talented and eclectic group of workshop participants she assembled.

I could not have completed this book without the aid and expertise of librarians and archivists at a variety of institutions including the University of North Texas, Tulane University, the University of Alabama, the New York Public Library, the Library of Congress, the National Agricultural Library, the Schlesinger Library at the Radcliffe Institute for Advanced Study, and the Archives Center of the National Museum for American History. I am especially grateful to the University of North Texas for funding through a junior faculty summer research fellowship and a research initiation grant, which made much of this travel possible.

John David Smith, the general editor of the American Ways series, has been an unfailingly helpful mentor and an excellent editor. He flooded my mailbox with news clippings and book reviews that helped shape this manuscript in a number of subtle and not-so-subtle ways. Niels Aaboe and Carrie Broadwell-Tkach also offered useful editorial suggestions. I am grateful to the American history editor at Rowman & Littlefield, Jon Sisk, and to assistant editor Darcy Evans for their skill and amazing efficiency in producing this book.

The incomparably generous Teresa Stack and Tom O'Keefe gave the wonderful gift of the use of their cottage in the Poconos, a serene setting that provided the perfect backdrop for writing the chapters on race and gender. They also provided my husband and me with wonderful food and companionship whenever we could tear ourselves away from the majestic natural environment of the home they lent us. My dear friends Sarah Gates and Matt Gates generously offered me a place to stay during research trips to Cambridge, Massachusetts. My husband, news junkie Charles Bittner, supplied me with a steady stream of media coverage about various food issues that has expanded my understanding of contemporary issues in countless ways. He also patiently listened to and helped me refine my ideas during long walks with our dogs Paulie and Darcy, whose companionship he rightly claims deserves to be acknowledged. Kelly Wisecup and Gretchen Hoffman helped me find some needed work-life balance during our weekly therapeutic happy hours at Hannah's. Jamie Jensen and Aaron Jensen read drafts of parts of the manuscript for flow and clarity, as did my indispensible editor, my mother, Carolyn S. Briggs, whom the book is dedicated to.

Introduction

In their classic 1972 book *The Taste of America*, food critic John L. Hess and food historian Karen Hess adamantly declared that "good food in America is little more than a memory, and a hope." They despaired about what they regarded as bland, processed, industrial food and the disappearance of cooking skills, acerbically proclaiming, "The Founding Fathers were as far superior to our present political leaders in the quality of their food as they were in the quality of their prose and intelligence." Although this book will shy away from romanticizing the past over the present or making evaluations about what constitutes "good food," it will endeavor to examine and explain the changes in American eating patterns that so disturbed the Hesses. It is an interesting thought experiment to ponder how a piece of industrially produced lasagna served on a paper tray and cooked in the microwave would have tasted to the gourmet Thomas Jefferson or how a harried modern urbanite would confront the task of raising and slaughtering animals for food. It is also important to remember that each food system is the product of a set of historical circumstances. An enormous array of issues ranging from technological innovations, to trade networks, to personal choices and beyond has influenced the dining decisions made by each generation of American eaters.

The unifying concept of the book is the subject of food and how Americans have filled their stomachs as a nonverbal way of articulating ideas about what it has meant historically to be an American or an outsider; a man or a woman; a modern or a conservative thinker; a member of a particular racial or ethnic group; or a pious, patriotic, or political person. This is a book about United States history, which covers the time period from the colonial era to the present, but readers should not expect to be marched decade by decade, major event by major event, through the nation's past. Although the broad arc of the book is chronological, taking the reader from European and Native American contact in chapter 1 to issues of food and ethics in the modern day in chapter 8, the intervening chapters are organized thematically and sometimes zigzag back and forth across time to show what a study of food habits can reveal about issues such as race, technology, or gender. Observant readers will encounter major social movements, U.S. presidents, military conflicts, migration and immigration, and other important issues that are the backbone of the conventional telling of the American story. However, they should not expect a synthesis of every usual issue or to read a neatly sequential tale. Food is at the center, and unwrapping its significance in the United States sometimes necessitates some pleasant meandering back and forth across the nation's history.

The study of food provides a compelling and, perhaps to some, an unexpected lens for examining this history, but it is an approach that makes sense considering what a central place the subject has played and continues to play in the lives of both individuals and larger social groups. In the most fundamental sense, food, or at least having access to it, *is* life. According to historian Felipe Fernández-Armesto it "has a claim to be considered the world's most important subject. It is what matters most to most people for most of the time." Yet despite its central place in the human consciousness and its status as necessity for human survival, the subject of food has traditionally received little scrutiny from historians. Eating has generally been thought of—when it has been thought of at all—as more of a biological action than a process of cultural creation. Although the study of food has traditionally held a place of importance in the work of many scientists whose careers are devoted to increasing or adapting the food supply and in the work of some social scientists who have examined food consumption as a marker of social status, students of the humanities have been slower to embrace the significance of eating practices. The processes of procuring and consuming food are often seen at best as a backdrop to other forms of human behavior. People must eat, after all, in order to wage war, form social movements, stage elections, and engage in other practices that are generally placed in the foreground of historical narratives. The topic of sustenance is so basic and so constant as to seem almost invisible.

However, it is because of the quotidian nature of the topic that students of the past ignore food practices at their peril. If food is indeed the most commonly thought about subject in human history, then studying these thought patterns may be a key to understanding the values and self-perceptions of entire societies as well as of subgroups who dared deviate from general eating patterns. Food studies scholar Warren Belasco balances eighteenth-century French gourmand Jean Anthelme Brillat-Savarin's often-quoted claim, "Tell me what you eat and I will tell you what you are," with a corollary. He notes that food aversions are often as revealing as food preferences. "Our tastes," he claims, "are as telling as our distastes." For as historian Hasia Diner points out, "Consumption of food has always been culturally constructed." Groups make decisions about what is edible and inedible, which foods have status and which are lowly, and what is delicious and what is disgusting.

Philosophers Ron Scapp and Brian Seitz argue that "eating is largely about creation and self-creation." When deciding when, what, and how to eat, human beings are not only attempting to sustain themselves, but they are also sending out powerful messages about who they are in cultural, rather than in merely biological, terms. Food habits are linked closely with the process of identity formation. While learning what to eat and what not to eat, children socialized into a given group are also imbibing a set of ideas about national-ity, religion, race, gender, and social class among other categories. A look at past and present eating decisions made by people living in the geographical space that we now call the United States will shed important light on many of these issues.

In recent years the field of American history has begun to benefit from the growing literature in the interdisciplinary field of food studies. Books like Hasia Diner's *Hungering for America: Italian, Irish, and Jewish Foodways in the Age of Migration* (2002) and Psyche Williams-Forson's *Building Houses out of Chicken Legs: Black Women, Food, and Power* (2006) have convincingly demonstrated that an understanding of American food habits and ideas is not merely ornamental, adding a layer of interest to our understanding of U.S. history, but fundamental. Throughout time, American food choices reveal a great deal about who people living in the United States were or sometimes wished to be.

Due to the complex American history of conquest, enslavement, and immigration, the United States has never developed a singular recognizable culinary tradition. U.S. food practices have been shaped by the various groups that have called this place home. However, more than fusion and friction between different racial and ethnic groups went into creating American food-ways. Technological innovations have also impacted what and how Americans eat. Additionally, the American diet is the product of more amorphous fac-tors, the outgrowth of both shared and competing values. An examination of food habits in the United States can reveal shifting and contradictory ideas about subjects ranging from politics and patriotism to gender.

This book brings together much of the existing research on United States food history to begin to tell the complicated and fascinating tale of how peo-ple have cooked and consumed, fasted and gorged, and accepted and rejected certain foods as a way to tell a story about their identities. Because the issue of food is so predominant in daily life, the study is far from comprehensive and represents only a starting point in this infinitely expansive subject. The over-view of food history that is presented here is also necessarily partial because of the fact that the study of United States food history is still in its infancy.

Many chapters have not yet been written. This book is designed to whet the reader's appetite for more.

Chapter 1, "The Cuisine of Contact," examines the origins of American styles of cooking in the fusion of English and Native American food habits, demonstrating that European settlers adopted foods that they identified as "savage" only reluctantly when their survival was at stake. It also examines the beloved myth of the first Thanksgiving, exposing the story as an example of wishful thinking about what American history had been rather than a true reflection of historical realities. The tale of cultural intermingling in the culinary realm continues in chapter 2, "Food and the Founding," which describes the influence of enslaved Africans on American eating habits. The nation's founding fathers had few qualms about eating food prepared by unfree hands and seemed not to notice the irony embedded in characterizations of the new country's food habits as the simple, republican food of free people.

American expansion across the continent after new territory was acquired by purchase and by conquest continued to transform American eating habits. These sweeping historical changes brought a number of different groups of people into contact with one another and challenged the developing ideas of what rightfully constituted "American" food. This subject is explored in greater depth in chapter 3, "Foodways in an Era of Expansion and Immigration."

The fourth chapter, "Technology and Taste," investigates how the second industrial revolution influenced eating habits in the United States. Citizens of the young nation made the choice to value inexpensive and convenient food produced using the latest techniques over food that was carefully prepared or pleasing to the palate.

Other categories of group identification are explored in chapter 5, "Gender and the American Appetite," and chapter 6, "The Pious or Patriotic Stomach." Women have been and continue to be the primary cooks in American households. While many have embraced that role, either by choice or necessity, others have struggled with deciding how to best use the kitchen to fight against limiting ideas of gender difference. Some middle-class women tried to escape the responsibilities of domestic life by outsourcing cooking and cleaning or by hiring servants. Others embraced the domestic role but tried to elevate it by transforming cooking and other household tasks into a scientific discipline of equal value to male-dominated fields of inquiry. Throughout time Americans have also used their dietary habits as a way to symbolize their religious ideas or moral virtue by eschewing certain foods. Furthermore, during times of war when food shortages were an issue, public denial of certain food items was a way to demonstrate patriotic fervor. Conversely, ignoring government recommendations about food conservation or buying black-market foods could be a way to symbolize a sense of alienation from the broader populace.

"Food Habits and Racial Thinking," the seventh chapter, explores the paradoxical fact that mainstream American society has been more willing to embrace the foods of groups deemed as racially other than it has been to accept the individuals who created the foods as first class citizens. Finally, chapter 8, "The Politics of Food," looks at conversations about the food supply in the twentieth and twenty-first centuries, which have become politically charged. Environmentalists, animal rights supporters, and health advocates have increasingly come into conflict with industrial food suppliers and governmental entities who are accused of knowingly creating a tainted food supply for the sake of convenience and profit.

An examination of United States food history from the colonial era to the present reveals a wide variety of shifting cultural concerns that can be uniquely isolated and studied by looking at eating patterns. It also substantiates Jeff Miller and Jonathan Deutsch's claim in defense of food studies that "looking at people's relationships with food can speak volumes about people—their beliefs, their passions, their background knowledge and assumptions, and their personalities." The volume that follows is designed to synthesize much of the groundbreaking research about American food history, to add new insights drawn from a variety of archival materials, and to encourage students of history to recognize that the study of eating, the most basic of human instincts, can yield insights into a seemingly endless variety of other human behaviors. The study of United States food history is surprising, entertaining, and guaranteed to make the reader hungry for more.

1

❧❦❧

The Cuisine of Contact

For the early European colonists who settled in what became the United States, their first culinary concern was simply having enough food to eat. They struggled to learn the secrets of how to produce familiar foods in their new environment and began, sometimes reluctantly, to adopt new food items. They frequently depended on the help of Native Americans who knew the local terrain both for food and for the information that they needed to develop a replenishable food supply. Colonists in both what is now New England and present-day Virginia had to balance the ideas they brought with them about what constituted an appealing and healthful diet with harsh realities that made it initially impossible to replicate familiar food traditions. For many, food choices could not be taken lightly because they believed that what a person ate impacted his or her health as well as his or her character. Unfamiliar foods might produce unexpected consequences. However, avoiding hunger necessitated an ability to adapt. The melding of the familiar with new food realities led to the creation of uniquely American culinary traditions.

THE LEGEND AND REALITY OF THE FIRST THANKSGIVING

Food plays a central role in the mythology surrounding the founding of the United States. In fact, few national origination stories are as cherished as that of what has come to be called "the first Thanksgiving," a three-day feast celebrated by a group of self-exiled English religious dissidents and a larger company of Wampanoag Indians that took place in present-day Massachusetts in the autumn of 1621. The event was designed to celebrate the European settlers' first harvest in their new home.

1

In 1620, the 102 passengers of the legendary ship *Mayflower* had made a ten-week voyage from England to North America. Some of the travelers aboard the ship made the journey seeking adventure or financial gain, but a substantial segment of the passengers were embarking on a religious quest. They shared a collective disdain for the Church of England, an institution they believed had distorted the beauty and the simplicity of God's word as revealed in the Bible with its elaborate rituals and liturgy. They were not the only seventeenth-century English worshipers to have doubts about the holiness of the wealthy, hierarchical Anglican Church, but they were among its staunchest critics. They were certain that the church was completely corrupt and could not be reformed, even by the efforts of devout believers like themselves. To avoid being compelled to support England's official religion, they fled the country. They traveled first to Holland and then later decided to take an even more radical step and try to form a new religious utopia in what was to them the "New World" of the Americas.

Their voyage across the Atlantic was a turbulent one, and they suffered not only from seasickness but also from infectious illness that thrived in the close quarters of their accommodations under the main deck. The settlers did not leave any detailed records about precisely what they ate during their journey, but they likely subsisted on a diet similar to that eaten on comparable voyages. When selecting the food that they brought with them, they would have made decisions based on economy, ease of storage, and durability. The most common food eaten while at sea was a simple bread known as "ship's biscuits." This staple item was easy to transport and long lasting. If kept dry, it could last for over a year. Because it was eaten over the course of weeks or months, ship's biscuits were subject to insect infestation, and they had such a hard texture that they often had to be soaked in liquid before they could be eaten. This standard nautical diet was generally supplemented by salted meat (both beef and pork) and dried legumes. The settlers would have likely begun their journey carrying some fresh fruits and vegetables, but they would not have taken up much valuable space with large quantities of perishable goods that would not survive a lengthy ocean voyage. Because of the lack of fresh fruits and vegetables, seventeenth-century travelers, including some aboard the *Mayflower,* frequently suffered from scurvy, a disease caused by a deficiency of vitamin C. Scurvy causes loose teeth, bleeding gums, skin sores, nausea, fatigue, and, if left untreated, eventually death. By the mid-eighteenth century, seafarers had begun to make the link between the consumption of citrus fruit and the absence of scurvy and made efforts to make sure that they provisioned themselves with life-saving foods such as citrus juice or sauerkraut. However, before this knowledge was widespread, the issue of having enough fresh drinking water and beer onboard was the primary dietary concern of the ship's crew. Even on well-provisioned ships, travelers were not at liberty to drink to their fill. Supplies had to be rationed due to space constraints, uncertainty about travel times and conditions, and anxieties about travelers' future ability to replenish dwindling resources. By the time the *Mayflower* made landfall, the settlers' supply of drinking water was perilously low, as was their precious supply of beer.

In addition to provisions for the sea voyage, the *Mayflower* would also have been stocked with supplies to feed the settlers as they worked to establish their new home. In addition to the staples of ship's biscuits, salted meat, and legumes, they also would have brought some spices that may have included sugar, cinnamon, cloves, pepper, and mace. They may also have brought ingredients like flour, oats, cheese, and vinegar. They certainly carried a supply of aqua vitae, a distilled liquor that was used partially as a medication. None of these items would have been carried in large enough quantities to sustain the settlers indefinitely, and upon arrival they would need immediately to find ways to augment their meager larder.

The colonists, who later became known as the "Pilgrims," arrived in North America in November 1620, landing first in Provincetown, on the tip of the thin Cape Cod peninsula. They were familiar with stories from European explorers who had preceded them to the continent, and they knew that they were likely to encounter Native Americans who might provide a source of opposition as they staked a territorial claim. Eager to find a site to plant their settlement, the arrivals sent out a small party to cautiously explore their new surroundings. After an arduous hike, they were delighted to discover a source of fresh water. Enthralled by their dreams of establishing a new society, the water they discovered seemed to be particularly thirst quenching. Pilgrim William Bradford later recounted this first taste encounter with the New World, claiming "being the first New-England water they drunke of, and was now in thir great thirste as pleasante unto them as wine or bear had been in for-times."

The Pilgrims' anticipated first interaction with the native inhabitants of the area was an indirect one, and it involved the issue of food. During these preliminary explorations of Cape Cod, the Pilgrims discovered a winter store of more than four bushels of dried Indian corn that had been carefully buried in reed baskets underground. Amazed by what the most religious among them likely saw as a providential discovery, they decided to carry away as much of the preserved grain as they could to replenish their dwindling food supplies. In retrospect, William Bradford, who later became governor of the colony the Pilgrims established, claimed that the explorers felt some pangs of conscience as they raided this food supply. To assuage their guilt, he reported that they repaid the Native Americans for the stolen corn six months later.

As the *Mayflower* passengers continued to familiarize themselves with their new environment, they found and took more dried corn and beans along with various other items, including some baskets and clay pots, which they found inside some empty Native American wigwams. As the Pilgrim explorers tramped around wintery Cape Cod, a group of local Native Americans kept a surreptitious but careful eye on their movements. One day they angrily surprised the trespassers with an attack by bow and arrow. The Pilgrims quickly grabbed their muskets to retaliate, and they managed to end this first cross-cultural encounter unscathed. Having invoked the ire of the indigenous people and having not yet found a plot of land that they found suitable for the site of their village, the Pilgrims chose to widen the scope of their exploration. They ultimately decided to build their community seventy miles inland on abandoned land that had already been cleared by Native Americans.

The original inhabitants had called this area Patuxet, a name that was also used to identify the people who had first lived there. Erasing the Native American identity of the place, the Pilgrims referred to the settlement they built as "Plimoth" after the name of the town in England where the *Mayflower* had begun its journey. Patuxet had been decimated by disease, perhaps smallpox. Before the famed passengers of the *Mayflower* arrived in the vicinity that they eventually referred to as "New England," other English vessels had already made landfall there, visiting temporarily while on fishing expeditions in search of cod, an important food in Europe. As they looked for a source of dried fish to augment their larders, the English and other European traders and explorers inadvertently brought European diseases, against which the local population had no immunity, along with them. The consequences of this biological exchange were devastating to the original North Americans. Between 1616 and 1618 the native population of New England was reduced from approximately 120,000 inhabitants to about 70,000. Patuxet and many other surrounding settlements were completely wiped out. Those who did not succumb to illness abandoned their homes in an attempt to escape the deadly plague.

The Pilgrims, like all Europeans, had more resistance to the diseases that destroyed most of their neighbors, and they were able to take advantage of Patuxet's misfortune and to claim this site that had already been cleared for agriculture. They began erecting simple housing structures in December 1620, but their efforts were slowed by inclement weather and by their own increasingly poor health. Of the original 102 immigrants to the colony, more than 40 died during the winter of illnesses such as tuberculosis and pneumonia. Scarcely half survived until the legendary first Thanksgiving celebration. In March, as some of the harshness of the New England winter began to fade, the survivors had just begun strategizing in earnest about how they would protect and improve their settlement and shore up their food supply when they were surprised by the sudden appearance of a visitor. A Native American ambled confidently toward them, shocking them when he uttered, "Welcome, Englishmen!"

In halting English, which he had learned from European traders, he introduced himself as "Samoset," and he assured the Pilgrims that his intentions were friendly. A few days later Samoset made a return visit to the settlement, bringing several other Native Americans with him, including a Patuxet named Tisquantum, whom the Pilgrims called "Squanto." Tisquantum spoke excellent English because he had spent several years in Europe after being abducted and enslaved by the captain of an English fishing vessel in 1614. Miraculously he was liberated from bondage and made his way back to his native home in 1619, working as a translator for another English explorer. When Tisquantum arrived back in Patuxet, he must have been shocked to discover the devastation that had been wrought by disease. However, by the time the Pilgrims arrived, he had pragmatically adjusted to the new reality. During this first meeting he immediately offered his assistance to his new neighbors.

Although Tisquantum likely had some mixed emotions about assisting the Pilgrims who had claimed the land that had once been inhabited by his people, his English skills made him a valuable resource to the Europeans and the local Indians alike, and he capitalized on his skill to ingratiate himself with both parties. At any rate, Tisquantum likely did not anticipate that the fifty-three sickly colonists he encountered would constitute a significant threat to the remaining Native Americans in the region. He offered to work as an intermediary and translator between them and Massasoit, the supreme sachem, or chief, of the Wampanoag confederacy of Indian tribes who lived in Massachusetts and Rhode Island. Ultimately the assistance that he offered went far beyond his skills as a translator.

When Tisquantum arrived, the surviving *Mayflower* passengers had already attempted to begin cultivating some seeds they had brought with them from England, but Bradford reported that this first attempt at planting was a failure, for the "wheat & pease . . . came not to good." Seeing that their English plants and ideas about agriculture were not well suited to the Massachusetts soil and climate, Tisquantum stepped in, teaching the Pilgrims to adopt native agricultural techniques. He urged them to set aside the seeds they brought from England to concentrate on those that would thrive in the local environment. Tisquantum patiently demonstrated how the local Indians planted corn in hills and then grew squash and beans alongside the staple crop. Corn provided a pole for the bean plants to climb, and the beans added nitrogen to the soil, which enhanced its fertility. As the squash began to cover the ground, it blocked the sunlight and prevented weeds from growing. He also demonstrated how fish could be used as a fertilizer, saying that they should be planted alongside the seeds of maize. In many accounts of native contributions to agricultural knowledge at Plimoth, the technique of fertilizing corn with rotten fish is described as a Native American innovation. More recently, some scholars have suggested that, ironically, Tisquantum may have learned how to do this while he lived in Europe. Thus, this knowledge was the result of Tisquantum's uniquely cosmopolitan background. Most local Native Americans regarded the use of fish fertilizer as unnecessary and tedious.

Tisquantum also advised the Pilgrims on how to forage for edible local plants. He may have introduced them to the cranberry, known as *sassamenesh* by the Wampanoag. The berry, which is indigenous to North America, grew in the region's bogs and would not have been recognizable to the Pilgrims. He also showed them how to catch a wide variety of local fish and seafood, including mussels, clams, and lobsters. He tutored them on which edible items could be found in the environment during each season of the year. Cranberries, for example, were harvested by Native Americans each fall. Spring was the time to catch herring because that was the season when they left the ocean to spawn in ponds, where they were easier to catch. The accumulated knowledge about local foods that Tisquantum conveyed to the Pilgrims was invaluable.

When William Bradford decreed that a celebration of the Pilgrims' first harvest should take place in 1621, the bounty that they were so grateful for was in large part the result of the charity of Native Americans who unwillingly shared the food that the Pilgrims took at Cape Cod and of Tisquantum and others who willingly passed on the information that the Pilgrims needed to produce their own food. William Bradford was cognizant of the Native Americans' contribution to their survival, but he directed his gratitude for their earthly help toward the heavens, declaring that "Squanto" was a "spetiall instrument sent of God for their good beyond their expectation."

Despite the fact that generations of American schoolchildren have reenacted imaginary scenes from the first Thanksgiving replete with dark Pilgrim hats and buckled shoes or feathered headbands made with construction paper, very little is known about the original event. There is only one brief surviving account of the actual feast, written by Plimoth resident Edward Winslow, who later served as a governor of the colony. Winslow recalls that following Bradford's proclamation, the men in the settlement went hunting and "in one day killed as much fowle, as . . . served the Company almost a weeke." He is also the source of the information that ninety Native Americans, including the Wampanoag sachem the Pilgrims called Massasoit, attended the three days of feasting and activities. The visitors contributed to the feast when they "went out and killed five Deere." Winslow makes no specific mention of turkey, the menu item that has become the most commonly associated with the holiday. Elsewhere Bradford documented the state of the Pilgrims' larder after the harvest, and he mentions accumulations of cod, bass, corn, waterfowl, and turkeys, leading most historians to believe that the wild bird was indeed served at the feast.

Peculiarly, this feast has a much larger place in the imagination of contemporary Americans than it had in the memories of the Pilgrims. The Pilgrims and their Puritan neighbors, thousands of whom began settling nearby in the 1630s, frequently celebrated days of thanksgiving, often after a good harvest or after a military victory, as did European colonists who settled elsewhere in the Americas. A group of French immigrants who made an ill-fated attempt to establish a colony in Florida celebrated a "thanksgiving" decades before the Pilgrims, in 1564. For the residents of Plimoth Plantation, their 1621 celebration was no more or less significant than other days set aside to show gratitude to God. They did not, as contemporary Americans do, commemorate this feast on an annual basis.

Modern ideas about Thanksgiving are instead products of the nineteenth century and the result of the campaign of Sarah Josepha Hale, the editor of the popular women's magazine *Godey's Lady's Book*. For seventeen years, Hale used her influential position to campaign for a national holiday of Thanksgiving to be held on the last Thursday of November. She wrote letters to five different U.S. presidents urging them to establish an official holiday, which she envisioned as a day "when the noise and tumult of worldliness may be exchanged for the laugh of happy children, the glad greetings of family reunion, and the humble gratitude of the Christian heart." Her efforts finally bore fruit in the midst of the Civil War. In 1863, Abraham Lincoln made a proclamation declaring the last Thursday of the month a day of Thanksgiving for the entire nation. In his Thanksgiving proclamation, Lincoln declared that even in the midst of civil war the nation had much to be grateful for. In addition to expressing thanks to God, Lincoln urged Americans to use the holiday "to fervently implore the interposition of the Almighty Hand to heal the wounds of the nation and to restore it as soon as may be consistent with the Divine purposes to the full enjoyment of peace, harmony, tranquility, and Union." Thus, this first nationally observed Thanksgiving was born in the midst of strife and turmoil, not completely unlike the tensions that emerged not long after the 1621 Plimoth celebration.

Although the English and the Wampanoag Indians shared food peacefully during their legendary harvest festival, the larger context of the relationship between the European settlers and their new neighbors was far less harmonious. Although many Native Americans living near Plimoth died of disease, others died in warfare as the different cultures battled over control of territory and over competing worldviews. With variations, this same struggle played out between Europeans and Native Americans across the continent of North America, and the native peoples were ultimately unable to stave off European domination of their ancestral territories. In many of these conflicts, access to food supplies was one of the causes of tension between the colonists and the native peoples.

In 1636, the Plimoth Colony and their Puritan allies went to war with the Pequot Indians. Although this conflict has not traditionally been interpreted as being related to the issue of food supplies, historian Katherine A. Grandjean has argued that one of the motivations for war was the desire of the English to seize native supplies of corn and to seek revenge on Native Americans for the killing of an English trader who brought food and information between spread-out English settlements. The timing of the conflict, Grandjean argues, was no accident. The confrontations began at a time when food supplies were perilously low in the colonies due to devastation to the harvest brought by a hurricane, an unusually cold winter that killed many cattle, and a rapid influx of English immigrants that strained already low food resources. The English settlers were ultimately victorious in the bloody conflict, and they indiscriminately killed even noncombatants, a fact that led historian Gary Nash to label their actions as "genocidal." Grandjean claims that although "nothing can justify the war's injustices . . . with scarcity and hunger in view, certain things about the war become more comprehensible." Fear of hunger may have made the English more concerned than usual about competing for resources with the Pequots, making finding a way to seize some of their stored food unusually tempting.

Decades later, Puritan minister Cotton Mather was still celebrating the victory over the Pequots, thanking God "that we have sent six hundred heathen souls to hell." Although a tentative peace followed this bloody war, it did not last indefinitely. In a conflict that began in 1675, an estimated two thousand English colonists and four thousand Native Americans lost their lives in a brutal war between the colonists and Indians led by Wampanoag sachem Metacom, the son of Massasoit, the Pilgrims' former ally. Thus, violence and competition were ultimately more characteristic of the relationship between the colonists and the natives than cooperation and joint celebrations.

Because European contact decimated Native American societies through both disease and violence, some—including many descendants of the original Americans—have criticized the Thanksgiving holiday, which they argue provides a false vision of colonial history. Although there were fleeting moments of interracial cooperation between the Pilgrims and the Indians, the Pilgrims were primarily the beneficiaries, not the benefactors, a fact that is hidden in accounts of Thanksgivings that depict the Pilgrims as beneficent hosts. Furthermore, the argument goes, the three-day feast must be contextualized within the larger history of the relationship between the outsiders and the native peoples. Robert Jensen contends that "Thanksgiving is a day when the dominant white culture . . . celebrates the beginning of a genocide." Interpreted in this light, sentimental stories of the first Thanksgiving reveal more about nineteenth- and twentieth-century imagined histories, ideas about what *should* have happened, rather than the stark reality of what *actually* occurred. A Thanksgiving mythology depicting interracial understanding and Edenic bounty has been understandably more appealing to some than the infinitely more complicated historical reality.

When Lincoln declared the first national day of Thanksgiving in 1863, he did not invoke the memory of the 1621 feast. In fact, the now familiar tale of the "first Thanksgiving" was not popularized until the end of the war. Historian Alexander Young discovered Winslow's account of the feast in 1841, and he erroneously assumed that the event provided the inspiration for local New England thanksgiving feasts, which were popular even before the creation of a national holiday. Using her editorial pen in *Godey's Lady's Book*, Hale made the supposed connection between the Pilgrims and contemporary Thanksgiving celebrations widely known for the first time in 1865. Her powerful storytelling caught on, and by the end of the century the tale was being retold in magazines, works of art, and children's schoolbooks. The heartwarming story has been used to teach an idealized version of United States history and values ever since. Food historian Andrew F. Smith argues that the growing popularity of the Thanksgiving holiday should best be understood within the context of the immigration of millions of people to the United States beginning in the late nineteenth century. The story was used as a vehicle for assimilation by the public school system that "needed to create an easily understood history of America." Not only was the true history of European colonization more complex, it was a far darker tale than that enshrined in the Thanksgiving tale.

The menu that has become associated with contemporary Thanksgivings was also developed beginning in the Victorian era. Some of the foods typically associated with Thanksgiving such as turkey, cranberries, and pumpkin may

Schoolchildren Reenacting the "First Thanksgiving" in 1911. The romanticized version of the feast was used to help create a sense of national cohesiveness during an era of massive immigration. *Source*: Library of Congress, Prints & Photographs Division, Bain Collection, LC-DIG-ggbain-10001.

very well have been served at the feast. However, if cranberries were on the menu, they were not served in a modern sugar-laden cranberry sauce, and the pumpkin would most likely not have been converted into pie because the settlers did not have either butter or wheat flour, two essential ingredients for baking. Potatoes, a modern holiday staple, would not have been served. Although potatoes, which originated in South America, had already been taken to England by the time the Pilgrims arrived in New England, they were not widely adopted in English diets and were probably known only by the wealthy, who may have encountered them as a novelty item. Similarly, sweet potatoes, another New World crop from Central and South America, had been transported to England, but they were not widely known or eaten. Because they were reputed to be an aphrodisiac, some well-off members of English society may have sought them out for that reason, but they would not have appeared on the tables of this feast. In 1621, the Wampanoags would not have been familiar with either crop. Thus, the Thanksgiving menu that has evolved pays homage both to many traditional, New England foods and to other dishes and preparations that were popular at the time the holiday was created.

Thanksgiving menus signify nostalgia for a past that is part reality and part fantasy. The Pilgrims who allegedly invented the feast may not have eaten now beloved foods like turkey and corn with as much relish as contemporary Americans do. Although the Pilgrims were no doubt grateful for the 1621 harvest that saved them from starvation, this fact does not mean that they necessarily enjoyed the food they were eating. Although some artists who have attempted to render imaginary images of the first Thanksgiving sometimes draw a large table overflowing with culinary delights, the original feast was far less refined. The Pilgrims, who had expended all of their energy on creating crude shelters and producing enough food to ensure their survival, likely would not have taken the pains to build an enormous communal dining table. Since there were only fifty-three surviving colonists but more than ninety native guests, most of the diners would have been seated on the ground. No one would have had forks, which were a rare luxury item even in England. Furthermore, much of the food that the Pilgrims would have eaten with only knives, spoons, and their hands would have seemed crude and unfamiliar to them. According to historian James E. McWilliams, it probably "offended the palate of any self-respecting English colonist." One colonial minister described fare similar to the food that was likely served at the first Thanksgiving as "exceedingly filthy and most execrable." The colonists, while being grateful for New World bounty that saved them from starvation, were still hungry for the English fare that they were accustomed to.

EARLY MODERN EUROPEAN IDEAS
ABOUT HEALTHFUL EATING

When the English colonists arrived in the territory that is now the United States, they brought with them concrete ideas about what constituted healthful and civilized eating habits. They hoped to replicate their previous dietary practices in what was to them a "New World." However, when faced with scarcity, as they often were during the early days of settlement, they were forced to eat foods that were unfamiliar to them or that they regarded as somewhat unpalatable. The settlers also had to adapt to the reality of living in a different geographical terrain than the one they were accustomed to, learning to eat foods that were available or could be produced in their new environment rather than foods that were the most familiar to them. However, their willingness to dramatically change their foodways had its limits, and the English colonists did what they could to continue to eat the foods that they preferred. They were afraid that they would be unable to maintain good health while eating alien foods.

Historian Trudy Eden points out that the people who created the first permanent English settlements in North America were still influenced by an understanding of physiology derived from the ancient Greek physician Hippocrates and the Roman scientist Galen. Hippocrates and Galen believed that the body was made up of four basic substances that became known as humors: black bile, yellow bile, phlegm, and blood. These substances became identified with certain organs of the body and with other attributes. Blood and yellow bile were considered to be warm, while black bile and phlegm were cool. Yellow bile and black bile were thought of as dry; blood and phlegm were considered moist. Humors were also associated with personality traits. Too much blood was thought to result in the courageous and amorous sanguine personality type. Excess yellow bile turned a person into an irritable choleric. The sluggish phlegmatic suffered from an abundance of phlegm; while the introspective melancholic personality had an imbalance of black bile. Both personality disorders and physical illnesses were thought to be the result of a disproportionate distribution of these humors, and early modern medical practitioners used various methods to help the patients regain humoral balance.

Bloodletting and induced vomiting were commonly used medical practices, which were designed to help patients rid themselves of excess humors. Significantly, diet was thought to be another way to help the body maintain humoral equilibrium. In the Jacobean mindset of the early settlers in Plimoth and elsewhere in North America, some foods were considered warmer and cooler, moister and dryer than others. If a person was too warm or too dry, she could regain internal balance by eating cooler or moister foods. Foods like garlic and pepper, for example, were thought to be choleric foods that would neutralize too much phlegm. Wine, which resembles blood, was thought to actually increase levels of blood. In ingesting an animal, a person was thought to be prone to taking on characteristics from the animal. For example, rabbits were thought to be fearful. Therefore, eating rabbits could increase black bile levels and thus contribute to a melancholy disposition. In this mindset, food was a vital medicine that if used properly could keep the body in working order.

Those who were inclined to heed the wisdom of the scientific establishment believed that food decisions could not be taken lightly. The overall well-being of a person was thought to be related not just to having a sufficient quantity of food but to having the right kind of foods to eat. It was no wonder then that the early English colonists suffered from anxiety as they tried, with varying degrees of success, to recreate English food practices, which they associated with good health. In their minds, the issue of what they would eat was not merely a matter of survival but one that engaged core understandings of how the body functioned.

Despite aspirations to eat a balanced diet, to some extent the luxury of humoral eating had been reserved for the gentry in Europe. Seventeenth-century British diets varied along class lines. The very poor had relatively little variation in their daily diets and may have subsisted largely on bread, cheese, small amounts of meat and fish, and whatever fruits and vegetables they could either grow, forage for, or purchase. They commonly ate one-dish meals made of grain and scraps of available vegetables and meat or fish. Like the early settlers in the Plimoth Colony, the poor in England were forced to eat what was available to them and could not always afford to eat according to what they thought was best for their health. Nonetheless, they may have been familiar with many of the dietary ideas of their day and if so may have aspired to following contemporary medical advice whenever possible.

The very wealthy were accustomed to opulent feasts and could eat in accordance with prevailing medical wisdom if they desired. They ate many kinds of meat, including lamb, beef, pork, rabbit, fish, and various types of fowl such as swans and blackbirds. The medieval English culinary traditions they had inherited prescribed ideal preparations for each kind of meat and specified the proper accompaniments. For example, rabbits were served with ginger and vinegar or with mustard and sugar, and venison was thought best with cinnamon and sugar. Thus, eaters came to expect to see foods served in certain combinations and were not accustomed to the variations and unpredictability of modern fusion styles of cooking.

Although medieval eaters who could afford to be choosy ate relatively few vegetables and even fewer raw vegetables, by the era of English colonization the consumption of vegetables by those who could afford to choose what they ate was becoming more common. The gentry enjoyed raw salads of lettuce and herbs, seasoned with vinegar and oil. They also ate a wide variety of vegetables, including asparagus, cauliflower, and globe artichokes, which were recent arrivals imported from France and Italy. Root vegetables such as turnips and carrots were consumed in varying degrees by English throughout the class spectrum.

The early modern English also ate fruits, including apples, pears, apricots, plums, cherries, and strawberries. However, they ate very few raw fruits, which they thought had the potential to dangerously heighten phlegm levels. Cooked fruit was considered less problematic, and they enjoyed fruits baked into pies and other desserts. It was not until the eighteenth century that fresh fruit completely lost its stigma as being potentially poisonous. Those who could afford it seasoned their food with spices like cinnamon and sugar, which did not grow in England and could be procured only by trade. Increasingly, foods from the New World such as chili peppers and potatoes were available to the wealthier classes, who began to experiment with them in their cooking. However, the introduction of these and other products via the Columbian Exchange of microbes, foods, and animals between the hemispheres had not yet radically altered English eating habits, which generally favored Old World ingredients.

Regardless of social position, bread was the backbone of the English diet. They made bread out of wheat, rye, barley, and oats. The poor sometimes also resorted to baking bread made of ground peas and beans. These breads varied in shape and consistency. Some were flatbreads. Others were leavened with either a sourdough starter or barm, the foamy yeast by-product from brewing ale. The loaves also varied in color. Not only did the color of the grain influence the shade of bread it produced, but in the case of wheat, so did the degree of processing it underwent between harvest and baking. The more bran that was left on a kernel, the darker the resulting bread would be.

Highly processed, leavened wheat bread was the most desirable and the most expensive option. Those who could not afford to eat loaves baked entirely of wheat would sometimes combine the grain with less-sought-after barley or rye flour. Wheat was also a favored grain because it produced superior pastry crusts and cakes, which were popular items on the contemporary banquet table. Despite the overwhelming preference for wheat, few could afford to consume large quantities of it. Some scholars estimate that in the seventeenth century less than 5 percent of Europeans were able to afford the desirable light-colored bread. Nonetheless, most Europeans aspired to eat white bread made from wheat, and the English brought this preference with them to the New World. One of the ways that they would measure the success of their colonial adventure was in their ability to produce and to eat coveted wheat.

In addition to a preference for white bread, English settlers in North America brought with them an enormous appetite for meat. The ability to consume large quantities of meat was considered a sign of prosperity. In comparison to other European countries, the English were known for being particularly partial to animal flesh. Their preference was for beef or mutton. Although the prosperous could enjoy choice cuts of the animal, the less well-off had to content themselves with offal and other scraps. These smaller cuts of meat often found their way into one-dish meals, thick stews called pottages. Pottages were an economical way to cook. They were eaten by all social classes but were a staple in the diets of the poor and middling English and of colonial-era Americans. Pottages could be prepared in a single cooking vessel and took advantage of available ingredients. A grain (frequently oats) was combined with liquid, scraps of meat, herbs, and vegetables and cooked slowly. A pottage could be utilitarian and dull or a culinary delight, depending upon the skill of the cook and the available ingredients.

Although they lacked the symbolic significance of bread and meat, fish and dairy products were other staples of the English diet. Fish, both fresh and saltwater, appeared frequently on English menus because religious custom mandated a number of fast days when meat was not to be consumed. Fish, which was considered to be phlegm inducing, was thought to subdue carnal desires during times of religious reflection. Fish such as herring and cod were often salted to preserve them, but those who could afford it preferred to eat fresh fish. At the time of European colonization in North America, many fishing vessels were equipped with tanks, which would allow the fishermen to transport live fish to market from great distances. Shellfish were also popular, especially oysters, which were enjoyed by the rich and poor alike.

The English also consumed many dairy products, including milk, cream, butter, and cheese. Dairy products, often called "white meats," were more important in the diet of the poor than of the wealthy. Dairy products were used widely in cooking in wealthy homes, but the prosperous were less likely to consume them in their raw state because medical professionals believed that milk was difficult to digest. For the rich, a diet heavy in meats and expensive spices was considered more desirable than one rich in dairy. The colonists, however, came to consider the ability to make butter and cheese to be a vital homemaking skill. Dairy products allowed for the consumption of animal protein on an ongoing basis as it did not necessitate the killing of the animal.

When English migrants came to North America they hoped to continue eating the foods that they had enjoyed in England but in larger quantities. Part of reimagining a new and better life for themselves meant improving their diet. They did not seek to replace the English staples with food items from their new environment. Paradoxically they hoped to become in some ways more English in dietary terms by consuming more and better-quality items than those they had traditionally valued. Middling and poorer immigrants hoped that coming to North America would enable them to eat more wheat bread, more meat, and abundant and high-quality fish and dairy products.

They held tight to their traditional food practices, not only because they linked English foods with good health, but also because they were also determined to distinguish their food habits from those of the indigenous inhabitants of their new land, whom they regarded as savages. Scholar Trudy Eden argues that they were afraid that "savage foods produced savage people." If they ate the same foods that the Native Americans they encountered ate, they were fearful that they might lose the cultural superiority they felt they had as English people. The colonists' idea that food and identity were linked was derived from ideas common in the popular dietary guides of the day, which claimed that foods had the power to transfer their properties to their owners. Coarse foods were for lower-class people, while more refined foods were for the wealthy. People could influence their social position and personal attributes, positively or negatively, in accordance with the food they ate.

AMBIVALENT ATTITUDES ABOUT INDIAN CORN

Although the English were sometimes willing opportunistically to befriend Native Americans, they made a strong distinction between their own customs, which they regarded as civilized, and the native way of life, which they considered to be savage. The Pilgrims were willing to adapt Native American foods and techniques of cultivation and hunting when their survival depended upon it, but they persisted in believing that their culture and the food practices that they brought with them were superior. Mary Rowlandson, a colonist who was held captive by a group of Native Americans for several weeks in 1675, was appalled by the food practices of her captors. She claimed that they ate what "a hog or dog would hardly touch."

The native food that initially caused the English the most anxiety upon their arrival in North America was corn, which ultimately became a commonplace staple in the American pantry. The plant that is commonly referred to as "corn" in the United States is known as "maize" in most of the rest of the world. The Spanish first encountered the grain after arriving in the West Indies in the late fifteenth century. They adapted the native Arawak word for the grain, *mahiz*, to their language, referring to the dietary staple as *el maíz*, which later became "maize" in English. However, that term was not widely used. For the English colonists, the term "corn" referred to any kind of grain or kernel, and the word was originally applied equally to wheat, rye, barley, and maize. They initially labeled maize as "Indian corn." Their association of Native Americans with the grain was so strong that they often referred to it in shorthand as simply "Indian." Eventually, "corn" became a widely used abbreviation as well.

Maize was a staple item in the diets of most native people. The Iroquois name for corn translates into English as "our life." The Delaware often referred to it as "Our Mother." It was originally cultivated in Mexico around 5000 BC and gradually worked its way north. By about 700 BC Native Americans were growing maize in New England. Corn was as significant to the various Native American peoples as wheat was to the English. It has a growing cycle of 120 days and produces high yields in a variety of climates. It is also, as the Pilgrims discovered when they stole preserved Indian corn shortly after their arrival, easy to store for long periods of time.

Aware of the significance that the grain had to native peoples, the English were ambivalent about incorporating it into their diets. Presumably, they did not want to share a common culinary "mother" with their neighbors.

Hopi Indian Girls Grinding Corn, 1903. For native peoples throughout the Americas, corn has always been a staple ingredient of their diet. *Source*: Library of Congress, Prints & Photographs Division, Stereograph Cards Collection, LC-USZ62-56416.

Historian Edmund Morgan summarizes European attitudes toward cultivating corn this way:

> And the very fact that the Indians did grow corn may be one more reason why the colonists did not. For the Indians presented a challenge that the Englishmen were not prepared to meet, a challenge to their image of themselves, of their self-esteem, to their conviction of their own superiority over foreigners, especially barbarous foreigners like . . . the Indians.

Furthermore, English herbalist John Gerard, whose 1597 *Great Herball, or Generall Historie of Plantes* was among the most definitive studies in botany of the day, was dubious about the digestibility and nutrition of Indian corn. He claimed that "the barbarous Indians, which we know no better, are constrained to make a vertue of necessitie, and think it a good food: whereas we may easily judge, that it nourisheth but little, and is of hard and evil digestion a more convenient foode for swine than for men." Not only was corn associated with savagery and thought to be lacking in nutrition in the colonial imagination, but bread made from the grain reminded the English of lower-class food. They still aspired to eat white bread made of wheat flour, which they associated with wealth and refinement. Corn simply did not fit into their hierarchy of acceptable foods.

Unsurprisingly, given their obsession with wheat bread, the colonists immediately put a great deal of their energy into wheat cultivation. Early attempts at growing wheat in New England met with only moderate success because the colonists soon discovered that wheat was highly susceptible to blast fungus. In contrast to corn, wheat simply did not thrive in the New England soil and climate, and the efforts that the colonists made in cultivating wheat were not proportionally rewarded. Each acre of corn produced double the yield of an acre planted in wheat. White New Englanders regarded their inability to produce large quantities of wheat as a hardship. Edward Johnson said that "the want of English grain, Wheat, Barley, and Rye proved a sore affliction to some stomachs who could not live upon Indian Bread." In the minds of many, English bodies were not designed to easily digest coarse "savage" food like maize.

Rye, a less important grain than wheat in the English hierarchy of prestigious eating, could be more readily grown in the new environment, and the settlers initially tended to prefer eating this more familiar grain to corn. They were stuck, however, in something of a predicament as year after year their corn crops thrived. Due to their recent experiences with hunger and scarcity, they could not afford to dispense with this reliable food source regardless of how unpalatable some found it. Instead they made some attempts to disguise corn and to process it in a manner as close to traditional English foodways as possible. Just as the English often mixed wheat with less expensive grains, the colonists began to combine rye and corn to make a peculiarly New World bread, which they referred to as "Ryaninjun." They also put corn to a familiar and cherished use by brewing beer with it. Forced to depend upon maize as a dietary staple, they still attempted to differentiate their food practices from those of Native Americans. In a compromise of sorts, they attempted to eat what they regarded as "savage" food in a "civilized" way.

Ironically, despite the fact that early European immigrants to North America were reluctant to adopt corn as a staple of their diet, in the nearly four centuries since the Pilgrims first consumed it, maize has been transformed into a quintessential American food. For many people living in the United States, corn is more likely to conjure up the image of a backyard Fourth of July barbecue than historical memories of Tisquantum, who taught the Pilgrims how to best grow it. Peculiarly, given the food's role in ensuring the Pilgrims' survival, corn generally is not considered one of the most important menu items for a modern Thanksgiving Day feast. Although it is often served, it does not carry the heavy symbolic connotations of turkey, cranberries, and pumpkins as a cornerstone of the meal.

Even if it does not automatically appear on Thanksgiving tables, generations of Americans with varied backgrounds have grown up eating cornbread, corn on the cob, and various other preparations, for many of these foods are seen as a proud part of the United States' culinary heritage, a belief that is reinforced by scores of proudly preserved family recipes. As the number of Native Americans in the eastern United States steadily decreased and as white settlers began to see them as a less serious threat to their physical safety, Indian foods began to appear less threatening, too. As the Indian presence disappeared or was minimized, so was the corresponding English fear that the Native American foodstuffs might somehow transform Europeans into savages. As the staple filled more and more Euro-American cooking pots, it slowly lost its culinary stigma. By 1766, Benjamin Franklin did not consider corn to be a specifically Native American food but an American one, and he bristled at English eaters who denounced the suitability of the grain for human consumption, indignantly claiming, "It is one of the most agreeable and wholesome grains in the world." Nicholas P. Hardeman has pointed out that corn eventually became the only crop that was grown in every colony and later U.S. state, making this once reviled food the nation's "great common denominator in agriculture." Despite its reluctant incorporation into the American diet, it rapidly became not only an important food for human consumption, particularly in times and areas in which wheat was scarce, but a crucial animal food as well.

The widespread adoption of corn contributed to an erasure of American collective memory about Native American culinary contributions to the history of the United States. One of the few places where the memory of Native American influence on American foodways is still preserved is in the name of the dish of "Indian pudding," a preparation reminiscent of boiled puddings frequently prepared by early colonists. Corn was a common item in the thick puddings of the era, and although it could be made plain, it was often combined with berries or fruit. A mixture of cornmeal and fruit or other ingredients was held together with water, tied up into a cloth bundle, and then boiled in a pot filled with water to create a filling meal or substantial side dish. A 1796 recipe by American cookbook author Amelia Simmons is representative of the kinds of corn puddings made during the early colonial period:

A NICE INDIAN PUDDING

No. 3 Salt a pint meal, wet with one quart milk, sweeten and put into a strong cloth, brass or bell metal vessel, stone or earthen pot, secure from wet and boil 12 hours.

Simmons also gives two more elaborate recipes similar to Indian pudding as it is eaten today. Her other versions are baked rather than boiled and contain milk and raisins or molasses. She generically calls for the use of "spice," which in today's recipes would most likely be cinnamon.

Today tourists visiting Boston can dine on Indian pudding in places like the Union Oyster House, the oldest continuously operating restaurant in the United States, which has been open since 1826. Another Boston institution, Durgin Park, located in historic Faneuil Hall, opened in 1827 and is equally famous for serving what is now considered to be traditional Yankee fare, including Indian pudding, to the city's visitors. Keith Stavely and Kathleen Fitzgerald have remarked that eating this traditional dish at one of these historic restaurants "has become merely one attraction among the many the area offers to [the] postmodern passerby." Most consumers of the dessert, which is frequently served warm with vanilla ice cream, probably have little idea about how accurately the peculiar name of the dish reflects the impact that Native Americans had on contemporary American food practices.

CULINARY ENCOUNTERS AT JAMESTOWN

The New England settlers were not the only European arrivals who simultaneously incorporated and rebelled against Native American food practices. Colonists in Jamestown, Virginia, the first permanent English settlement in North America, had earlier learned to eat corn and other Native American foods. However, their culinary encounters have not been enshrined in a myth with the equivalent power of the first Thanksgiving story. Much like the Pilgrims who came after them, the colonists who arrived in Jamestown in 1607 needed to adjust their former ideas about what to eat and how to obtain food in order to survive in what was to them a harsh New World.

Unlike the settlers in Massachusetts, the 120 men and boys who came to Virginia on the *Susan Constant*, the *Godspeed*, and the *Discovery* did not come to create a religious utopia but instead hoped primarily to make a profit for themselves and the investors who funded their journey. Because the search for wealth was their most important motivation, upon arrival they spent most of their energy searching for gold and other riches rather than trying to establish a sustainable settlement. Their hopes were disappointed when they did not quickly discover gold, silver, or any other easily obtained commodity that they could appropriate to make a quick fortune.

The adventurers chose to build a village on a peninsula thirty miles from the mouth of the James River, a space they thought they could easily defend in the case of an attack from either local Indians or from their Spanish rivals, who had staked substantial territorial claims in the Americas beginning the previous century. The low-lying, marshy land proved to be a breeding ground for mosquitoes and disease. The suitability of this location for settlement was further compromised by the fact that they arrived in the midst of a severe drought. The period between 1606 and 1613 was the driest of the past 770 years. The dry conditions meant that potable drinking water was scarce. The brackish local water contributed to dysentery, which, along with other health problems, decimated the settlement. Nine months after their arrival, only thirty-eight of the original settlers were still alive.

Some of the initial colonists who came seeking riches and adventure considered themselves to be gentlemen with a status above that of common laborers. The self-perception of this segment of the population meant that many were not willing or able to engage in the hard work of building a settlement. Many lacked even very basic agricultural knowledge and literally did not know how to grow the food they needed. They expected those of lesser social standing to build houses and to clear and till the soil. The combination of poor health, disappointed expectations, and class tensions nearly caused the colony to fail. Captain John Smith, one of the members of the governing council appointed by the investors who funded the Virginia settlement, took control of the situation by instituting harsh military discipline. Smith forced everyone to work, regardless of their class status. His relentless determination earned him the hatred of his men, particularly members of the gentry who resented taking orders from Smith, who was the son of an English tenant farmer. Undaunted by their grumbling, the ever-confident Smith led explorations of the surrounding environment, initiated contact with Native Americans, and busied himself trying to solve the ever-present problem of finding enough food to ensure the colonists' physical survival.

The Jamestown settlers were living alongside a powerful Indian confederation. Thirty local tribes were led by a chief whom the English referred to as Powhatan. The English were vastly outnumbered by the Native Americans whom they quickly became dependent on for food. The colonists were pleasantly surprised to discover that the native people initially not only gave them a warm welcome, but also fed them. As they explored their new environment in the summer of 1607, the settlers recorded that they were "entertained with much Courtesy at every place." Local Indians, whether in accordance with local traditions of hospitality or in the hope of securing military alliances with these newcomers, gave the Europeans a wide variety of things to eat, including dried oysters, fruit, corn, and beans. Native women produced many food items that the English learned to value, including bread made of tuckahoe, a tuber that grew in local marshes and was labor intensive both to harvest and to process. They also made rendered "dears suyt [suet] made up handsomely into Cakes."

Despite receiving gifts of food, by the autumn of 1607 the settlers' supplies were dwindling, and most were too sick to scavenge for supplies. Smith despaired, "Though there be fish in the Sea, fowls in the Air, and Beasts in the woods, their bounds are so large, they so wild, and we so weak, and ignorant, we cannot much trouble them." Almost miraculously, from the point of view of the settlers, Powhatan noticed their suffering and sent men with food and supplies to sustain them. Thus fortified, the colonists were able to survive until a company ship arrived carrying fresh supplies and new colonists. Smith readily acknowledged their debt, writing "Had the Salvages not fed us, we directly had starved."

This Native American generosity was, however, not enough to end the settlers' insatiable hunger. The colonists consumed their supplies quickly and had not yet solved the problem of producing their own food. Smith tried to encourage the Native Americans to keep up a vigorous trade with the colonists. However, due to the drought, the Indians were short on winter supplies, and some were understandably reluctant to part with large quantities of the corn that they had put aside for their own survival. Powhatan told John Smith that corn was more precious to him and to his people than the copper that the English wished to trade for food because "he could eate his corne, but not his copper." Smith resorted to burning Indian villages and fields in an attempt to establish a trading relationship by force. When he could not coerce them into engaging in commerce, Smith led raids on Indian villages, where he stole food and indiscriminately killed whoever got in his way. Realizing that the English were completely dependent on his people for food, Powhatan advised Smith to take another course, asking, "What will it availe you to take that by force you may quickly have by love, or to destroy them that provide you food. What can you get by warre, when we can hide our provisions and fly to the woods? whereby you must famish by wrongdoing us your friends."

Despite Powhatan's words of caution, tensions between the settlers and the Native Americans whose charity had saved their lives grew. Powhatan eventually decided not to trade with the English and indeed to let them starve. Once again, in the winter of 1609, in what became known as the "starving time," the colonists nearly perished. This time Smith, who had returned to England that autumn, was not around to initiate a survival plan. The starving settlers resorted to eating horses, cats, dogs, rats, and mice. They even ate human flesh. One survivor of the harsh winter confessed, "a Savage we slew, and buried, the poorer sort took him up again and eat him . . . boiled and stewed with roots and herbs." In desperation, another starving man resorted to murder and cannibalism. He "murdered his wife, ripped the child out of her womb and threw it into the river, and after chopped the mother in pieces and salted her for his food." By withholding their charity and trade, Native Americans had nearly starved the colonists into submission. However, supply ships and new colonists saved the precarious colony from extinction, and hostilities between the English and the Native Americans continued.

The English came to depend not only on donated or stolen food but also on acquired knowledge of Native American foodways. They carefully watched their neighbors to see which foods were edible and how they could best obtain them. They must have noticed that the local Indians had a different idea about what it meant to have an adequate food supply. The Native Americans in Virginia suffered from periods of food scarcity on a regular basis and were, unlike the English, psychologically accustomed to the idea of periods of hunger. Their food supply was even more insecure than usual during the early years of colonization in Jamestown because of the severe drought. Nonetheless, for most of the year they ate an ample, diverse, and nutritious diet, which included corn, beans, squash, game, fish, wild plants, and nuts. During his period of leadership of the colony, Smith ordered the settlers to emulate the natives and to forage for food. They did so only reluctantly because they considered gathering to be a savage way of procuring food and because the food items that could be gathered this way did not necessarily *look* like food to them. According to historian Trudy Eden, they craved provisions that would enable them to produce "a good pottage" such as oatmeal and beef. They were less comfortable with wild foods, which they thought were best suited for those they regarded as wild people.

The Virginians shared their northern neighbors' prejudice against corn, which they saw as savage or animal food. To the horror of native peoples, English settlers in both regions sometimes fed the precious grain to their animals. In times of scarcity, the Jamestown settlers were willing to eat stolen Indian corn, but they were reluctant to cultivate their own supply. They stubbornly preferred to grow English crops during the early years of the settlement, ignoring the overwhelming evidence that corn was a key food in their new environment.

The colonists eventually embraced corn out of necessity. They also learned to follow the example of their Native American neighbors and to hunt for local game. The majority of the meat supply in England came from domesticated animals at the time of colonization in North America. Hunting was considered a leisure activity and was one that could be enjoyed only by those wealthy enough to own a landed estate. Ironically, then, the colonists had to contend with the contradiction of competing beliefs. They saw game as either an aristocratic or a savage food, depending on the geographical context. In an odd attempt to reconcile the two ideas about the suitability of food procured by hunting, the English repeatedly articulated the belief that Native American men were lazy.

Native American women were generally the chief agriculturalists in their communities, and the labor they performed cultivating crops was a kind of work that the English recognized and respected. They could, however, not initially shake their associations of hunting and leisure. In 1630 Frances Higginson observed, "Men for the most part live idly, they do nothing but hunt and fish. Their wives set their corn and doe all their other work." In spite of these prejudices, the English learned how and what to hunt from the Indians' example. They were, however, initially only willing to consume game that had a similar appearance to animals they had been familiar with in England.

The English in Jamestown and elsewhere adopted native food practices only reluctantly and only when starvation was the only alternative. As soon as each colony was stable, the residents expended enormous energy and resources growing and cooking familiar foods. Sometimes, as was the case with maize, they conveniently forgot their associations between a particular food and savagery. Despite the fact that in times of great hunger, such as the "starving time," the English showed their willingness to consume just about anything, they continued to differentiate their ideas about suitable food from those of the Indians. In this regard, they had a great deal in common with English colonists in Massachusetts.

After being held captive by Native Americans for several weeks, New Englander Mary Rowlandson made this report about what and how her hosts ate:

> They would pick up old bones and cut them to pieces at the joints, and if they were full of worms and maggots, they would scald them over the fire to make the vermin come out and then boil them and drink up the liquor. . . . They would eat horses' guts and ears, and all sorts of wild birds which they could catch; also bear, venison, beaver, tortoise, frogs, squirrels, dogs, skunks, rattlesnakes yea, the very bark of trees.

Despite her use of the third-person "they" in this passage, Rowlandson consumed some of the wild foods that she found repulsive during her period of captivity. For example, she confessed to gratefully eating portions of a deer fetus and a bloody horse liver. Like the Virginia colonists during the starving time, she found that her ideas about what constituted suitable food were not equal to the pain of severe hunger:

The first week of my being among them I hardly ate any thing; the second week I found my stomach grow very faint for want of something; and yet it was very hard to get down their filthy trash; but the third week, though I could think how formerly my stomach would turn against this or that, and I could starve and die before I could eat such things, yet they were sweet and savory to my taste.

Her descriptions of Native American food practices were aimed at a Euro-American audience who she hoped would forgive her for consuming savage food. She likely felt that her readers would be titillated by her culinary descriptions, which would reassure them of their own cultural superiority. Because of her European ancestry, she had been trained to prefer eating domesticated animals over those acquired by hunting, for as Thomas Wessel notes, "Hunting and savagery were synonymous in the frontier mind and no one doubted the savagery of the Indians." Therefore, she was not necessarily expecting her audience to recoil merely at the thought of tasting bear or beaver but also at the method by which these foods were acquired. Although dogs were domestic animals, they were not animals that Rowlandson would have recognized as being edible for they did not appear on English tables. Interestingly, venison, another item in her litany of objectionable Indian food choices, had often been enjoyed by the English aristocracy, who frequently hunted for the animal. She must have known then that the ultimate source of her readers' disdain was not from the foods themselves but rather for those who prepared and consumed them.

Despite her revulsion for the food practices of her captors, she found herself "stand[ing] in admiration to see the wonderful power of God in providing for such a vast number of our enemies in the wilderness, where there was nothing to be seen." The fact that Indians were able to survive on things that seemed to her to be inedible amazed her. Although Rowlandson admits to eating native foods, in the most detailed passage in her narrative about the food practices she observed while a captive, she is careful to avoid using the inclusive "we." Instead she chooses to separate herself from these foods by use of the pronoun "they." After she had returned to her family in Massachusetts, she desperately needed to separate herself from savagery by reclaiming English foodways. She does this by recalling a moment during her captivity when she had the opportunity not only to eat something familiar, something she recognized as food, but also to prepare the meal herself. She remembers, "A squaw gave me a piece of fresh pork, and a little salt with it, and lent me her pan to fry it in; and I cannot but remember what a sweet, pleasant and delightful relish that bit had to me, to this day."

Rowlandson may have felt a need to declare her allegiance to English food habits because in returning to Massachusetts, she was reentering a social world where ideas about acceptable eating practices were taken very seriously.

No group did more to adopt a set of foodways that they hoped would separate them not only from savages but also from sinners than the Puritans in Massachusetts.

FASTING AND FEEDING IN THE CITY ON A HILL

The Pilgrims were soon joined in Massachusetts by groups of Puritans who began arriving a decade after the *Mayflower*'s voyage. The Puritans, too, had come to the New World to conduct a social experiment. Unhappy with the religious practices of the Anglican Church, which they thought too closely resembled corrupt Catholicism, the Puritans hoped that they could encourage the institution to adopt what they regarded to be much-needed reforms. By 1630, however, many, like the Pilgrims before them, had determined that the Anglican Church was beyond redemption. Thousands from the sect decided not only to give up on their vision of a restructured church but also to abandon England itself. They set out to create what became the Massachusetts Bay Colony. By the 1640s, more than 16,000 reformers had arrived in Massachusetts.

The Puritans hoped to create what they labeled "a city on a hill," a settlement that would be organized around their version of Christian values. Although they came seeking religious liberty, ironically, they were not advocates of religious tolerance for others. Instead they demanded strict communal adherence to core beliefs. In their holy experiment Puritans not only endeavored to perfect their own individual behavior, but they also charged themselves with scrutinizing the activities of others. Those found guilty of violating local laws and religious beliefs might be expelled from the church or even banished from the settlement.

Because white settlers in New England were initially unified around the same goals, the colonists were willing to cooperate with one another as they endeavored to create a new kind of society. They did not believe that individuals had the freedom to behave however they wanted to but rather that individual actions had larger consequences. God might punish the entire community for the sins of a small number. Therefore, they held one another accountable for misfortunes the community faced. They believed that God's displeasure could be felt in a variety of ways. Wars and disease could be interpreted as divine messages, as could weather patterns. God might send droughts, floods, or pests to damage the community's food supply as a way to punish the wayward. Thus the ability of the community to feed itself was linked to its collective willingness to follow God's rules and to lead upright lives. A sin like fornication was not seen as merely a matter of conscience between the involved parties and their deity; it was a matter of shared communal concern because everyone might suffer as a result of God's judgment.

Puritan foodways also reflected these communal values. The community often dictated when individuals could and could not eat. Life in seventeenth-century New England was punctuated by literally hundreds of formal days of fasting or thanksgiving, collective occasions when the community begged God's forgiveness, asked for divine help, or expressed their gratitude for the heavenly gifts they had received. Because the Puritans were perpetually afraid of angering God or of losing his blessings, fast days, where they abstained from food in order to better concentrate on prayer, were more common than feast days of thanksgiving. For example, a day of fast was declared to ask God to save their precious wheat from the mildew that threatened to destroy it. Ironically, in that instance they believed that they had to temporarily stop eating in order to assure themselves of a future food supply.

Fasts were also more common than thanksgivings because one of the sins that the colonists were particularly fearful of was that of gluttony. Fast days were commonly practiced by both Catholics and Anglicans, but Puritans were scornful of the terms of those religious observances. On fast days in Europe, believers were asked to abstain from eating meat, but fish was consumed as were other rich dishes. The Puritans were unimpressed by ritualistic deprivation of this limited kind and called for a more rigorous style of fasting where neither water nor food of any kind was consumed. Although they prayed that God would provide them with sufficient food, many simultaneously maintained the belief that having an empty stomach brought them closer to God.

Famed minister Cotton Mather declared, "He that would have a Clear Head, must have a Clean Stomach." While studying at Harvard, young Mather may have flirted with the idea of becoming a doctor before he claimed his destiny of going into the ministry. He maintained a dual interest in theology and medicine throughout his life. Frederick Kaufman claims that his "devotion to Christ Almighty, his devotion to medicine, and his devotion to the stomach cannot be separated." Following the best medical advice of his day, Mather advocated purging the body of its impurities by vomiting. He recommended induced vomiting for almost every ailment and seemed to feel both holier and healthier when his stomach was empty.

In their daily lives, the Puritans hoped to distinguish themselves from what they regarded as the corrupt English upper class, who they thought gorged themselves on heavy and elaborately prepared food. They regarded eating practices such as these as ostentatious and prideful, and as a form of opposition they came to value simply prepared foods. By advocating moderate and uncomplicated eating, the Puritans were demonstrating their separation from the sinful, who could not show similar restraint. Overindulgence, they believed, could not only cause God's displeasure but could also lead to sickness. Puritan deacon Robert Cushman told his congregants that not only was simplicity in eating a form of humility that would be pleasing to God but also that gluttony could be harmful to the health, saying that "health is much endangered by mixtures in the stomach."

The custom of eating simply was fundamental to many Puritans' sense of who they were. It became as central to their identity as the seventeenth-century fasts and thanksgivings. They thought that neither their bodies nor their souls could function properly without these observances. Martha L. Finch argues, "They believed that ritually avoiding or consuming food literally produced alterations in members' bodies and souls." Mather urged people who indulged in harmful or immoderate eating to learn an important lesson from their mistakes. He declared, "Let thy bad stomach put thee in mind of neglecting to digest that Word that should be more to thee, than thy necessary food." Their most important source of sustenance, Mather reminded them, was spiritual and not temporal. The religious beliefs of the Puritans that favored simple eating were supported by contemporary cooking technology that increased the likelihood that colonials would prepare simple dishes.

The earliest settlers had very large fireplaces, so large in fact that cooks could stand inside them. The space was ample enough that separate dishes could be cooked at different temperatures on different fires, and the cook could move between them. She could, on special occasions, prepare multiple dishes using separate flames. However, regulating the heat of several fires was arduous, making one-pot meals appealing to busy housewives. Tending to fires was one of the colonial cook's most important chores, and the task required a great deal of skill. The women in a household had to make sure that the fires never went out, that the last embers were never quite extinguished, so that hotter flame could quickly be produced. Colonial women also had to learn how to gauge the heat of the flame and to learn when and on what part of the fire to cook certain dishes. One-pot boiled dishes could be cooked for a long time over a moderate fire without danger of burning. Because these meals did not require constant supervision, they were a popular choice for the perpetually busy colonial housewife.

The first generation of settlers aimed for survival, not elegance, a fact that is reflected in their meager household possessions. Initially most homes had only the most basic kitchen supplies, such as a heavy pot, a skillet or two, a spit, and a gridiron. Each family would have possessed some knives and spoons and wooden plates called trenchers for use by the diners. In the seventeenth century they may not, however, have had spoons or trenchers for every member of the household. Early colonists ate with spoons, knives, and fingers, frequently partaking out of common dishes or bowls. Many households did not contain a dining table or enough chairs for everyone in the family. The early colonists, who often ate with their hands while sitting on the floor, were, for the time being at least, happy to have enough food to eat. As long as the food paid homage to the English cuisine they were accustomed to, they were content. After all, their ability to feed themselves in this new environment was of primary importance; their holy experiment in the New World depended on it.

Many families in the seventeenth century subsisted almost entirely on pottages, one-dish meals made with grains, scraps of meat, and available vegetables. Ironically, given the English fear of becoming savage by eating food similar to that consumed by the Native Americans, the local Indians commonly ate one-dish meals as well. Both colonists and Native Americans ate succotash, a boiled dish made from corn and beans whose contemporary name is derived from the Narragansett word *sukquttahash.*

Another common one-dish meal with origins in both Europe and North America was baked beans. Since medieval times, the English had made pottages of beans and bacon. Sometimes this dish was baked in an earthenware pot rather than boiled like most pottages. The Indians, too, commonly baked beans in clay pots, which they placed into pits and covered with ashes. Drawing on these two different traditions, New England colonists often ate boiled beans. They also ate beans that had been baked in ovens built into their fireplaces. The baked beans were soaked overnight, rinsed, boiled, and then baked with fatty pork for several hours. Sarah Josepha Hale, the founder of the modern Thanksgiving holiday, gives a recipe for simple baked beans similar to the dish that early colonists would have prepared in her 1857 *Mrs. Hale's New Cook Book*:

> *Pork and beans* is an economical dish, but it does not agree with weak stomachs. Put a quart of beans into two quarts of cold water, and let them stand all night near the fire. In the morning, pour off the water, rinse them well with two or three waters poured over them in a colander. Take a pound of rather lean pork, salted, score the rind, then place the beans just covered with water in the kettle, and keep them hot an hour or two; then drain off the water, sprinkle with a little pepper and a teaspoonful of salt over the beans: place them in a well glazed earthen pot, not very wide at the top, put the pork down in the beans, till the rind only appears; fill the pot with water till it just reaches the top of the beans; put in a brick oven and bake three or four hours.

Another version of the dish, "Boston baked beans," often contains onion and molasses in addition to the basic ingredients. Cooks began adding molasses to their beans in the eighteenth century, when New England began importing large quantities of the substance, which was used to make rum in the region's numerous distilleries. Boston baked beans are still eaten today and are considered to be symbolic of simple Yankee cooking.

The colonial pottage diet was augmented by bread and other baked goods, beer, cider, and cheese. Although bread was a dietary mainstay, not all colonists baked bread in their own homes. Ovens required a great deal of fuel and were expensive to use. As a result, in the early days of English colonization nearby households sometimes pooled their resources and shared an oven to make loaves of wheat, rye, or a combination of these grains and cornmeal. They also frequently made a simple cornmeal flatbread, which became known as a "Johnny cake," a name that may have evolved from the phrase "journey cake." These small breads were easy both to make and to transport and would have provided convenient nourishment while traveling. Native Americans likely taught Europeans how to make these simple flatbreads, which in their simplest form consisted only of cornmeal and water. They could be cooked on a board placed in front of the fire, fried in a skillet, or baked in the oven. Johnny cake was eaten frequently as it was the most versatile and straightforward bread to prepare.

New England housewives were adept at making beer, cider, and cheese. The Puritans brought the techniques of cheese making and brewing with them from England. Along with the knowledge of how to produce cheese, they also brought cattle and cheese-making equipment. The colonists used small pieces of rennet from a calf's stomach to curdle milk in order to make both soft and hard cheeses. The milk and rennet were heated until curds formed. To make soft cheese, the curds were simply drained, leaving behind the cheese. Herbs and salt might be added to flavor it. Making hard cheese was a more elaborate process as the curds had to be not only drained but also put into a mold, washed repeatedly, pressed, and then aged. While soft cheese provided immediate gratification to the cheese maker, hard cheeses could be preserved for the future.

Most early colonial women knew not only how to make cheese but also how to brew beer, which in its crudest form required only a malted cereal grain and water to make. In Europe beer was generally made with malted barley, which was flavored by hops. The colonists, out of necessity, also learned to brew beer with corn. Although beer could be made relatively easily and reliably at home, some colonists preferred to purchase it. By the late seventeenth century many industrious home brewers began establishing businesses called "ordinaries." Housed in the proprietors' homes, these small establishments sold beer or hard cider. In areas with an ordinary nearby, some housewives stopped brewing their own fermented drinks, choosing to purchase them instead.

Colonial Americans also made and consumed large quantities of hard apple cider. The English brought apple seeds and plants with them when they came to North America, and by the mid-seventeenth century, thousands of apple trees had been planted. The press needed to reduce apples to pulp was beyond the means of most individual families. Thus community cider meals soon sprang up to meet local demand for the drink. Going without beer or cider in apple-growing areas was not considered an acceptable option. Not long after his arrival in the Massachusetts Bay Colony in 1631, a colonist wrote to his father back in England, begging, "Loving father, I would entreat you that you would send me . . . a hogshead of malt unground, for we drink nothing but water." Beer or cider was commonplace in daily diets of the English, and to early New Englanders these beverages were seen as necessities rather than luxuries. Alcohol was considered healthful. It allegedly aided in digestion and was thought to be useful in curing a variety of ailments. The colonists, who each drank on average more than twice the amount of alcohol consumed by a contemporary American, scorned or pitied the local Native Americans for drinking only plain water.

The early Puritans would also have had seasonal access to fresh fruits and vegetables. In addition to corn, beans, and squash they also grew asparagus, peas, cucumbers, and cabbages and other greens. They ate fruits such as apples, pears, plums, and berries. Some colonists, no doubt, were squeamish about eating fresh fruit, fearing that it was harmful and difficult to digest. Evidence suggests that others freely ignored the advice of medical experts and consumed it as it was available. Simple colonial cooking would also have been enhanced by imported sugar and spices, depending on a family's budget. Salt and pepper were the most common seasonings for foods. Nutmeg, cloves, and cinnamon were also popular and were used by those who could afford them.

As the decades progressed, the colonists saw improvements in their kitchens, and their eating habits became more refined as a result. In 1796 Benjamin Thompson from Massachusetts designed a more efficient fireplace called the Rumford. The large fireplaces from the early days of settlement had correspondingly large chimneys, and a great deal of heat escaped through the large openings. The new fireplace design was smaller, used less wood, and produced more heat. Cooking tasks could be completed more quickly and efficiently using better-designed fireplaces. During this same period, many families became prosperous enough to purchase more household goods. Europeans had begun using forks instead of their fingers to eat with in the seventeenth century, and the innovation finally became commonplace in the colonies during the era of the Revolutionary War. As the decades passed, colonial kitchens became better equipped with a larger variety of pots and utensils, and wooden serving platters were replaced by pewter, pottery, or china. However, even with the introduction of these greater refinements, many New Englanders maintained their fondness for simple dishes.

As the Puritans became more affluent, succotash and bean pottages, which were generally cooked with only scraps of meat, were transformed into boiled dinners. Boiled dinners contained larger pieces of beef or pork boiled alongside vegetables such as potatoes, carrots, or turnips. Although the amount of protein and the variety of ingredients improved in the transition from pottage to boiled dinner, the adherence to simplicity in cooking techniques was maintained. Both dishes can be prepared in a single pot and would have been seasoned only very mildly, perhaps with a little salt and pepper.

The Puritans were remarkably ambivalent about food. They were fearful of both abundance and scarcity. They disavowed the significance of earthly sustenance in contrast to spiritual nourishment at the same time that they squeamishly tried to separate their diet from that of the Native Americans. Their obsession with food reveals its cultural significance. As they celebrated their numerous thanksgivings, the Puritans set about helping to create a unique American cuisine. In the southern United States, other elements of what was to become American cooking were emerging at the same time, and the food culture that emerged in that region was to bear the strong imprint of another recent arrival to the Americas, the African. The melding of the influences of Native Americans, Europeans, and Africans led to the creation of a unique American cuisine, one that was ultimately eaten by many with patriotism and pride, rather than with the reluctance that characterized many of the first cross-cultural culinary encounters.

2

~~~~~~

Food and the Founding

In his classic study *American Slavery, American Freedom: The Ordeal of Colonial Virginia,* historian Edmund Morgan argued that by racially unifying wealthy and poor whites, the institution of slavery made the development of the ideas that inspired the American Revolution possible. He claimed that the institutionalization of slavery solved the problem of class tensions that might have prevented the development of ideas of egalitarianism. Because people of African descent were perceived as being less human and thus not entitled to the natural right of personal freedom, a form of republican thinking developed where "zeal for liberty and equality could go hand in hand with contempt for the poor and plans for enslaving them." Thus in Morgan's analysis, the arrival of Africans in the New World was a necessary prelude to the political experiment that became the United States. African slavery and American freedom were conceived side by side and interdependent on each other.

The African presence was also a vital component in creating a unique American culture, the bedrock of which was the creative cuisine created by enslaved cooks who combined African, Native American, and European ideas to create a new style of cooking. Although their contribution to American foodways was an involuntary one, African influence was central in the creation of food habits that signaled a departure from English customs. Staking a claim to a unique food identity was important to a new nation that wished to distinguish itself as a distinctive political, social, and cultural space. However, citizens of the young country did not always recognize or appreciate the cultural contributions of enslaved Africans, and not all African Americans had equal opportunities to influence cooking styles. Africans' influence varied regionally in proportion to their percentage of the population. Furthermore, some enslaved people had few foods to experiment with and often went hungry. Their suffering, too, is an emblem of Morgan's reminder that the freedom and prosperity of some was purchased with the suffering of others. An understanding of America's founding foodways must begin with an examination of the arrival of the African.

THE EMERGENCE OF A MULTIRACIAL CUISINE

The white Virginians who paradoxically both depended upon Native American food and regarded it with some skepticism soon had to respond to yet another set of ideas about food and cooking, which were introduced to the colony by people of African descent. In describing the origins of the food habits of the United States, culinary historian Jessica Harris has said that "three is a magic number" because the cuisine that emerged was the result of the intermingling of the foods and cooking techniques of various European, Native American, and African peoples. The first documentation of Africans arriving in the Chesapeake comes from records kept by the Virginia Company, the investors who began the colonial enterprise. A brief passage refers to a Dutch ship that visited the colony and traded its cargo—twenty Africans who were likely from Angola—with the Virginians. The human cargo was "bought for victual." By 1619 the colony had a more stable stock of food than in the previous decade, and they used their surplus food to purchase these human beings. The origins of slavery in the Chesapeake are thus intertwined with the history of the colonial food supply.

The earliest African inhabitants of Virginia held an ambiguous social position. They were not yet automatically considered slaves for life and likely had a status similar to that of white indentured servants, poor Europeans who exchanged their labor for a chance to improve their lives in the New World. Under this arrangement, in exchange for passage, food, lodging, and the future promise of land ownership, indentured servants would pledge their labor for a set time period, often seven years. They worked under harsh conditions, clearing forests, planting the soil, and performing various domestic tasks. Working conditions were so brutal that many died before their term was over. Those who endured had to live under harsh rules. Servants could not leave their employers without receiving severe penalties, and they could be corporally punished for even slight infractions. Not only did they have to contend with grueling physical labor and strict rules, but they also had to make do with crude accommodations and coarse food.

Elizabeth Sprigs, a servant in the Chesapeake in the eighteenth century, wrote a letter home to England complaining of the conditions she labored under, saying, "What we unfortunate English People suffer here is beyond the probability of you in England to Conceive, let it suffice that I one of the

unhappy Number, am toiling almost Day and Night . . . and then tied up
and whipp'd to that Degree that you'd not serve an Animal, scarce any thing
but Indian Corn and Salt to eat." For Sprigs, being physically punished was a
fate as cruel as being forced to subsist primarily on Indian corn, an item that
a new arrival from England would not have recognized as proper food for
human consumption. Richard Frethorn similarly grumbled about hard labor
and insufficient food, reporting that he had to "work hard both early and late
for a mess of water gruel and a mouthful of bread and beef." Conditions were
so bad that English authorities considered indentured servitude a suitable
form of punishment and transported undesirable elements of English society,
debtors and criminals, to places like the Chesapeake. To some, imprisonment
in the Old World would have been preferable to unremitting labor and possible early death in Virginia.

Evidence suggests that like their white counterparts, early African arrivals to Virginia could earn their freedom if they survived a term of indenture.
Because their living conditions were so similar, poor whites and blacks often
felt a sense of class solidarity in opposition to government officials and large
landowners. They socialized with each other, engaged in interracial sexual
relationships, and sometimes cooperated by attempting to escape from bondage together. James Revel, a seventeenth-century English convict who was de-
ported to the colonies as a punishment for theft, later wrote of the similarity in
status between the white and black underclass, poetically recording, "We and
the negroes both alike did fare, Of work and food we had an equal share." The
relationships between white and black servants were so close that the ruling
classes became fearful of the possibility of the development of a large, angry,
and unified working class, which could threaten their control over the colony.
They decided that they needed to find a way to break this potentially powerful
alliance and to begin to make distinctions between white and black laborers.

They drew upon their prejudices toward people with darker skin as
a justification for making differentiations between these groups. In 1640
John Punch, a black man, ran away from his master along with two white
companions, but the three were captured by colonial authorities. His friends
were sentenced to whippings and had additional years added to their terms of
indenture. For Punch, however, the penalty was much harsher. The judge declared, "Being a negro . . . John Punch shall serve his said master or his assigns
for the time of his natural life here or elsewhere." Soon all people of African
descent living in Virginia were enslaved. Not only were they condemned to
spend their lives in bondage, but a 1662 Virginia law decreed that children
were to inherit the status of their enslaved mothers.

The temptation to debase African American laborers was particularly
strong in the final decades of the seventeenth century because the supply of
white indentured servants was beginning to shrink. Economic opportunities
for the poor were improving in England. Furthermore, numerous horror

stories about harsh conditions in the colonies reached Europe, and potential indentured servants were growing more reluctant to sign several years of their lives away. At the same moment, the price for African laborers, who could be procured through the already well-established transatlantic slave trade, decreased. The temptation of an abundant, permanent labor supply pushed the colonists into the institutionalization of racial slavery.

The colony had an insatiable appetite for labor due to the recent introduction of tobacco cultivation into the region. The first adventurers in the colony may not have found gold, but they found something that had the potential to earn them tremendous profits when they discovered that tobacco grew well in the climate. Cultivating the plant was, however, incredibly laborious. Because of the demand for workers, decade by decade the number of Africans in Virginia increased from 25 in 1625 to more than 210,000 by 1775. The vast majority of these enslaved workers labored growing tobacco, but many played vital roles in making sure that the colonials—both those who worked in the fields and those who benefited from their labor—were fed. Africans worked at cultivating food crops and in colonial kitchens, making a tremendous impact on the foodways of the American South in the process.

Culinary encounters between Europeans and Africans began on the coast of Africa. European slave traders, with assistance from their African trading partners, designed an elaborate system for procuring, temporarily housing, and then transporting African captives to lives of slavery in the Western Hemisphere. Captured Africans were marched from the interior of the continent to the coast, housed in holding facilities, packed into cramped slave-trading vessels, and taken to New World plantations to work. The valuable human commodities had to be provided with sufficient food on every leg of their journey, and a complex trade network was created to provide the vast quantities of food necessary to fuel the slave trade. Various coastal African peoples, many who were enslaved themselves, were enlisted to grow crops and to provide animal protein to not only sustain the enslaved Africans who were to make the Atlantic crossing but also feed European traders and military personnel.

Unsurprisingly, the Europeans first tried to grow their own traditional staple foods but found that grains like wheat, barley, and rye were not suited for a tropical agricultural environment. They turned instead to the local grains of sorghum and millet and to indigenous African foods like yams and black-eyed peas. Interestingly, they also cultivated with great success manioc and maize from the Western Hemisphere. Both manioc and maize flourished on the African coast, and many African societies began cultivating these foods to augment their own diets. Maize quickly became a particularly important food in the Gold Coast, where it helped make up for the shortfall in the food supply between the harvest cycles of other local crops. Thus, some enslaved Africans who were bound for North America, where corn was to become one of their staple foods, first encountered the grain either in their own villages or on the transatlantic voyage. Regardless of when they first encountered the grain, it was an emblem of European intervention in Africa.

Judith A. Carney and Richard Nicholas Rosomoff have pointed out that in this context maize "can be seen as a symbol of the dehumanizing condition of chattel slaves, who were no longer able to exercise dietary preferences. . . . A serving of maize was a daily reminder that one no longer held the fundamental right to eat the food that had traditionally defined membership in a culture." In the culinary triangle of European, Native American, and African foodways, maize emerged as a highly charged symbol for each group. For the Native Americans it signified life itself, for the Europeans it was initially equated with savagery and later with a uniquely American culinary tradition, and for Africans the grain first conjured up associations with slavery and attempts at cultural domination.

European slave traders were deeply concerned with the mortality of their human cargo. Every captive who died reduced the profit margins of their slave-trading venture. Because of this, the captains of slave ships traded advice with one another about how to manage their operations. They exchanged opinions about how tightly to pack their ships with human bodies, how to improve sanitary conditions below deck where the chained captives were held, and how they should exercise, control, and care for the health of their cargo. Traders hired surgeons to travel on the vessels and to monitor the health of their captives. These surgeons brought with them the prevailing medical sensibilities of the day, and they may have supported the idea that emerged that the slaves fared the best on the voyage if they were fed familiar foods. Once again, food and identity were seen as synonymous. Certain foods were seen as best suited for certain people, and eating foods that were not appropriate for one's particular constitution, social class, or racial group might have disastrous health consequences. One trader was reluctant to feed his captives maize despite its enthusiastic and rapid incorporation into African cuisines. He preferred to feed them African yams, saying, "No other food will keep them." Even the ubiquitous maize was, in his observation, "disagreeing to their stomachs."

Captains of slave ships thought carefully about what kinds of food they should feed their captives. Historian Marcus Rediker claims that some even took into account the specific regions in Africa where the enslaved came from when choosing their menus. Slaves from rice-growing Senegambia and the Windward Coast might be given rice, while slaves from the Bights of Benin and Biafra may have been fed yams, an important food in the local diet. Slave ships were also stocked with sorghum and black-eyed peas, foods of African origin, along with manioc and corn, plants that were introduced to the continent as part of the Columbian Exchange.

Even when familiar foods were served, they were not prepared in the customary style of any West African cooking tradition. The slave traders were fixated on the idea of serving familiar food items but did not attempt to adopt cooking techniques that the enslaved people would have recognized. During the journey from Africa to the Americas, the enslaved were often fed a gruel that became known as "Dab-a-Dab," which consisted of boiled grains and beans of whatever variety was available combined with yams. It was often seasoned by a condiment the sailors referred to as "slabber sauce," made of palm oil and malegueta pepper, two ingredients widely used in African cooking. Some of the flavors of the African continent were thus represented in the food served onboard slave trading vessels, but the food was designed for ease of preparation and did not pay homage to traditional recipes. Sometimes enslaved women were given the job of cooking meals, either on their own or alongside the ship's cook. In those instances, it is possible that African culinary traditions were more discernible in the final product.

Surprisingly, sailors aboard slave ships frequently complained that the enslaved ate better than they did, and one reported that he in fact felt "obliged to beg victuals of the slaves," whose food was generally both more abundant and of better quality than that of the crew. The sailors subsisted on salted beef, which slowly deteriorated into its brine throughout the course of the voyage, ship's biscuits that were often filled with vermin, dried peas, and grog, a drink made with water, weak beer, and rum. When supplies were running low, the men were often put on "short allowance" and would have to perform their laborious tasks while hungry. Common sailors represented a lower-class element of English society, and the typical slave trader cared far more about the health of his valuable cargo than about the fate of the crew members, who could be easily replaced should they succumb to illness.

Despite the attempts of many slave traders to keep the captives healthy by providing them with the foods that the traders believed they were the best suited to eat, the issue of eating became a source of contention onboard. Many captives resisted their enslavement by refusing to eat. This was such a common occurrence on these voyages that a special tool, a *speculum oris*, a metal mouth opener, was designed. The contraption would hold open the mouth of slaves who refused to eat so that sailors could force gruel down their throats. Alexander Falconbridge, a surgeon on a slave-trading ship, described even more brutal means for forcing the enslaved to eat:

> Upon the Negroes refusing to take sustenance, I have seen coals of fire, glowing hot, put on a shovel, and placed so near their lips, as to scorch and burn them. And this has been accompanied with threats, of forcing them to swallow the coals, if they any longer persisted in refusing to eat. These means have generally had the desired effect. I have also been credibly informed that a certain captain in the slave trade poured melted lead on such of the Negroes as obstinately refused their food.

In these slave voyages, enslaved people refused food as a form of resistance to circumstances that were otherwise beyond their control. By their actions they showed their oppressors that they preferred starvation and death to captivity. On their part, the slave traders used food as a tool of oppression as they appropriated the bodies of Africans as a way to make a profit, stripping them of volition even in the most basic decision of whether they chose to live or die.

James McWilliams convincingly argues that "America's culinary history is inextricably linked with suffering." The transatlantic journey of enslaved people from Africa to the Americas is one of the most brutal among the historical circumstances that brought about these New World culinary encounters. More than ten million African Americans made it across the Atlantic in what has become known as the "Middle Passage," the second leg of a trade network that went from Europe to Africa, to the Americas, and then back to Europe. Not only did the captives aboard the ship have to cope with the psychological turmoil that came from being taken away from their homes and families and the culture shock of encountering not only Europeans but Africans with different cultures and different languages, they also endured physical pain. Slave quarters on ships were hot, filthy breeding grounds for diseases. Slaves had little physical space to move or to perform bodily functions. Their skin was often rubbed raw by the friction of the boat's movement. In describing the horrendous conditions onboard ship, surgeon Alexander Falconbridge employed a culinary metaphor, writing that the floor in the area where the slaves were housed "was so covered with the blood and mucus which had proceeded from them in consequence of the flux, that it resembled a slaughter-house."

When the enslaved people disembarked to their new homes in various places throughout the Americas, they showed a remarkable resiliency. They formed new family and kinship networks and created a hybrid African American culture, which had strong antecedents in the societies that they left behind. One of the places where traces of African cultural continuity were the most obvious was in the culinary realm. The enslaved people not only brought memories, religious beliefs, and traditions of art and storytelling with them, they also clung to physical traces of Africa in the form of the foods that they brought with them. Sometimes deliberately and other times unintentionally, slave-trading vessels brought African botanical gifts to the New World. African millet, sorghum, black-eyed peas, okra, watermelon, species of sesame, and African rice were soon cultivated in garden plots grown by enslaved people throughout the Americas. Many of these foods also found their way into local recipes still prepared throughout the hemisphere.

The ability of enslaved people to shape the cuisine of a particular region varied from place to place, typically in proportion to their percentage of the population in a given area. In Virginia, where Africans constituted a minority of the population, the English imprint on the region's food was more predominant than the African one. John L. Hess and Karen Hess also suggest that European food practices may also have been even more prevalent in households that had access to English cookbooks. Thomas Jefferson's wife, for example, often read printed recipes to her enslaved cooks, limiting their ability to utilize traditional African techniques. Nonetheless, the English-derived cuisine of the region quickly took on certain aspects of an African culinary sensibility. This happened despite that fact that slaves in the Chesapeake were not as frequently permitted to plant their own gardens and thus to cultivate preferred foods as enslaved people living in, for example, the Carolinas or the Caribbean. They generally had to depend on rations given to them by slaveholders, who, unlike the traders, did not feel compelled to feed them traditional African foods but instead furthered their transformation into becoming African Americans by feeding them North American foods.

The ruling class had incentive to make sure that enslaved people had a reasonably adequate diet, but they did not take pains to make sure that enslaved people were given varied or preferred foods. They carefully doled out allotments of corn, which became the backbone of the slave's diet, and much smaller quantities of meat, generally fatty pork or sometimes, particularly in the colonial period, salted fish. Planters wanted to make sure that their slaves' food would provide them with sufficient energy to perform the arduous tasks related to tobacco cultivation, but the planters did not want to spend a penny more than necessary feeding slaves. The slaves' diets were designed to be enough to keep them alive but were certainly not sufficient for keeping the enslaved eater satisfied or well nourished.

Children who were not old enough to be productive laborers were fed an even more meager diet of cornmeal mush or cornbread, vegetables, sour milk, and various kitchen scraps. They typically ate their meals communally out of a trough similar to that used to feed animals. Robert Shephard, who had been enslaved in Kentucky, recalled that the children, who were often dirty because they were minimally supervised while their parents worked, ate with filthy hands. "Sometimes dat trough would be a sight . . . what was in de trough would look like real mud what had come off our hands."

Slave diets improved between slavery's seventeenth-century origins and the institution's nineteenth-century zenith. During the latter period, corn remained the most significant item in the slave diet, but enslaved people began to eat larger quantities of meat. Historian Sam Bowers Hilliard estimates that average slave rations during this era consisted of about a peck of corn per adult enslaved person per week. Pork allotments varied, depending upon the whims and resources of owners, the time of year, and the arduousness of the work being performed at any given time but generally ranged from between two and five pounds a week. These staple items might be augmented by vegetables such as collard greens, sweet potatoes, cabbages, and turnips. Enslaved people might also be given some fruit if it was grown on the plantation as well as small and occasional quantities of things such as molasses, tea, coffee, salt, and alcohol. The price of slaves increased after the 1808 end to the transatlantic slave trade. Around the same time, a radical and outspoken abolitionist movement emerged in some Northern states. These factors caused slave owners to improve the material conditions of their slaves, including their diets. The slaveholding class made these improvements out of necessity rather than benevolence in order to protect its valuable investments and to bolster pro-slavery claims that the institution was a "positive good." However, even during this period, some slaves went hungry.

While he was enslaved in Maryland, Frederick Douglass remembered receiving "less than half a bushel of corn-meal per week, and very little else, either in the shape of meat or vegetables." Even those who received a sufficient quantity of food often suffered from malnutrition because of the lack of variety in their diets. Enslaved people suffered from conditions related to poor nutrition, such as pellagra, scurvy, and anemia. Both hunger and a desire for diversity in their diet caused slaves to scavenge for wild foods, hunt, fish, and steal from their masters. Douglass was loath, however, to call the act of hungry slaves taking food from their masters "stealing." After all, when slaves took additional food, their actions inevitably benefited the master since "the health and strength derived from such food were exerted in *his* service."

Given the monotony of their food rations, enslaved cooks had to find creative ways to diversify their diets and learned to become expert cooks with available ingredients. Even in areas where they were not allowed to grow their own gardens, they could emulate traditional Native American techniques and collect wild foods like greens, fruits, and berries. They also hunted and fished. Archeological evidence reveals that in addition to the domesticated animals that slaves received in their rations or took from their master's food supplies, enslaved people ate a variety of fish and wild animals, including catfish, opossums, squirrels, and various birds. Many of the wild greens and animals that enslaved people encountered reminded them of similar food products they had known in Africa. Speaking specifically about Igbo transplants to the Chesapeake, historian Frederick Douglass Opie argues that they "did not have that much adapting to do. . . . They only had to find an alternative to palm and kola nut oil for frying fish and poultry and making soups and stews." Julia Banks, who was a slave in Texas, recalls fish fries that exemplified Americanized African techniques: "The men used to go up to the lake, fishin', and catch big trout, or bass, they call 'em now; and we'd take big buckets of butter . . . and we'd take lard too, and cook our fish up there, and had corn bread and hoecakes . . . it sure was good."

The hoecakes that accompanied Banks's fish fry were a Southern equivalent of the Johnny cake and were ubiquitous in the slave diet. They received their name from the alleged fact that enslaved people with scarce kitchen equipment sometimes cooked the cakes, which in their most basic form contained only cornmeal and water, over a fire using the back of an agricultural hoe as a cooking surface. Simple foods like corn flatbreads and fish could be pleasing to the palate if well prepared, and many enslaved people prided themselves on their ability to make the most of what was available to them. Frederika Bremer, a Swedish visitor to a plantation in South Carolina, had the opportunity to sample a lunch prepared for slaves by an enslaved cook, which consisted of beans and hoecakes. Afterward she raved that she "had seldom tasted better or more savory viands."

The slave owners themselves were the primary beneficiaries of the culinary imaginations of their enslaved cooks. In the master's kitchen slaves had a much wider variety of ingredients to work with and could create elaborate feasts. Even in the Chesapeake, where English foodways predominated, African ingredients made inroads into the local diet. Because more than a hundred edible greens flourish in Africa, African cooks came to the Americas knowing how to prepare them and how to temper their bitterness. In the American South they slow-cooked collard greens, a plant that originated in Africa and quickly became popular in Southern cooking, and seasoned them with small pieces of meat. They urged the consumption not only of the greens themselves but also the nutritious liquid they were cooked in, which became known as "pot-likker." Okra, another vegetable that originated in Africa, also was widely adopted into the Southern diet. Mary Randolph's classic 1824 cookbook *The Virginia House-wife* includes a recipe for stewed gumbo prepared with onions, butter, and tomatoes.

Regardless of the specific ingredients they used, African American cooks prepared the dishes their masters ordered using what Charles Joyner has called "African culinary grammar." By using familiar techniques and ingredients and subtly altering European recipes, enslaved cooks were able to exercise creativity and to pay homage to their traditional culture. In so doing, they were able to demonstrate that although their labor had been stolen from them, intangible things, such as cultural expression, could be altered over time and circumstances but never completely usurped. For example, they seasoned foods liberally with pepper, introducing an African preference for spicy foods into many Southern dishes. The fact that spicier foods are still more prevalent in regions of the country where slavery was the most entrenched than in many other areas is confirmation of a lingering African influence. Fried chicken, which has became a quintessential American food, was developed in part by enslaved cooks. African cooks commonly fried fowl in vegetable oil, and African Americans combined this tradition with European recipes that called for breading pieces of chicken and briefly frying them before stewing them. The breaded, deep-fat-fried chicken that emerged from plantation kitchens united these techniques.

In areas with a black majority population, such as the colony of Carolina, African American influence on the cuisine of the region was even more pronounced. The majority of the white settlers who came to Carolina in the late seventeenth century came from the island of Barbados, an English colony where sugar was cultivated. Because of its small geographical size, the sugar plantations could not expand indefinitely to provide holdings for succeeding generations of white Barbadians. Therefore, many younger sons who would not inherit substantial property came to Carolina in search of new opportunities. From the very beginning, they built their society on slavery. Their dependency on enslaved labor was so pronounced that by 1710 the colony had a black majority.

Like their neighbors in the Chesapeake, the white settlers in Carolina originally struggled to find a commodity or staple crop that would make them wealthy. They produced tar and turpentine and bred cattle with some degree of success. However, the key to the economic development of the region was ultimately the cultivation of rice. The decision to grow rice was directly tied to the large African presence in the colony. Planters in Carolina encouraged their slaves to cultivate garden plots and to take a much larger responsibility for feeding themselves than in the Chesapeake. Furthermore, enslaved people were often permitted to sell the surplus foods they produced and the animals they raised at market. Inspired by the desire to supplement their diets as well

African Americans Carrying Food to Sell in a Savannah, Georgia Market, 1875. People of African descent contributed both specific ingredients and particular cooking techniques to United States culinary history. *Source: Harper's Weekly,* May 29, 1875, p. 436, Library of Congress, Prints & Photographs Division, LC-USZ62-102153.

as to earn money, slaves planted a variety of African foods in their garden plots, including okra, sesame, sorghum, and African red rice. Historian Judith Carney speculates that Carolinian planters may first have experimented with rice cultivation after seeing the plant growing in their slaves' gardens.

Initial experiments in rice cultivation were done using the red African variety of the grain. Ultimately, Asian varieties were imported into the colony, and white rice became predominant. Regardless of the origin of the rice, it was cultivated using African techniques. Enslaved Africans taught their owners how to irrigate fields and how to engineer necessary controlled flooding. They introduced the planting technique whereby a worker in a rice field would use his or her foot to open up a hole, drop a seed in, and then close the hole with the foot. They also made the baskets used in winnowing, the process where the rice was tossed so that the hull would separate from the grain. The hull had already been loosened from the grain by a large pestle of the kind used in West Africa. Planters in Carolina were so dependent upon enslaved people for their knowledge of rice cultivation that they began deliberately importing enslaved workers from regions of Africa where rice was grown.

Not only did Africans introduce the idea and the process of rice cultivation in Carolina, they also showed the ruling class how to cook it. They favored boiling rice, removing it from the heat, and letting it sit long enough for the grains to fully absorb the moisture. They preferred eating grains that were separate and identifiable rather than a mass of indistinguishable gluey rice. African cooks also developed dishes that drew on ancestral techniques and ingredients. For example, "Hoppin' John," a classic Carolina dish containing rice, black-eyed peas, and salt pork, was developed by enslaved cooks. Jessica Harris argues that the dish is similar to a Senegalese dish, *chiebou niebe*, that contains black-eyed peas, rice, and beef. The use of meat as a condiment or a seasoning rather than as a main component of the meal is a common technique not only in "Hoppin' John" but also in other classic dishes from the Low Country. This style of cooking is another manifestation of "African culinary grammar," for West Africans did not share the English obsession with large quantities of meat with their meals. They were accustomed to using meat as a condiment or seasoning for a starch-based meal.

Despite the fact that racial slavery was predicated on a belief in black inferiority, white culinary stereotypes of Africans were not as negative as those associated with Native Americans. While Native American eating habits were seen as savage, Africans quickly gained the reputation of having, as one slaveholder put it, a "natural genius" for cooking. Planters took great pride in the talent of their African American cooks, and many allowed them a great degree of latitude in running the kitchen and in deciding what to prepare. These freedoms could be, and certainly sometimes were, taken away by the plantation mistress who supervised the household servants. Nonetheless, the tenacious belief that black cooks had innate ability to prepare good food took root. The emergence of this favorable stereotype may be attributed in large part to the fact that black cooks, unlike Native American ones, operated under white supervision and within a mostly European paradigm of which ingredients constituted acceptable foods. Regardless, from the establishment of slavery until structural changes in the southern United States as the result of the civil rights movement in the twentieth century, mostly female cooks of African descent played an unparalleled role in the preparation of Southern meals and in the creation of the unique cuisine that emerged from that region of the country. The role of African American cooks in creating the founding foodways of the United States cannot be overstated. In fact, many of the men who gave birth to the idea of an independent nation, including George Washington and Thomas Jefferson, grew up eating food prepared by African American cooks.

FOOD AND THE FOUNDING

Seventeenth-century European American eaters had been, out of necessity, more concerned with survival than with elegance in dining. The precariousness of their food supply led them to adapt and, albeit reluctantly, to eat foods that were available rather than foods that were preferred. From the perspective of the Puritans, the simple eating habits that had been born of necessity also had a sound theological basis. Plain cuisine did not reflect false pride or gluttonous indulgence that might distract eaters from concentrating on their spiritual lives. Despite the attempts of New Englanders to glorify American food habits that originated due to scarcity, hungry American eaters expanded their meager early diets as soon as they had the means and the available resources to do so. In the eighteenth century, new attitudes about food were revealed in a proliferation of kitchen equipment and in a new concern about creating a designated cooking space.

Inventories of eighteenth-century households reveal that as soon as early Americans achieved a reliable subsistence they began purchasing more kitchen and dining equipment. Many cooks now had access to more specialized cooking utensils, such as devices made to toast bread or specifically to cook fish. Particularly prosperous householders might own tin kitchens, imported from England. These barrel-shaped devices contained a spit and were placed next to the fire and used for roasting meat. By the eighteenth century, those who could afford it built kitchens that were separated from the rest of the house. No longer was the kitchen the center of a family's living space, a place where cooking took place only incidentally alongside other household tasks. In these newly designed spaces, food preparation was considered a significant enough activity to require its own room.

As items used for cooking increased in quantity and quality, so did implements used for eating. Except in the very poorest houses, diners expected to eat off of their own plates with their own forks and increasingly to benefit from other refinements. Genteel diners ate off of china at designated dining tables covered by white cloths. They would be served tea out of a teapot and might even have their meal warmed with a plate warmer. Their food might be illuminated by candles displayed in silver or brass candlesticks, and those who could afford it could enjoy drinking wine and other beverages out of separate and distinct glasses. In comparison with the customs of early arrivals to Massachusetts and Virginia, these improvements were substantial and embraced enthusiastically by those who wished to use material goods to reflect their growing economic success.

Culinary historian James McWilliams argues that the colonists, who were sheepish about their reputation as rough frontier dwellers, used their more sophisticated kitchens and dining spaces to prepare food that would elevate their status, food that would make them feel like "proper Englishmen." Now that their basic survival was more certain, the colonists could afford to think more about the issue of social status. They bought English cookbooks and used their growing financial means to purchase English goods, often importing food items and cooking utensils from the mother country. Like the wealthy in England, well-off colonials imported wine and brandy to elevate their dining experience and to supplement their supply of locally produced beer, cider, whiskey, or rum. One of the most dramatic changes in eating habits was the gradual inclusion of more wheat in the American diet. Although the grain did not grow well in New England, it thrived in Virginia and in other regions of the expanding North American colonies such as New York and Pennsylvania. Increasingly, New Englanders could afford to buy imported wheat, and throughout British North America, consumption of this most favored grain increased. It never completely replaced corn, which had made quick and permanent inroads into the American diet, but the increasing availability of wheat gave colonial Americans the opportunity to better imitate the British by incorporating more white bread, pies, and cakes into their menus.

At last many Americans had the means to do what the Pilgrims had wished to accomplish—to replicate an English diet in the colonies. This mission was complicated by the fact that most eighteenth-century Americans had not been born in England and thus had only secondhand knowledge of eating habits in that country. The desire to eat the foods of the mother country was also compromised by the impact Native American and African traditions had already made on American eating habits. However, this lack of firsthand knowledge about England and the multicultural influence of native and African eaters did not stop status-conscious Americans from seeking to adopt the foods, customs, and fashions of the English. William Eddis, a resident of Maryland, remarked with wonder, "I am almost inclined to believe that a new fashion is adopted earlier by the polished and affluent American than by many opulent persons in the great metropolis."

The desire to emulate the style of both the cuisine and the clothing of their country of origin, albeit in an inevitably modified fashion, was strongly felt by many Americans. Trudy Eden claims that typical American eaters sought to eat foods that symbolized their identification "with other British Americans, and indeed with other British people all over the world." Refined American eaters sought to design menus that would be largely recognizable and palatable to the most distinguished British guest. However, the preference for all things English became challenged and complicated during the lead-up to the Revolutionary War, when American attitudes underwent a profound transformation.

Although fashionable Americans wanted to emulate certain aspects of British culture, they sought to do so as equals. By the eighteenth century colonials had become accustomed to a great deal of independence in governance, and Americans looked to their assemblies that made local laws for guidance and generally felt less connected to far-off Parliament. From the perspective of many colonists, particularly those from a British background, ties to the mother country based on cultural affinity and affection were unthinking and natural. However, colonial elites expected to control the local political arena and found ways to exert considerable influence even over royally appointed governors, who found it expedient to cooperate with the local assemblies that had the power to vote on taxes and other expenditures. For the first half of the eighteenth century, the Crown and Parliament allowed the colonies to largely govern themselves through a policy of "salutary neglect."

This delicate relationship changed in the aftermath of the Seven Years' War, which ended in 1763. Great Britain's victory over France and its new territorial acquisitions had come at great financial cost, and the government in London became determined to force the American colonies to help share the cost of the war and of administrating the empire. They sought to do this by enforcing tax and trade regulations, which the colonials had openly flouted during the period of salutary neglect, and by imposing new taxes. One of these new measures was named after a precious food commodity. The Sugar Act of 1764 reduced an earlier tax on molasses imported into the colonies from the French West Indies, but the measure infuriated many Americans because it included strong measures to prevent smuggling. The previous tax on molasses had not troubled colonial merchants, who had consistently managed to avoid paying it. This new measure, however, had the potential to increase the price of molasses, which was a vital ingredient for American rum manufacturers. Molasses was, John Adams argued, "an essential ingredient in American independence."

The 1765 Stamp Act sought not only to regulate trade but to levy a direct tax on materials printed in the colonies. This mandate enraged many Americans, who argued that Parliament had no right to impose taxes on the colonies that did not have a representative in the legislative body. As a response to the Stamp Act, the mainland colonies agreed to boycott British goods, signaling a modification to their tendency to seek cultural affinity with the British by the mass importation of items from the motherland. From this point on, to be an American patriot meant to eschew British goods, to wear simple homespun fabric rather than the latest London fashions, to abandon foreign luxuries in favor of items made in the colonies, and to find other ways to distinguish oneself from the British. Although many merchants found it economically disastrous to stop importing British goods, widespread pressure to thwart British attempts to regulate trade and to collect taxes grew year by year. Customs officials, merchants, and royal appointees became increasingly vulnerable to violence and intimidation from angry American colonials. Those considered disloyal to the antitaxation, anti-British cause might find themselves subject to mob justice by being tarred and feathered and then publicly humiliated by being wheeled through the streets. The habit of boycotting British goods became so entrenched for some that the habits persisted even after the end of the Revolutionary War. In 1789 George Washington declared his decision to only buy beer or cheese that had been produced in America, claiming, "We have already been too long subject to British prejudices."

One of the most symbolically charged imported British items to become part of the battle over competing ideas about Parliamentary authority was, of course, tea. Parliament passed the Tea Act in 1773, which was designed to save the East India Company, one of Britain's largest businesses, from financial ruin. The measure allowed the company to sell tea directly to the colonies rather than through English merchant middlemen. The result of this measure would have been cheaper, legal tea for American colonials to drink. At this point, three-quarters of the tea drunk by Americans was smuggled and thus tax free. Under the Tea Act, the price of legal tea for the colonists would have been competitive with or even cheaper than the smuggled tea. However, the direct importation of legal tea would cut out the merchants who had formerly imported it and would threaten the lucrative business of tea smuggling. Furthermore, if the colonials accepted this taxed tea, they would be acknowledging Parliament's right to tax them without representation.

Local residents of Boston responded dramatically and memorably to this latest perceived British imposition on December 16, 1773, when a group of men, some wearing disguises to resemble Mohawk Indians, boarded ships carrying tea from the East India Company that were docked in the Boston Harbor. They threw over three hundred chests of tea into the Atlantic. The event that became known as the Boston Tea Party cost the company ten thousand pounds and inspired the British to take even more extreme measures to reassert their weakening control over the colonies.

The Boston Tea Party also proved to be a boon to coffee consumption in the United States. In England, coffee was drunk most frequently in public by men who congregated to socialize or to conduct business in coffeehouses. Following the trend of emulating English customs, Boston had two coffee-houses of its own by 1690. However, in both Great Britain and her American colonies, tea was widely served at home and was the hot beverage of choice in the first half of the eighteenth century. Although American tea consumption outpaced that of coffee during the colonial period, during the Revolution and its aftermath, coffee came to be considered a more patriotic beverage. By 1830, Americans drank six times as much coffee as tea. By 1860, coffee was consumed nine times more frequently. In a letter to his wife, Abigail, future American president John Adams recounted asking his landlady for a cup of tea in 1774 "provided it has been honestly smuggled, or paid no Duties." She patriotically served him coffee instead. Despite his obvious preference for the beverage, Adams agreed that "tea must be universally renounced." Although it is unknown to what extent his memories of the American Revolution influenced his palate, late in his life Thomas Jefferson, Adams's successor to the presidency, declared that coffee was "the favorite drink of the civilised world."

Although some Americans drank coffee to differentiate themselves from the British, most aspects of the American diet remained unaltered during the Revolution and its aftermath. James McWilliams intriguingly argues that although what Americans ate did not change in this era, in the early national period residents of the newly formed United States learned to think differently about their food. He argues, "America's culinary declaration of independence was an *intellectual* declaration of independence more than a revolution in specific culinary style." British colonial cuisine became republican food.

Due to Native American and African American influences, American cuisine was not identical to British cuisine even during the late colonial period when the American drive to imitate British manners was at its height. It should also be noted that British menus were not static and unchanging either, and eating habits in that country came to bear the imprint of culinary influences from throughout the empire. However, in the eighteenth century, standard American and British diets were still largely based on similar ideas and ingredients, which had their roots in medieval English cooking.

Many British recipes popular during the era were inscribed in Hannah Glasse's *Art of Cookery Made Plain and Easy*. Written in 1747, Glasse's cook-book was widely used on both sides of the Atlantic. It remained popular even after American independence. However, as a manifestation of changing times, an 1805 edition of the book, which was published after the author's death, contained a section on "Several New Receipts Adapted to the American Mode of Cooking." What made most of these dishes "American" was the use of ingredients indigenous to the Americas, such as cranberries or corn. The first published cookbook written by an American, Amelia Simmons's *American Cookery*, published in 1796, is derived largely from British cookbooks. She, too, shows the influence of her American environment by including recipes using ingredients such as blueberries and squash. Simmons also introduced her readers to the use of pearl ash, a chemical leavening agent extracted from wood ashes that was widely used in colonial households. Despite these unique elements, most of the dishes for which Simmons gives her readers preparation guidelines would have been equally recognizable in both London and Boston. However, it should be remembered that cookbooks are not always an accurate reflection of what people ate on a daily basis. They might instead represent the kind of meals that were cooked on special occasions or foods people aspired to eat.

When Americans during the Revolutionary era or early national period extolled the virtues of American cooking, they, like Simmons, sometimes trumpeted specific American ingredients or preparations. The significantly named Hominy Club of Annapolis, a late eighteenth-century gentleman's supper club, reverentially dined not only on hominy made from Indian corn but also on other traditional American ingredients "in imitation of our ancestors, whose memory we shall ever respect." At other times, American republican cuisine was described as being distinct and more virtuous than British food due to its simplicity rather than because of the usage of specific ingredients. Luxury and extravagance in eating and in all areas of life became associated with decadent British aristocrats. In contrast, patriotic Americans prided themselves, in the 1778 words of David Ramsey, on "frugality, industry, and simplicity of manners."

Restraint in eating and drinking was considered a virtue, an earmark of a good citizen. Some of these ideas were articulated before the Revolution in Benjamin Franklin's popular yearly publication *Poor Richard's Almanack*. Franklin, who notoriously did not always follow his own advice, claims, "Cheese and salt meat should be sparingly eat," and "Eat few suppers, and you'll need few medicines." He also warns against excessive drinking, writing, "Drink does not drown care, but waters it, and makes it grow faster." Some Americans took this advice to heart, and for many plain cooking, much like that which had been favored by the Puritans, came to symbolize American superiority over frivolous Europeans. Lydia Maria Child codified these beliefs memorably in her 1832 cookbook, *The American Frugal Housewife*, which she dedicated to "those who are not ashamed of economy."

Even as residents of the United States set out to differentiate their style of eating from the English and other Europeans, foreign visitors to the new nation also noted culinary differences between the two continents. What Americans regarded as simplicity in eating was seen as barbarous behavior by some observers. The American diet was even heavier on meat than the protein-heavy English diet that it was based on. A nineteenth-century English visitor to the United States remarked with a measure of disgust that "as a flesh-consuming people, the Americans have no equal in the world." He recalled feeling shocked as he watched an American eater consume seven or eight different kinds of animals in "half a dozen minutes." Other foreign visitors also commented upon the rapidity with which Americans ate their food. In 1841 an Englishman expressed dismay that while dining in the United States, "All manner of good things are set before you, but no time for reflection or selection is allowed—promptitude of decision is your only chance." A 1794 English tourist who may also have competed with hungry American eaters for his dinner more charitably remarked, "The Americans know the value of time too well to waste it at the table."

Frenchman Constantin-François Chasseboeuf, comte de Volney, who toured the country in 1804, concurred with the observations of the English sightseers about the haste with which his hosts ate, observing, "They swallow almost without chewing." Unlike the diner who complained that he did not have enough time to make a considered selection of "good things" on the table, the Frenchman was disgusted by the quality of food that he was served. He complained of "turnips and potatoes that swim in hog's lard, butter or fat." He was equally unimpressed with the pumpkin pie he encountered, describing the pie crust as "greasy paste, never sufficiently baked." In the estimation of French traveler Fréderic Auguste Bartholdi, who visited the country in 1871, things had not improved much in several decades. He described the food at a hotel in New York as consisting of an "enormous amount of badly cooked food." In Baltimore, too, he noted the large quantities of food being served, noting that "one eats all day—a great deal of green corn, with cabbage." Apparently Bartholdi's French traveling companion was less horrified by American eating habits than he was. However, Bartholdi felt certain that his position would change "when he returns to French cooking and French customs," which he was certain would appear vastly inferior in contrast. Thus, what some regarded as simple republican fare was viewed by others as a culinary disaster.

Given the legendary attention that French culture has placed on the development of the national culinary tradition, it is unsurprising that harsh criticisms of American food would come from visitors from that country. However, some Americans felt equally critical of French food. Many of these negative views had come by way of the young nation's British culinary inheritance. The eighteenth-century British had ambivalent attitudes about the cuisine of their French military rivals. The aristocracy frequently hired French chefs to cook for them, and many French ideas about food were widely adopted in the country. For example, the French perfected transforming a thin pottage into *soupe*, a dish that became popular among the gentry during this era. French chefs also taught the English how to concoct richly flavored sauces made of flour, lard or butter, and broth, which could be used to flavor meat and fish. French techniques of baking bread and pastry had also elevated the quality of baked goods available in England. However, despite their obvious debt to French cuisine, many English regarded certain aspects of French cooking with suspicion. They recoiled at the thought of French consumption of snails and frog legs, items the British did not regard as food. Many worried that an enthusiasm for French cooking represented a lack of patriotism. Hannah Glasse mourned "the blind folly of this age, that would rather be imposed on by a French booby, than give encouragement to a good English cook!"

Americans felt similarly ambivalent about French food. The French had, after all, been allies of the colonials during the Revolutionary War. However, rich, heavily sauced, multicoursed French menus seemed to many to be the antithesis of simple republican cuisine. Prejudice against French food was sometimes based on the fact that many Americans had no idea what it consisted of, their knowledge having been derived primarily from British jokes about what their rivals ate. Nathaniel Tracy, a wealthy resident of Cambridge, Massachusetts, ordered his servants to catch green frogs in the swamps surrounding the city in 1778. He then served the creatures in their entirety inside a soup to a group of amused and horrified French naval officers at a formal dinner. John Adams, who was fond of French food and wine, disdainfully blamed the British for teaching Americans to view French cookery with disgust. Thomas Jefferson, too, became enamored with French cooking after serving as an ambassador in the country between 1785 and 1789. However, his partiality for the cuisine did not escape the notice of fellow patriot Patrick Henry, who criticized him in 1775 of having "abjured his native victuals."

Jefferson, an aesthete and an intellectual who lived in a rarified strata of American society, can hardly be considered a representative eighteenth- or early nineteenth-century American eater. However, his food preferences represented the possibility of the broadening of the American palate. While he was in the White House, Jefferson became a trendsetter when he hired a French chef. Before long, French cooking became, as it had already become in Great Britain, the preferred food of the American elite. During the early national period, most Americans ate at home. Dining elsewhere, at a tavern or an inn, was an event primarily associated with travel. However, restaurants began appearing in cities in the United States in the late eighteenth century. The most famous of these new establishments served French-inspired cuisine, such as New York's famous Delmonico's Restaurant, which originally opened in 1827. Signaling a new openness to French food at least on the part of elite American eaters, the restaurant's eleven-page menu was written in French with English translations.

Jefferson's admiration for French food was undeniable. However, in spite of Patrick Henry's criticism, he did not entirely reject American food items in favor of French ones. While living in Paris, he planted corn in his garden. He also craved Virginia ham and even tried unsuccessfully to illegally import some to France. At home, Jefferson was an avid gardener, and his enslaved laborers grew a wide variety of fruits and vegetables at his Virginia estate. Jefferson romanticized the American agriculturalist, whom he saw as an embodiment of national virtue. Jefferson also took pride in serving locally produced foods and beverages to his guests. His slaves worked hard not only to grow fruits and vegetables but also to brew beer and to produce a unique Monticello version of the American specialty of hard apple cider.

When he returned home to the United States, Jefferson brought elegant French copper cookware with him, ensuring that he would have the best-equipped kitchen in Virginia if not in the United States. He also brought home food items such as cheese, anchovies, vinegar, pasta, olive oil, and an astonishing 680 bottles of wine. While serving as president, Jefferson, a wine connoisseur, spent an astonishing $10,955.90 on wine, a figure that food writer Dave DeWitt calculates would be roughly $175,000 today. The end result of Jefferson's love for products produced in Virginia as well as foods he discovered in France led him to adopt a style of menu at his Monticello home that Daniel Webster described as "half Virginian, half French."

In Jefferson's mind there was nothing unpatriotic about his love of good food and wine from France. He felt a political kinship to the French, who were in the verge of their own revolution as Jefferson was leaving Paris in 1789. He did, however, like many other patriots, feel free to express his disdain for certain aspects of British culture and cuisine. In a 1785 letter to Abigail Adams, he harshly speculates, "I fancy it must be the quantity of animal food eaten by the English which renders their character insusceptible of civilisation." While Jefferson rejected the "animal food" consumed by the English, he did not necessarily embrace every aspect of French haute cuisine, which entailed elaborately prepared and dramatically presented multicourse meals. Jack McLaughlin has argued that Jefferson brought French *cuisine bourgeoise*, French home cooking that emphasized simple ingredients that were expertly prepared, home with him. Thus the concept of French food that Jefferson embraced may not have been far removed from other ideas about simple republican foods.

French food Jefferson style was inevitably served with a peculiarly American twist because much of the food that Jefferson ate was grown or prepared by enslaved laborers. At Monticello, not only did slaves grow food items at Jefferson's behest, but he supplemented his larder by buying vegetables from his enslaved workers, which they had grown in their scant free time. While living in Paris, he even paid to have his slave, James Hemings, the brother of his enslaved mistress Sally, who also resided in Paris, trained in the art of French cooking. James studied first with Combeaux, a cook in the Jefferson household who also managed a restaurant in Paris, and later with the cook for a member of the royal family who taught him the art of making French pastry. After completing his training, he became chef de cuisine in Jefferson's diplomatic household, a position of tremendous responsibility, for which he was paid the prevailing wage.

Because slavery was not recognized in France, Jefferson's relationship to both Hemings siblings was complicated by the fact that they could seize their freedom and refuse to return to Virginia with him. Jefferson's negotiations with Sally were largely of a private nature, but he purportedly promised to free any children that would come out of their sexual union if she returned home with him. His arrangement with James was more clear-cut. If he would agree to return to Virginia with Jefferson and train another slave in French culinary techniques, Jefferson would offer James his freedom. Even though James had hired a French tutor to help improve his language skills and was likely planning to stay in France when Jefferson left, he ultimately accepted the offer, perhaps to avoid being permanently separated from his family.

Both men made good on their promises. James trained his younger brother Peter Hemings in the art of French cooking. After fulfilling his end of the bargain, he left to start a new life in Philadelphia, a city that was home to many free African American caterers. Far from his native home, Hemings struggled to adjust to the new realities of life as a free black man in a country steeped in racial hostility. He reportedly drank heavily and had difficulty establishing a fulfilling professional life despite his considerable skill as a chef. Tragically, he gave up on his new life altogether when he committed suicide, an event that Jefferson was shocked to learn about in 1801.

Like Jefferson, George Washington also benefited from the cooking skills of an enslaved African American cook. Hercules worked first at Washington's home at Mount Vernon and later in the kitchen of his presidential residence. Observers reported that Hercules ran both kitchens with considerable skill and efficiency. He was described by a contemporary as a "celebrated artiste." Despite his skill in the kitchen, for which he received recognition infrequently given to enslaved workers, he was not reconciled to a life of unpaid labor, regardless of how well known his master was. Culinary historian Jessica Harris speculates that Hercules may have had the privilege of selling leftover food from the kitchen and thus had money of his own. While living in Philadelphia and working as chef to the president, Hercules used his funds to escape from bondage. He disappeared, choosing the uncertainty of life as a free black man over a certain future of coerced labor. Washington, who valued his extraordinary culinary skills, was distraught and confused by Hercules's choice and went to great lengths and much expense to try to locate him.

The stories of James Hemings and Hercules Washington illustrate one of the key paradoxes of American history. Virginians like George Washington and Thomas Jefferson articulated ideas about American liberty in opposition to what they saw as British tyranny at the same time that slavery was being entrenched as the economic and social foundation of life in the American South. Much of the cuisine that was touted as virtuous republican fare was ironically prepared by enslaved laborers.

Embedded in America's founding foodways is a complicated history of colonization, conquest, and slavery. It is also the story of religious and political idealism and the outgrowth of early modern medical knowledge and theological concerns. America's founding foodways are the product of both human rigidity and remarkable creativity and ingenuity. From these foundations, food habits in the United States have continued to be reshaped in response to particular historical circumstances and evolving ideas of what it meant to be an American. As the nation struggled to find a distinct identity, American expansion across the continent was to have a further impact on the kinds of foods Americans ate and the meaning they assigned to their meals.

3

꘠

Foodways in an Era of Expansion and Immigration

During the colonial and early national periods, the traditional English diet was the predominant European food influence in what became the United States. However, it is important to remember that other European groups also helped shape what Americans ate, including the Dutch. In 1626 the Dutch, who financed Henry Hudson's 1609 exploration of the river that would later bear his name, created a settlement that they called New Amsterdam in what is now Manhattan. Like their English neighbors to the north, they had to struggle to adapt the cuisine of their homeland to their new environment. They, too, pragmatically cultivated and consumed a great deal of corn, eating a cornmeal mush that they called *sapean*. They also grew rye, which they made into bread that was a frequent accompaniment to simple pea or bean soups. However, like the English they saw wheat as a higher-status grain; thus their most prized baked goods and many of their most enduring culinary contributions to the United States involved wheat.

Wheat was so highly valued that during times of scarcity, residents of the New Netherlands were forbidden from trading it with Native Americans so that the precious staple could be reserved for European consumption. The grain was used to make not only bread but also a variety of baked goods, many of which were associated with holidays. For example, a spiced cake known as *speculaas* was served on St. Nicholas Day. The Dutch also prepared pancakes, which eventually became popular with Americans from a variety of backgrounds, and a deep-fried bread they called *olykoeks*, the predecessor of the contemporary doughnut. Dutch culinary contributions to American cuisine, however, were not limited to baked items. Another Dutch specialty that eventually became popular with eaters from different backgrounds was coleslaw. The Dutch origin of the contemporary dish is evidenced not only in the technique used to prepare it but also in its name, which is derived from the Dutch words *Kool* (cabbage) and *sla* (salad).

By the time the British claimed the colony for themselves as "New York" in 1664, the unique foodways of the region were already established. People of Dutch heritage tended to eat more shellfish than colonists of English descent and were particularly fond of clams and mussels, which were generally less esteemed in the foodways of the new colonial power. Although New Englanders eventually claimed the clam as a symbol of regional identity, in the early days of settlement clams were foods negatively associated with the poor and with times of food scarcity. Until the image of the clam was resuscitated in the early nineteenth century, it was a food some considered more fit for swine than for humans.

Dr. Alexander Hamilton, a Scottish physician who immigrated to Maryland in 1738, recalled encountering an unfamiliar dish during a visit to New York, which was served to him by his "landlady [who] spoke both Dutch and English." He recalled, "I dined upon what I never had eat in my life before, a dish of fried clams, of which shell fish there is abundance in these parts." Hamilton complained that the unfamiliar dish, which was served with rye bread and butter, "took such a deal of chewing that we were long at dinner." In this cross-cultural exchange, his host may have been equally uncertain about how to evaluate her guest's ideas about proper foods and proper behavior, particularly after he spilled the pot of clams while reaching for a mug of beer.

Similarly, German-speaking immigrants who began arriving in Pennsylvania in the early eighteenth century brought a set of recipes that differed from those of the predominant British food habits. Native English speakers corrupted the German word for their language, *Deutsch*, into "Dutch," soon referring to this group of settlers as the "Pennsylvania Dutch." This group also created a cabbage dish that eventually made inroads in the American diet. They preserved the cabbage that the Dutch enjoyed as coleslaw by transforming it into sauerkraut. First the cabbage was cut into thin slices using a specially designed mechanism for shredding cabbage by passing the vegetable back and forth over a sharp blade. The sliced vegetable was then put into a crock along with salt and allowed to ferment, a process that transformed the cabbage into a soft, sour-tasting dish containing lactic acid that could be kept for months without refrigeration.

Another notable contribution to the foodways of the United States was the invention of the dish of "scrapple," which combined the New World ingredient of corn with Old World techniques of preserving meat. Scrapple was an American adaptation of the central European dish *panhaas*, or "pan rabbit," which was prepared with rabbit and buckwheat flour. In Pennsylvania the dish was modified to contain pig offal and other scraps from butchering along with spices such as sage and cornmeal to create a pudding that was poured into molds, covered with lard to preserve it, and later prepared by baking or frying. Although sauerkraut became widely eaten by Americans from other ethnic backgrounds, scrapple has remained a regional specialty most frequently enjoyed in the areas where the Pennsylvania Dutch first settled.

The food traditions of Dutch and German Americans demonstrate yet another dimension of the recipes from the initial period of European settlement in what is now the United States. They indicate that from the very beginning, cuisine in the United States consisted of techniques drawn from a variety of cooking traditions. During these early days, the American diet had a unique regional character and varied from place to place according to which outsiders had settled there and in what proportions. However, all new arrivals to the continent had to adapt their cuisine to the ingredients available in their new environment. All adopted ideas about food preparation from people with different backgrounds, beginning with European and Native American culinary fusions. However reluctant some initial settlers were to make changes to their preferred diet, they adapted by necessity and set a precedent for a style of American eating that was ultimately able to embrace diversity and change.

American cooking, which was multicultural from the very first encounters between Europeans and Native Americans, became even more varied during the nineteenth century as the country expanded geographically across the continent and as millions more immigrants joined the descendants of the original colonists. In 1803, Thomas Jefferson gained control of the Mississippi River and nearly doubled the size of the young nation when he purchased territory from France. The Louisiana Purchase consisted of approximately 827,000 square miles and of proportionately equal new food possibilities due to the different flora and fauna of the area and, equally significantly, due to exposure to the culinary inventiveness of the people living in the territory. The territorial ambitions of the expanding country were further realized in 1848 when the Treaty of Guadalupe Hidalgo ended the Mexican-American War and ceded 500,000 miles of territory in the Southwest to the United States. American conquest not only enabled the nation's empire builders to realize their dream of acquiring territory that spanned the continent, it also resulted in the introduction of an entirely new set of food practices to the United States. The newly incorporated foodways were themselves the product of a complex history and the outgrowth of another imperial project, that of Spanish colonization in the Western Hemisphere.

This rapid territorial expansion was soon followed by an explosion of population growth as twenty-eight million immigrants, mostly from Europe but also from places such as the Caribbean and Latin America, came to the United States seeking new lives and better economic opportunities between 1860 and 1920. They brought along with them knowledge of elaborate food traditions that long predated the founding of the United States and that added still more diverse influences to the development of American food habits.

FOODWAYS AND THE LOUISIANA PURCHASE

The acquisition of Louisiana brought New Orleans, the center of a unique, sophisticated, and multicultural cuisine into the United States. In contrast to many of the European settlers in the original thirteen colonies, the inhabitants of this region did not have a culinary heritage of celebrating simple, unadorned, republican cuisine as a means of reinforcing a distinct political identity. Instead, many of the settlers of the area proudly used their elaborate cooking traditions as a way to demonstrate a unique regional character. In contrast to the admonitions to limit indulgences recorded by Benjamin Franklin in his *Poor Richard's Almanack*, many Louisiana Creole proverbs encourage consumption. Lafcadio Hearn, a Greek immigrant who lived in New Orleans for a decade in the late nineteenth century, published a book of Creole sayings, which he tellingly titled *Gombo Zhèbes* after a local stew made with a variety of greens. One proverb wisely and cheerfully proclaims, "When the sweet potato is cooked, it must be eaten." Another declares, "Lagniappe," which the editor defines as a small treat such as a candy or a cake given to customers along with a purchase at a retail store, "is lawful booty." In their classic book *Eating in America*, Waverly Root and Richard de Rochemont celebrate this joyous local food culture, humorously describing the Creole cooking in Louisiana as being "cheerfully unconscious of the very existence of Anglo-Saxon cooking."

Like other New World cuisines, cooking in Louisiana bore the imprint of many different influences, combining eighteenth-century French, Native American, African, Spanish, and German ingredients and styles of cooking with the cuisines of other groups such as Italian immigrants who arrived in Louisiana in large numbers in the late nineteenth century. Because Louisiana had been a French colony, locals drew heavily on French culinary techniques. This heritage led to a style of cooking different from that developed by their American neighbors to the east, who had traditionally eschewed French cuisine as too elaborate and adorned for a nation intent on casting off the taint of alleged European decadence. However, French cuisine as it was reinvented in Louisiana would not have been recognized in the home country. Food writer Bethany Ewald Bultman has observed that contemporary visitors who travel to New Orleans to sample the city's Creole food are eating the results of a complex and multicultural culinary history. She writes:

> In a pot of gumbo served today in a traditional New Orleans house, there is a French roux, African okra, Indian *filé*, Spanish peppers, Cajun sausage, and oysters supplied by a Yugoslav fisherman, all served over Chinese rice with an accompaniment of hot French bread made by one of the city's finest German bakers.

The French began exploring and claiming territory in North America in the sixteenth and seventeenth centuries. The city of New Orleans, which was later to become one of the culinary capitals of the continent, was founded in 1718. Its first settlers, like the Europeans who reached the continent before them, developed a cuisine of compromise. French people living in Louisiana soon discovered that their preferred staple grain of wheat would not grow in the local muggy climate. Initially, flour had to be imported from abroad, and at times the colonists went for as long as two years without receiving a shipment of this precious commodity. As the colony of Louisiana became more well established, farmers in the sparsely populated French territory of Illinois Country, where the grain thrived, grew it to export to southern Louisiana. Short-term Louisiana resident Marc-Antoine Caillot reported that grain shipments from Illinois Country seldom lasted for more than six months. Therefore, most people could afford to eat wheat bread for only part of the year, and the first explorers and colonists had to learn to survive eating relatively little of this once-staple element in their diet. Like Europeans elsewhere in North America, they became dependent on Native American knowledge about the local environment as they sought to develop a food supply.

Initial settlers learned to eat corn rather than wheat, and the earliest accounts of culinary encounters between the French and local Native Americans record the European discovery of a dish that became known to the French as *sagamité*. The recipe primarily consisted of ground corn made into a stew. In addition to maize, the dish could also contain animal fats (particularly bear fat), beans, wild rice, and vegetables. Naval captain Jean-Baptiste Le Moyne de Bienville reported as early as 1706 that male settlers in Louisiana were learning to eat it, but he claimed that the female colonists were more squeamish about corn consumption, claiming "the women who are for the most part from Paris eat it reluctantly." Although some French settlers were hesitant to eat any more of this unfamiliar food than was necessary to ensure their survival, many seemed to learn to appreciate the grain. The historian and naturalist Antoine-Simone Le Page du Pratz, who lived in Louisiana between 1718 and 1734, grew fond of *sagamité*, and he generously proclaimed that to his "taste [it] surpassed the best dish in France."

Historian Shannon Lee Dawdy has argued that the French colonists were generally more open-minded about embracing Native American food practices than the English, who were more notorious for their culinary xenophobia. One French military officer reported that while interacting with Native Americans whose favor he hoped to gain, he ate dog, "not through preference, but in order to not offend my host." Other colonial French eaters embraced Native American foods for less pragmatic reasons as well. Some, like Marie Madeleine Hachard, who reported, "We accustom ourselves readily to the wild foods of this land," seemed to enjoy the culinary adventure of savoring the new tastes of unfamiliar foods such as raccoons, persimmons, and crawfish. Others even suspected that "wild" native foods might actually be healthier than domesticated French agricultural products. However, Dawdy argues that French culinary adventurism had its limitations. French eaters embraced these foreign foods most readily if they were prepared using French culinary techniques. Bear or beaver tail was best enjoyed if served with a comforting French sauce or transformed into a familiar pâté. The method of preparation could transform a "savage" food into a "civilized" one in the imagination of these colonial eaters. However, an open-mindedness about local foods never displaced a desire for familiar ones, and settlers continued to buy as many imported foods and wines as they could afford.

Residents of Louisiana who lived outside of the port city of New Orleans had even less access to preferred European foods, most significantly wheat, than those who resided in the city due to the expense of transporting it over land rather than via water. The Acadians, a group with a common French ancestry who lived in Canada until the British expelled them in 1755, began settling in Louisiana, primarily in the area west and north of New Orleans, beginning in 1764. Like the French settlers who preceded them, they too learned to eat *sagamité* in the absence of wheat. In fact, they adopted corn into their cuisine so readily that it remained the backbone of the Acadian diet until the late nineteenth and early twentieth centuries. It was often served three times a day. For breakfast it appeared as a variation of *sagamité*, a fried cornmeal mush known as *couche couche*. It was served as bread for the other meals. These and the other food traditions of the Acadian settlers in Louisiana were eventually named for the English corruption of the settlers' place of origin, the colony of New France known as "Acadia," becoming known as "Cajun."

Because rice has been a ubiquitous accompaniment to Cajun food for more than a century, the early dependence of Cajuns on Native American maize is sometimes forgotten. Rice was cultivated in Louisiana beginning in 1716, and soon enslaved Africans grew rice in abundance along the Mississippi River, making it a staple in the diet of Creoles in the region. However, Cajuns who did not live near the river initially experimented only halfheartedly with rice cultivation, occasionally scattering seeds in low-lying areas as an agricultural insurance policy in case the corn crop failed to thrive. In the late nineteenth century immigrants in the region from Germany or the Midwestern United States began experimenting with complicated irrigation systems and better tools for harvesting and milling rice. This development encouraged Cajun farmers to cultivate the crop, too. Very little rice was harvested as late as the era of the American Civil War, but by the turn of the twentieth century, 2.8 million bags were being produced annually. Production nearly doubled again by 1910, making local rice a food item that was vital to the cuisine throughout what was by then the state of Louisiana. Corn never disappeared from Cajun tables and is, in fact, a key ingredient in the iconic stewed corn dish known as *maque choux*, but it was eventually superseded in significance by rice.

Native Americans contributed another equally enduring ingredient to the hybrid cuisine of the region when the Choctaw people introduced the Europeans to ground young sassafras leaves, a product that became known as *filé*. The substance imparts an earthy flavor to the dishes it is added to and came to be used as a thickening agent in the unique New Orleans dish of gumbo. The first printed references to "gumbo" do not appear until the early nineteenth century, but the antecedents of the classic stew go back much earlier. The dish is inherently adaptable and reflects the varying availability of ingredients and the particular culinary heritage of the person assembling the treat. Regardless of the specific combination of ingredients in the stew, today it is always served over rice.

The Picayune Creole Cook Book from 1901 gives these directions for making "Gumbo *Filé*":

1 Large Tender Chicken.
2 Large Slices or ½ Pound Lean Ham.
2 Tablespoonfuls of Butter or 1 of Lard.
1 Bay Leaf. 3 Sprigs of Parsley.
3 Dozen Oysters.
1 Sprig of Thyme.
1 Large Onion.
2 Quarts of Oyster Water.
2 Quarts of Boiling Water.
1 Half Pd of Red Pepper, Without the Seeds.
Salt and Pepper and Cayenne to Taste.

Clean and cut up the chicken as for a fricassée. Dredge with salt and black pepper, judging according to taste. Cut the ham into dice shapes and chop the onion, parsley, and thyme very fine. Put the lard or butter into the soup kettle or deep stewing pot, and when hot, put in the ham and chicken. Cover closely and fry for about five or ten minutes. Then add the onion and parsley and thyme, stirring occasionally to prevent burning. When nicely browned add the boiling water and throw in the oyster stock, which has been thoroughly heated. Add the bay leaf chopped very fine, and the pepper pod, cut in two, and set the gumbo back to simmer about an hour longer. When nearly ready to serve dinner, and while the gumbo is boiling, add the fresh oysters. Let the gumbo remain on the stove for about three minutes longer, and then remove the pot from the fire. Have ready the tureens, set in a "bain-marie" or hot-water bath, for once the Filé is added, the gumbo must never be warmed over. Take two tablespoons full of the Filé and drop gradually into the pot of boiling hot gumbo, stirring to mix thoroughly; pour into the tureen, or tureens, if there should be a second demand, and serve with rice. (See recipe.) The rice, it should be remarked, must be boiled so that the grains stand quite apart, and brought to the table in a separate dish, covered. Serve about two spoonfuls of rice to one plate of gumbo.

The above recipe is for a family of six. Increased quantities in proportion as required. Never boil the gumbo with the rice, and never add the Filé while the gumbo is on the fire, as boiling after the Filé is added tends to make the gumbo stringy and unfit for use, else the Filé is precipitated to the bottom of the pot, which is equally to be avoided.

Where families cannot afford a fowl, a good gumbo may be made by substituting the round of the beef for the chicken.

Filé is primarily valued because it acts like a thickening agent and transforms a watery soup into a thicker stew. It may have been popular initially in part because *roux beurre*, a thickener common in French cooking, was made with flour and butter. Because wheat was so scarce in colonial Louisiana, dishes involving *roux* were reserved for special occasions. Some cooks may have viewed *filé* as a partial substitute for the traditional French technique of using flour to add substance to a dish. While Native Americans introduced *filé* to the gumbo pot, enslaved Africans, who were imported into the colony in significant numbers beginning at around the same time that the city of New Orleans was established, introduced another vital element to some versions of the dish in the form of okra, a vegetable of African origin, which can also be used to thicken the stew. The identification of okra with this particular meal was in fact so strong that the name "gumbo" is derived from a Bantu word for okra, *kingombo*.

Not only do the three primary thickening agents associated with gumbo, *roux*, *filé*, and okra, have clear antecedents in the culinary traditions of three separate groups, but other aspects of the soup point to still more culinary influences reflected in varying degrees throughout the region. The food of New Orleans is known as "Creole" cuisine from the term initially used to describe Louisianans who had been born in the colony and settled primarily along the Mississippi River rather than those who had been born in Europe or in Africa. Although their food habits shared a great deal in common with the Acadian traditions, these two groups had different historical experiences, which are partially reflected in some aspects of their cuisine.

Cajun cooks traditionally lacked the same kind of access to fresh ingredients enjoyed by their more urban neighbors. In an era when transporting ingredients by land was slow and expensive, Creoles who lived near the port of New Orleans had access to cheaper foods that had been shipped by water. Cajuns were thus more dependent on developing methods of food preservation.

For example, they famously developed techniques to preserve hot peppers with vinegar. A distinctive Louisiana hot sauce was being produced by the mid-nineteenth century. Cajun cooks tended to take greater advantage of local spicy ingredients than were used in the more subtle Creole food. Hard-scrabble early Cajun settlers had to make do with a variety of ingredients scavenged from the local environment. Food writer Bethany Ewald Bultman speculates that "the flavors of foods, from old raccoon meat to 'mudbugs' (crawfish), were greatly enhanced by the addition of a little salt and a dose of red pepper."

Contemporary Louisiana chefs and food writers caution against conflating the cuisines developed by two distinct groups of French settlers in conjunction with various other ethnic influences despite their similarities. Cajun gumbo and other foods are often spicier than Creole variations. Some food critics have simplified this distinction by explaining that Cajun food is generally somewhat rustic home cooking while Creole is restaurant cuisine. The two styles have used somewhat different ingredients as well. For example, before the invention of refrigeration, the use of seafood was uncommon in inland Cajun parishes. Because of the expense of transporting the highly perishable shellfish needed to make seafood gumbo, most Cajun gumbos were originally made with chicken, duck, squirrel, or rabbit seasoned with ham or sausage. In contrast, Creole cuisine has always featured shrimp and oysters in particular as staple ingredients.

The more cosmopolitan Creole cooking in New Orleans has always been far more likely to contain tomatoes than Cajun food. France lost control of Louisiana to Spain at the conclusion of the Seven Years' War in 1763, and the Spanish, too, made their imprint on the local cuisine. Their previous colonial adventures in the Americas had familiarized the Spaniards with peppers and tomatoes, foods that quickly made inroads into Spanish cuisine and were re-exported to Louisiana. The tomato is indigenous to Central America, but after discovering it there, the Spanish quickly brought the plant to the Caribbean and to Europe, where it was consumed in Spain and in Italy by the mid-sixteenth century. The English and the French, however, were less welcoming of the strange new plant, which many suspected to be poisonous. The fruit did not appear on dinner tables in those countries until at least the mid-eighteenth century in France and the late eighteenth century in England. Thus French colonists in Louisiana did not bring the tradition of eating tomatoes with them to the New World. The Spanish likely introduced the food item into the Creole melting pot, where it was embraced with enthusiasm.

A dish that is sometimes prepared differently by Cajun and Creole cooks, which, like gumbo, reflects the diversity of Louisiana's culinary heritage, is jambalaya. Lafcadio Hearn, who recorded recipes as well as proverbs, gives this basic recipe for jambalaya in his 1885 cookbook *La Cuisine Creole*:

JAMBALAYA OF FOWLS AND RICE

Cut up and stew a fowl; when half done, add a cup of rice, a slice of ham minced, and pepper and salt; let all cook together until the rice swells and absorbs all the gravy of the stewed chicken, but it must not be allowed to get hard or dry. Serve in a deep dish. Southern children are very fond of this; it is said to be an Indian dish, and very wholesome as well as palatable; it can be made of many things.

Curiously, Hearn, who was a fascinated student and chronicler of New Orleans culture in the late nineteenth century, claims that this classic dish was of "Indian" origin. Culinary scholars, however, disagree with this claim, arguing that jambalaya was most likely a local variation of the Spanish *paella*. Like jambalaya, which Hearn claims "can be made of many things," *paella* comes in a number of varieties. The most classic form of the dish originated in Valencia and generally contains snails, chicken, rabbit, saffron, paprika, tomatoes, lima beans, and green beans. In other variations, both jambalaya and *paella* are often made with shellfish.

Although Hearn was incorrect in his attributions of the dish's origins, his willingness to give credit for the dish to non-European cooks is typical among even the earliest chroniclers of Creole cuisine, who typically exhibit a keen understanding of the multicultural origins of their local food and even applaud the diverse influences in their collective kitchen. The name of the dish proudly reflects its origins, although there is some disagreement about exactly which influences it pays tribute to. "Jam" is a diminutive for the French word for ham, *jambon*, and *ya-ya* is derived from a West African word for rice. Others have suggested that the name of the dish is a combination of the words *jambon* and *paella* or a melding of *jambon* with the Choctaw word *falaya*, which means "long" and could refer to a meal designed to feed many people using only scraps of protein. Whichever etymology is true, its name acknowledges its hybrid nature.

Cajun cooks generally made a jambalaya similar to the one Hearn describes, the end result of which was brown-colored rice, which had absorbed juices from the slowly cooked meats. Although not acknowledged by Hearn in this recipe, Creole cooks sometimes added tomatoes to their jambalaya, reflecting not only a greater adherence to the Valencian dish but also perhaps an alternative source of culinary origination in the West African dish of *jollof* rice, which can contain a variety of meats added to a basic dish of rice, tomato, and red pepper. The 1901 *Picayune Creole Cook Book* records four recipes for jambalaya, three of which contain chili pepper. Two call for cayenne. These spicier versions of the dish may very well point to African as well as Spanish antecedents.

The pride that local residents had in their cuisine and the importance that their culture ascribed to eating well was exemplified in the development of a rich local restaurant scene. Until the nineteenth century, Americans ate the vast majority of their food at home, dining out at inns and taverns primarily only when traveling. In addition to feeding travelers, taverns also served local men who congregated there to socialize and who sometimes ate the simple food served at these establishments while drinking. Food at these venues was an afterthought, which could be nicely or indifferently prepared depending upon the availability of ingredients and the skill and interest of the cook. Because it was fed to captive and perhaps also intoxicated audiences, the food was often notoriously poor. While traveling through Rhode Island in 1704, Sarah Knight recalled being served a meal of cabbage, pork, and corn bread so unappealing that despite her hunger she only "gott down a little." She remembered that "what cabbage I swallowed serv'd me for a Cudd the whole day after."

Food that was designed either primarily to soak up liquor or to quickly feed hungry travelers was not conducive to the development of a sociable dining culture for more than a century after Knight's unappetizing supper in Rhode Island. While traveling in the United States in 1842, Charles Dickens was appalled both at the quality of much of the food he was fed and at the manners of his dining companions. To his taste, the ubiquitous corn bread was "almost as good for the digestion as a kneaded pin-cushion." He was equally unimpressed with the table manners of many of the Americans he met. While dining aboard a steamship traveling from Pittsburgh to Cincinnati, he complained, "Nobody says anything, at any meal, to anybody. All the passengers are very dismal, and seem to have tremendous secrets weighing on their minds. There is no conversation, no laughter, no cheerfulness, no sociality, except in spitting; and that is done in silent fellowship round the stove, when the meal is over." Dickens was briefer in his description but less disparaging of the dining scene he encountered in St. Louis, a city, like New Orleans, with French origins. He enjoyed staying at the Planter's House and with uncharacteristic generosity proclaimed, "It is an excellent house, and the proprietors have most bountiful notions of providing the creature comforts. Dining alone with my wife in our own room, one day, I counted fourteen dishes on the table at once."

Although Dickens did not visit New Orleans, a glowing description of the food options available in antebellum New Orleans appeared in Dickens's journal *All the Year Round* in 1874. When recalling the bounty available in New Orleans before the Civil War, the anonymous author described the ambiance in the French Market, where shoppers could purchase raw ingredients for cooking along with cups of strong coffee and accompanying snacks, as being marked by "a great clatter of coffee-cups, a cheery chumping, as of chopping meat, various cries and polyglot invitations to buy, an omnipresent hum and bustle. . . . It contrasts remarkably with what one might see at some of the minor markets of New York City, say Jefferson, with its horrid avenues of bleeding and greasy carcasses; its bawling butchers, its shouldering, pushing, and crowding purchasers; its noisome and rat haunted floors." Not only was the atmosphere among the shoppers purportedly different from elsewhere in the United States, but the quality and variety of food items for sale in the city was alleged as being superior as well:

> Groves of bananas of various colors, from green, through pale yellow, up to deep red and purple black, apples, oranges, limes, and lemons, grapes, cocoa-nuts resembling the eggs of monstrous unknown birds, with a great deal of hairy nest adhering to them, onions curiously bound on little sticks, yams, potatoes, cabbages, celery, carrots, spinach, and flowers environ us. . . . The display of shellfish is amazing. There are enormous oysters, many of which it would certainly be of necessity to cut up into four mouthfuls, before eating; tubs full of live crabs and lobsters, hold- ing onto each other with desperate tenacity; and shrimps alive and dead.

The writer interestingly contrasts New Orleans with New York, but de- spite his disparagement of the quality of New York markets, the city had a remarkably well-developed dining scene in comparison to many other parts of the country. In cities like New York, with large enough populations to sup- port such establishments, taverns were soon joined by more respectable, but still male-dominated, dining spaces. By the late eighteenth century, travelers in New York City could augment the meals provided by boarding houses with trips to the oyster bar, street vendors, and a variety of other casual eating es- tablishments. Patrons of fine hotels could eat in an increasingly large number of dining rooms, where French cuisine was dominant by the early decades of the nineteenth century.

History was made in New York when two Swiss immigrants opened up a coffee and pastry shop in 1827, which they named after themselves as Delmonico's. By 1830 it had morphed into a fine dining establishment. By 1837, the restaurant had an impressive eleven-page menu, all in French, and a clientele consisting of not only well-to-do travelers but also members of New York's elite, who were learning to view dining as entertainment and as something that could be done with elegance and style, rather than with mere expediency, outside of private homes. Even Dickens felt obliged to eat his previous words about the crudeness of American cuisine and table manners after dining at Delmonico's on a return visit to the United States in 1868, where he recalled being greeted by "unsurpassable politeness, delicacy, sweet temper, [and] hospitality."

Dining experiences of the caliber of Delmonico's, and indeed freestand- ing restaurants devoted to fine dining, were exceedingly rare in most of the United States even as Dickens gorged at Delmonico's. In contrast, New Orleans had a much longer and much better established dining culture than

Antoine's Restaurant, New Orleans. Antoine's has been serving French Creole cuisine continuously since 1840, a time when most American cities had not yet developed an extensive upscale dining culture. *Source*: Photo by Charles Bittner.

much of the rest of the nation. By the time it was annexed to the United States in 1803, the city had an established café culture, giving patrons not only a chance to fill their stomachs but also a chance to converse. The Café des Refugiés was established in 1791 and frequented by exiles who fled to New Orleans during the Haitian Revolution and who came to enjoy live entertainment, food, coffee, and alcoholic beverages. During that same era, cafés sprang up on surrounding streets in the French Quarter, giving residents places to congregate over carefully brewed coffee, often blended with chicory in adherence with a French custom for stretching coffee, along with other carefully prepared foods and drinks.

In addition to these casual gathering places, New Orleans developed a sophisticated restaurant scene in the first half of the twentieth century. Antoine's, which has operated continuously since its founding, began serving elaborate French Creole cuisine in its elegant dining rooms in 1840. Among its other culinary contributions, chefs at the restaurant invented the legendary dish *huitres en coquille à la Rockefeller*, otherwise known as oysters Rockefeller, in 1889. The recipe calls for oysters on the half shell to be lightly browned with a topping of a combination of greens and herbs and New Orleans's own anise-flavored liqueur known as Herbsaint. Since it was invented, other cooks in New Orleans and beyond have tried to replicate the dish, whose recipe is a carefully guarded secret. This and the culinary contributions from landmark restaurants such as Madame Begue's and Commander's Palace, which were also established in the nineteenth century, gave the city of New Orleans the reputation for being a dining destination at a time when the United States was known for mediocre restaurant food of the kind Dickens complained about. In the 1850s the visiting English novelist William Thackeray declared that New Orleans was "the old Franco-Spanish city on the banks of the Mississippi, where, of all the cities in the world, you can eat the most and suffer the least."

THE FOOD OF WESTERN EXPANSION

The American migrants who began creeping westward across the continent to stake claims to some of the lands the nation had acquired by purchase and conquest encountered other foods as unfamiliar to them as Louisiana cuisine, but they typically did not discover it in settings as cosmopolitan as New Orleans with its well-established café scene. Settlers who wished to make the arduous overland journey from the eastern United States to the West Coast needed to think carefully about how they would feed themselves on a journey that might last more than six months. By the 1840s a number of guides were available that gave emigrants suggestions about how much food they needed to carry with them. One guide recommended carrying 200 pounds of flour,

150 pounds of bacon, and smaller quantities of staples such as sugar, salt, and coffee. These were to be augmented by items such as dried meat, dried beans, lard, and dried fruit. Because the length of the journey was unpredictable and their chances for purchasing new supplies were few and far between, migrants had to conserve their resources and demonstrate ingenuity in replenishing their supplies. Before the 1840s and 1850s when trading posts became well established on the most commonly traveled routes, settlers found few opportunities to purchase supplies. However, even where shops selling supplies existed, food prices were high and beyond the means of many travelers, who needed to stretch scarce resources to finance the journey and to begin their new lives upon their arrival.

Travelers often made up for shortfalls in their original store by trading with Native Americans or by scavenging for food using information that they gained from the indigenous inhabitants they met along the route. Since European contact, travelers in the American West were reliant on Native Americans for information about how to transform foods indigenous to the area into palatable recipes. The Blackfeet, for example, were adept at utilizing nearly every scrap of bison flesh in their cuisine, even transforming the blood into sausages, which they seasoned with berries and other local ingredients. They also made the otherwise hard-to-digest fat into a tasty delicacy by slowly smoking it and converting it into a delicacy known as "dupuyer," a food that European traders in the region coveted. Reginald Horsman observes that "a great deal has been written about the dangers that Indian resistance presented to American settlers; far less has been said about the extent to which Indian knowledge of American natural resources and their willingness to share this knowledge and food with settlers contributed to the European settlement of the continent." Migrants learned to forage for wild greens as they traveled, to fish when they came upon water, and to hunt for buffalo and antelope to bolster their food supply.

Because many European American migrants were farmers who ate only domesticated animals, some had difficulty learning how to hunt. This group was particularly dependent on the willingness of Native Americans to trade with them, and indeed trading between Native Americans and European Americans was exceedingly common. In 1853, emigrant Celinda Hines wrote nonchalantly in her diary about such a transaction, which to her was a commonplace part of the journey, recording: "A great many Indians came to camp with fish which they wished to exchange for clothing. We bought a number." Similarly, emigrant Francis Sawyer recalled trading "a string of beads to an Indian boy for some fish."

In the Southwest, Americans who traveled there both before and after the region was annexed to the United States expressed interest and amazement at the Mexican food they discovered, which significantly differed from both English-dominated eating practices in the eastern part of the United States and the French-inspired cooking in Louisiana. The foodways of that region were the product of a cultural fusion of Spanish and Native American cooking techniques.

When the Spanish began their campaign to conquer Mesoamerica in 1519, the Aztec food that they encountered was remarkably different from what they were accustomed to eating in Spain. The Aztecs had developed a sophisticated cooking style and had cultivated dozens of varieties of the chili pepper, which is still strongly associated with cuisine in much of Mexico and the southwestern United States today, including well-known varieties such as the serrano and poblano. Talented cooks were already making items such as tamales and salsa, variations of which have been eaten ever since.

Maize was the staple of the Aztecs' diet, and they made the grain more nutritious through nixtamalization, a process whereby the grain is soaked and cooked in a solution of lime. This procedure makes the maize easier to grind; it also makes the corn more nutritious because the process converts the niacin in the corn into a form that the body can more easily absorb. Combined with beans, corn that has been prepared this way constitutes a complete protein, which means that the combination contains proper proportions of all of the amino acids essential to human health.

The corn, beans, and chilies that were mainstays in the Mesoamerican diet were supplemented with ingredients such as squash, tomatoes, chocolate, and fruit. The people indigenous to the region did not domesticate animals besides turkeys and small dogs. As a consequence, their nutritious and flavorful diet was largely a vegetarian one. They did occasionally supplement the protein from beans with animal protein from turkey, deer, rabbits, seafood, and insects, but meat was not the backbone of their diet as it was for many Europeans. The far more carnivorous Spanish were appalled by the paltry use of animal flesh that characterized Mesoamerican cooking, and upon arrival they immediately introduced cattle, sheep, and pigs into the region. The ready availability of domesticated animals had a transformational impact on the cuisine, which became far more meat intensive. Soon *masa*, the dough used to make tamales and tortillas, was being combined with lard to give it a richer flavor and a creamier texture.

The Aztec cooking that formed the soul of what would develop into Mexican cuisine diffused to the regions north and south and morphed into several distinct regional cooking styles. Areas near the coast adopted more seafood-intensive diets than inland areas. Building upon the basic maize and beans template, particular subregions developed their own unique flavor combinations and utilized particular local ingredients like acorns or the prickly pear. Zalkier Janer argues that cuisine in what is now the southwestern United States was influenced even more by the Spanish than Mexican food in regions outside the area of the United States and Mexico borderlands. Janer describes food in this region as being "mild, hearty, and relatively simple." In contrast to other regions, beef and wheat became common ingredients in that area's style of cooking.

Beef from cattle introduced to the area by the Spanish is still utilized in many recipes that originated in this area. Because the arid landscape proved to be less suitable for cultivating a wide variety of crops, fewer herbs, fruits, and vegetables grow in the region than in areas farther south. As a result the cuisine that developed is less varied and has a simpler flavor profile than that of places with a more favorable agricultural climate. The strong Spanish influence in this area is still manifested by the fact that wheat tortillas have been consumed more widely in the Southwest than elsewhere where the ancient and labor-intensive practice of processing and grinding corn remained predominant for far longer.

The Spanish were initially uncomfortable—like new European arrivals throughout the hemisphere—about the idea of substituting corn for their preferred grain of wheat. Conquistador Bernal Díaz del Castillo bemoaned the "misery of maize cakes." Like the English in Massachusetts or the French in Louisiana, the Spanish found cultivating wheat in a climate not suited for it to be difficult. However, instead of abandoning wheat altogether, the scarcity of the substance only increased its desirability in the minds of transplanted European eaters. One Spanish missionary urged the indigenous people to imitate Spanish eating habits, telling them to eat "that which the Castilian people eat, because it is good food . . . they are strong and pure and wise. . . . You will become the same way if you eat their food." In an interesting modification of the idea later adopted by the Pilgrims and the Puritans who had initially resisted eating corn in New England because they thought that the "Indian," as they labeled the grain, would make them savage, the Spanish urged Native Americans to eat wheat in order to become more European and thus more civilized.

Mexican cooks partially followed this advice and ultimately adopted ingredients that the Spaniards brought with them like wheat, meat, chickpeas, onions, garlic, sugar, and bananas. However, they used these items to modify, but not replace, traditional foods like salsas, moles, tortillas, and tamales. Strictly speaking, they had not followed the advice of adopting a diet just like the Castilians'. Nonetheless, the acceptance of these foreign ingredients, even when they were adopted in a modified fashion, came about only gradually and often with a great deal of ambivalence if not hostility. For example, Donna R. Gabaccia claims that the southwestern Pueblo Indians "hated wheat, which symbolized conquest, and they burned the missions' wheat crops during their last major revolt in 1680 against Spanish domination."

In his study of the cooking styles of the ensuing generations of the offspring of Native American and Spanish parents, historian Jeffrey Pilcher examines the impact that the Spanish preference for wheat had on indigenous cooking styles that were centered on corn consumption, and he concludes that neither grain ultimately won the battle for the culinary soul of Mexico and the American Southwest. Instead he claims that the end result of these competing culinary visions was a "fusion of both; wheat and corn came to be seen as a complementary pair, each an authentic representation of a mestizo national cuisine." He argues, however, that this dualistic culinary identity was not solidified until the twentieth century, when Mexican elites finally abandoned their crusade to denigrate those who consumed corn. Interestingly, however, indigenous ideas about food preparation survived even when the core ingredient of corn was replaced with wheat, as this wheat was more often transformed into a tortilla than into European-style leavened bread.

The Anglo Americans who visited the Southwest in the mid-nineteenth century maintained similar ideas about the inherent inferiority of the mestizo cuisine that they encountered to those held centuries earlier by the Spanish conquistadores who first encountered Aztec cooking. Just as the Spanish encouraged Native Americans and their joint offspring to eat more meat and consume more wheat, Anglo American eaters in the Southwest in the decades after American conquest critiqued the foodways of the region as being unhealthful and less civilized. They, too, used foodways as a marker of race and class and as evidence that they were more civilized than the Mexicans who had been incorporated into the United States at the end of the Mexican-American War.

Anglo tastes were eventually reflected in modifications of traditional southwestern dishes, which were adapted to be less spicy for this new group of consumers. By the 1890s, restaurants in cities like San Antonio, Texas, were serving Anglos "combination plates" of rice, beans, and items like enchiladas and tacos, which had been originally designed to be served separately and in more subtle and sophisticated preparations. These dishes were now also made with prepared chili powder (consisting of chilies, pepper, cumin, and oregano) in the place of superior freshly ground spices. This made Anglo-oriented Mexican food, which became known as Tex-Mex, not only more palatable to different culinary sensibilities but also easier to prepare.

These Anglo eaters were left to reconcile the contradiction implicit in the reality that many grew to like this allegedly "uncivilized" food. Waverly Root and Richard de Rochemont note that after these initial culinary encounters, Anglo eaters discovered that "somehow *tamales* of cornmeal, chopped meat, and hot pepper, wrapped in a cornhusk and steamed, had more to offer than hoecake, johnny cake, or pone." For most, the acclimation to new food items came only gradually. Susan Margoffin traveled in the Southwest prior to American annexation. Initially, she was reluctant to eat a highly spiced mixture of meat and chili, which she was instructed to scoop up using a corn tortilla, and was instead relieved when she was able to secure a more familiar meal of fried chicken. However, she slowly grew to appreciate the food she encountered and even asked to be taught how to make her own tortillas. She also decided to document the new foods she ate in a recipe book because, she reasoned,

"All of their dishes are so fine 'twould be a shame not to let my friends have a taste of them too." The kinds of culinary compromises many made during the period after the U.S. conquest of the region may be represented by the cooking style of a widow of an American army surgeon who was killed in the Mexican-American War. She opened a boarding house in Albuquerque to support herself, and she boarded only Anglo men, not people of Mexican descent, but the food she fed them was distinctly cross-cultural. Potatoes and apple pie were served alongside homemade tortillas and Mexican-style beans.

Whatever initial misgivings some Anglos may have had about eating southwestern foods, they were able at best to modify but not to destroy this Spanish and Native American fusion cuisine. As historian Richard Horsman observes, "Ultimately the food of the Southwest was to have a greater impact on the entire United States than the foods of the Anglos had on the Mexican population of the Southwest." California resident Encarnación Pinedo wrote a Spanish-language cookbook in 1898 to try to preserve his culinary heritage even as the demographics of his native land were changing due to new Anglo arrivals. He may have articulated the antipathy many felt for the food habits of these invaders when he described their diet as "the most insipid and tasteless that one can imagine." Some countered European allegations that their cuisine was unhealthful or uncivilized with antithetical ferocity and clung to their food habits as a way to perform a shared collective identity. Brett Williams has argued that for Mexican Americans living in Texas, "to prepare their own foods when possible is to reaffirm the dignity of Tejano identity in an Anglo world which offers it little respect."

Territory could be conquered, but not culture. Ancient food habits had been modified in response to various cross-cultural contacts, but their core ideas had remained intact. Because Tex-Mex food became nationally prominent after it was highlighted at the 1893 Columbian Exhibition in Chicago and continued its ascendency until salsa became more popular than ketchup in 1991, one could argue for a partial culinary conquest of the rest of the United States by southwestern Mexican American traditions. However, this triumph of food culture is accompanied by the irony that the biggest profits from the industrialized Tex-Mex foods of the late twentieth century, such as jarred salsa, packaged tortilla chips, and fast-food items like those sold at Taco Bell, are going to Anglo entrepreneurs rather than to the descendants of those who created the cuisine.

IMMIGRATION AND THE EXPANSION
OF THE AMERICAN PALATE

Some aspects of the nineteenth-century clash and melding of already-established American styles of cooking and the customs of the newly incorporated

Southwest were replicated in culinary encounters between European immigrants and already-established Americans beginning in the late nineteenth century. Rapid industrialization in the United States in the late nineteenth century created an enormous demand for labor to staff the quickly expanding network of factories. Some of this newly needed industrial workforce was supplied by migrants from rural areas of the nation, but the need for workers was too insatiable to be met by a reshuffled domestic labor force alone. Millions of immigrants, most of them from Europe, flooded into the United States in large numbers beginning shortly after the end of the Civil War and ending when Congress passed harsh laws restricting immigration in 1921 and 1924. Because of the demand for labor, Americans were temporarily willing to let economic concerns override xenophobic fears and to provide some measure of welcome for these newcomers. Most who came did so, to one degree or another, because they were hungry or had reasonable fears about their ability to continue feeding themselves in their countries of origin.

Between 1880 and 1920 more than four million Italians immigrated to the United States. They came fleeing poverty brought on by overpopulation, high taxes, and a concentration of land ownership into few hands. Most of the Italian immigrants who came to the United States were peasants. Some owned and attempted to eke a living out of tiny plots of land, but most were *contadini* who worked as tenants on someone else's property. Even this disadvantaged group was better off than the day laborers, who held no claim to permanent employment. Due to the exploding population, food was scarce, and it was expensive. The average family spent the vast majority of its income, sometimes as much as 85 percent, on feeding itself.

Despite its tremendous cost, the food that the poor ate was monotonous and meager. Regionally specific staples such as wheat, corn, or rice provided the backbone of the diet. These core ingredients were supplemented by produce grown by those lucky enough to have space for a garden or by foraging by those fortunate enough to work for generous landowners who allowed them this privilege. Most consumed meat only two or three times a year on feast days. Most ate relatively little pasta, the most iconic of all Italian foods.

Historian Hasia Diner argues that although poor Italians lived in a country whose cuisine is now among the most celebrated in the world, many gained firsthand knowledge of the local culinary traditions only through tastes that landowners granted them during feast times, which were generally Christmas, Easter, and during the annual celebration of the local saint. Some acquired secondhand knowledge by working in the kitchens of the well-off or from jobs processing regional specialties like olive oil or cheese. They lived a life on the edge of survival. The average Italian immigrant who reached the United States in 1901 had a net worth of less than nine dollars. It was the promise of filling their bellies with food purchased with the relatively high wages offered by American jobs that propelled them to immigrate.

Although few planned to stay in the United States, many did. However, as many as 30 percent returned to their home country, and they did so with a less tolerant attitude toward the subsistence diet they had fled. They used savings from their American earnings to purchase foods like chocolate and coffee, which would have been perpetually out of reach had they stayed in Italy. They also brought home tales of American abundance that seemed fantastical to those who had never left. One of the things that most amazed them about life in the United States was the abundance and the affordability of food. Even immigrants who constituted the lowest end of the economic spectrum and who worked at the most dangerous and dirty jobs in the United States could afford to eat a diet that was unimaginably luxurious by working-class Italian standards.

Ironically, many Italian immigrants were able to first enjoy some of the specialties of the regions they had come from upon arriving in America. Many purchased imported olive oil and Italian cheeses and transformed pasta, which had been a special occasion food, into one that was consumed casually and with great regularity. Most importantly, Italians living in the United States purchased previously unimaginable quantities of meat, transforming that rarest of commodities from something that had been eaten only a handful of times a year into something that was consumed on almost a daily basis. Working-class Italians could aspire to enjoying multicourse meals that contained both pasta and meat even on a weeknight. Italian American families soon began to replicate the once rare Italian feast days on a weekly basis with elaborate Sunday family meals, which featured multiple meat courses, salads, pasta, and desserts. Jane Ziegelman observes that, "The American larder was so immense that it could literally feed the working class on a diet once reserved for Italian nobility."

In a peculiar way, the experience of immigration created a new Italian identity as sojourners and settlers from various parts of the peninsula encountered each other and discovered that their shared language and cultural similarities now seemed more significant than regional differences had back at home. Although Americans came to recognize that immigrants from places like Sicily were generally poorer than those from the northern regions of the country, they generally paid scant attention to regional distinctions beyond that broad outline. Italian Americans shared regional recipes with those from other parts of the country and often adopted these new culinary ideas into their diet. For example, immigrants from Naples shared the recipe for the regional specialty of pizza, a flatbread topped with tomato sauce and cheese, with their neighbors who collectively transformed it into one of the staples of Italian American food. They also adapted their cuisine to reflect the wider availability of ingredients. Most notably, they began using larger quantities of meat in their dishes. Although many traditional pasta sauces were vegetarian, meat sauces became wildly popular in the United States and a universally acknowledged marker of an accomplished cook. The Italian American invention of "spaghetti and meatballs" is the most iconic manifestation of the new culinary landscape, as it reflected the widespread availability of both pasta and meat, which were served together in a style unknown in Italy.

The mainstream American population were perfectly happy to allow these newcomers to perform undesirable jobs that the native born scorned, but such low-status occupations and generalized poverty often reinforced negative stereotypes about these culturally different foreigners. Many Americans regarded Italian immigrants, particularly those from the southern part of the country, as lazy, uneducated, and violent. In 1875, an opinion writer for the *New York Times* opined that it was "hopeless to think of civilizing them." Some of these prejudices were transferred from the people to their food. In the early twentieth century, social workers were infuriated when their poor clients refused to abandon traditional food and to adopt a blander, more mainstream diet. For many, food was transformed into a measure of assimilation and a marker of whether or not the eater was truly American. Social reformers were particularly appalled at the proportion of their income that poor Italian Americans spent on food and on the decision many made to import beloved Italian ingredients rather than purchasing cheaper American substitutes. Many were offended by the strong smells of garlic and other unfamiliar scents emitted from Italian kitchens. John F. Mariani has observed that to this day, kitchen slang keeps alive the association of Italians with pungent garlic, by labeling the seasoning "Italian perfume" or "Bronx vanilla."

In 1876 the *Cook* magazine printed a recipe for pasta and meat sauce that contained beef, veal, chicken, butter, celery, carrots, nutmeg, salt, pepper, tomatoes, parsley and other greens, and wine under the subject heading "An Overwhelming Recipe." Although the magazine printed the elaborate recipe in its entirety, it followed the directions with a chastisement of the creator of the dish, who was identified as "Signor Barottoni." The magazine deemed the recipe, which would have seemed commonplace to a proficient Italian home cook, as being "too difficult and costly for common use." The staff of the magazine was, the writer claimed, "too practical a people to blindly adopt, for our home often needlessly and injuriously elaborated merely to make a seeming mystery of the palatable preparation of food and to magnify the office of the imported *chef.*" Intriguingly, in the column below the one harshly criticizing the recipe that Signor Barottoni had generously allowed them to publish, the editors evaluated the morality of violating one of the most entrenched culinary taboos in the United States, that of eating dog, concluding half seriously, "Maybe it isn't either bad taste or immoral to eat dog." Even if written half in jest, it is interesting that the magazine found the idea of consuming canine preferable to indulging in the allegedly decadent dish of pasta and meat sauce.

In spite of the reservations of their newly adopted neighbors to their style of cooking, Italian Americans insistently continued to practice their traditional cooking habits and those that evolved by the process of regional Italian fusion in the United States. Although some schoolchildren were snickered at by classmates who did not appreciate their home-cooked meals, most Italian Americans became convinced at an early age that their way of eating was superior, and these customs became an important marker of identity. One Italian boy proclaimed his ambivalence about claiming an American identity for himself, disdainfully proclaiming, "Americans were people who ate peanut butter and jelly on mushy white bread." He understandably found a lunch of crusty bread, imported Italian cheese, and cured meats preferable. Italian immigrants showed remarkably little inclination to change their food habits and remained proud of their unique culinary identity. Using their American money to purchase once scarce and coveted ingredients had transformed them into fiercely proud Italian American eaters.

Italian Bread Peddlers, New York, circa 1900. Italian Americans clung tenaciously to many of the food habits of their country of origin and eventually helped make a meat- and pasta-intensive Italian American cuisine into one of the nation's most popular ethnic foods. *Source*: Library of Congress, Prints & Photographs Division, Detroit Publishing Company Collection, LC-DIG-ppmsca-4a09005.

In spite of, or perhaps even because of, the disdain that many Progressive Era reformers held for Italian styles of cooking, artists and writers in the late nineteenth century began venturing into Italian neighborhoods and happily sampling the cuisine. These initial timid culinary encounters expanded decade by decade until even less-daring eaters learned to crave Italian American restaurant food, which was then dominated by pasta and red sauce. Hoping to ease lingering anxieties about this still unfamiliar style of cooking, the owner of a Chicago restaurant offered patrons lessons on how to properly consume potentially messy spaghetti noodles in 1910.

The United States' entry into World War I finally made Americans more open-minded to the cuisine of their allies, and women's magazines in the 1920s contained numerous recipes for spaghetti, which underwent a transformation from something eaten only rarely in restaurants into a dish mainstream enough that home cooks were willing to prepare it. Not only did Italian American food find a permanent place in the homes of American cooks, but the Italian restaurant with its trademark red-checkered tablecloth and straw-encased bottles of Chianti wine became iconic markers of special restaurant meals. By the 1930s, there were ten thousand Italian restaurants in New York City alone. As was the case with Tex-Mex, the American appetite proved an able match to American food prejudices.

Another group whose food insecurity led them to the United States were Jewish immigrants from eastern Europe. They were drawn to the United States in part due to anti-Semitism in their native lands, particularly in Russia, where Jewish residents lived under the threat of being beaten or killed during periodic pogroms. As a despised minority, Jewish people faced many restrictions about where they could live and how they could earn a living. They were forbidden from owning land, so many worked selling or crafting various goods. However, due to overcrowding in the densely populated Jewish districts, many had difficulty eking out a sufficient livelihood. One immigrant remembered, "There were ten times as many stores as there should have been, ten times as many tailors, cobblers, barbers, tinsmiths." Thus, for many, economic concerns proved to be even more pressing than the problem of persistent persecution. Hasia Diner claims that "the search for work that would enable them to buy good food propelled [their] exodus" to the United States.

More than two million Jewish settlers immigrated to the United States between 1880 and 1924. When they arrived, they discovered a previously established community of Jewish immigrants from Germany, many of whom had become well assimilated. Although some early Jewish arrivals continued to practice *kashrut*, the Jewish dietary laws derived from the Torah, others had abandoned these rules prior to immigration or shortly after arriving in the United States. Among other things, *kashrut* forbade consuming blood, eating sea creatures that do not have fins and scales (such as shellfish) or animals that do not chew cud or have split hooves (such as hogs), and consuming dairy products and meat together.

Some immigrants who stopped abiding by kosher rules were influenced by the growth of Reform Judaism in the nineteenth century. This movement sought to liberalize Jewish religious practice in a variety of respects and no longer mandated adherence to dietary laws. Others failed to adhere to *kashrut* due to the difficulty of finding the proper foods. This was particularly true for immigrants who settled in areas with few other Jewish residents. Others abandoned these traditions as a means of furthering their process of assimilation and to cast off the taint of being a "greenhorn." One migrant remembered, "When they used to call me names like 'greenhorn,' I felt that I'd rather die than hear it again." Some sought to assert their new American identities by quickly adopting new styles of dress, learning English, celebrating new holidays like Christmas, and adapting their traditional diets to their new surroundings. "By adopting abundance," historian Ronald Takaki observed, "the immigrants were adopting America."

Like the German Jews who preceded them, the second and much larger wave of Jewish immigrants who arrived in the late nineteenth century also had to decide how to combine a Jewish and an American identity. Unlike many Italian immigrants who planned to return to their homeland after saving some money, Jewish immigrants from eastern Europe planned to stay. Therefore, these decisions would have lasting consequences for the succeeding generations of this transplanted community. All had arrived from areas where Jewish laws were widely observed and where food practices were considered sacred. They were not accustomed to consuming food thoughtlessly but always had to know the source of their food, the means by which it had been prepared, and whether or not it was lawful to eat under their strict dietary code. Not only were foods themselves considered holy or unholy, kosher or *treyf* (forbidden), but the vessels that cooked the food and the dishes from which the food was served also had to be kept ritualistically pure. Meat and dairy meals could not be cooked or consumed in the same receptacles. The holiday of Passover required its own set of dishes. Adhering to these restrictions was one way to symbolize a Jewish covenant with God and a shared communal identity.

While still living in Europe, the poor had the greatest difficulty in adhering to these laws. For example, animals with defects were not considered kosher and could not be consumed. For a poor family, to have a rabbi declare one of their few precious geese as *treyf* due to signs of illness or imperfection would have a much more significant impact than the same event would have had in the life of the better-off family, who could simply consume another animal. Furthermore, the necessity of owning cooking vessels and utensils in triplicate was also a financial hardship to the poorest in the community. Broken or contaminated dishes that had to be replaced could cause something of a financial crisis. The poor also suffered disproportionately from the *ko-robka*, the tax placed on kosher meat. Like many Italians, most poor eastern European Jews ate little meat. Many were dependent on the charity of their better-off neighbors, who were required to give to the poor in the community and were particularly likely to do so around traditional Jewish holidays. For those who longed for more abundance and greater self-sufficiency, immigration became an increasingly attractive option.

Upon arrival in the United States, Jewish immigrants had more food choices than ever before. Like migrants from other impoverished regions, they soon became more carnivorous, adding greater quantities of meat to their diets and sometimes conflating the ability to eat meat with the American dream. The majority of immigrants in this second wave of migration settled in New York City, particularly in the Lower East Side, which soon became the most crowded neighborhood on the planet. The vastness of the city and the proximity of residents to New Yorkers from other ethnic and religious backgrounds emboldened many to abandon or modify their adherence to *kashrut*. According to Hasia Diner, "*Kashrut* became one of the most divisive issues in the American Jewish world, turning Jews against each other, sundering families." Some abandoned all traditional restrictions, others adopted a modified set of standards and created separate rules for eating in and outside of the home, and others struggled to maintain their previous dietary traditions.

Particularly devout Jewish migrants made their desire for religiously acceptable dining options known both onboard the ships that brought them to the United States and immediately on their arrival. When the kosher food supplies that they brought with them from their countries of origin ran out, they had to face the problem of resupplying themselves in a world that was initially insensitive to or ignorant of their requirements. Kosher food options were generally meager or nonexistent at various stages of their journey. Responding to lobbying from the Hebrew Immigrant Aid Society, Ellis Island, the famous immigration intake center, finally established a kosher kitchen in 1911. From that point onward new arrivals would no longer have to face the dilemma earlier immigrants had faced of eating forbidden foods in the dining hall or starving. As soon as they were settled in the United States, those who were determined to maintain their traditions began establishing a system that would assure them of regular access to kosher foods. The significance that many transplanted Jews continued to attach to ancient dietary practices was manifested in the proliferation of shops that catered to orthodox eaters. In the early years of the twentieth century, there were more than ten thousand kosher butchers in the United States, most of them in New York.

For those who abandoned kosher laws or adhered to them partially, doing so could represent a wish to assimilate, culinary curiosity, or a desire for convenience. Jewish Americans living in New York City were influenced by the food habits of their neighbors. They carefully observed what Italian Americans ate and ventured into their shops and restaurants to sample their specialties. Jewish eaters were also among the first Americans not of Chinese descent to begin frequenting the Chinese eateries that began cropping up in urban areas in the nineteenth century. Eating Chinese food, particularly on the Christian holiday of Christmas, when most other restaurants were closed, soon became a tradition for many Jewish Americans. The trend soon became so pronounced that it inspired the establishment of kosher Chinese restaurants, which were frequented by strict adherers to *kashrut*. Others showed a greater dietary flexibility. Some Jewish Americans who kept kosher to some degree or another at home soon learned to make exceptions for Chinese food, embracing the concept of what Don Siegel, the author of *From Lokshen to Lo Mein: The Jewish Affair with Chinese Food*, refers to as "safe treyf." He explains that some Jewish eaters learned to rationalize eating shellfish or pork in Chinese restaurants believing "that if they couldn't identify the food as it's chopped up . . . as an ingredient in, say, eggrolls . . . then it was considered safe." Gaye Tuchman and Harry Gene Levine note that the alteration of forbidden ingredients in new forms had a very practical appeal to Jewish eaters who wanted to experiment with non-Kosher foods but whose bodies rebelled at their experiments. In Chinese food "forbidden substances were so disguised that dishes did not reflexively repulse and so undermine their ability to rebel."

Not only did Jewish Americans adopt food ideas from other ethnic groups, they also created a multiethnic Jewish American cuisine by adopting the traditions of Jewish people from a variety of different geographical locations. Jews from eastern Europe quickly became enthusiastic consumers of German delicatessen foods such as corned beef and salami, which were previously unfamiliar to them. Jane Ziegelman explains that delis became central gathering places in Jewish communities precisely because eastern European Jews had come from a "meat-scarce society." Its greater availability came to represent the "unlimited bounty of their adopted home." Deli meats became a cornerstone of a pan-Jewish American diet.

Foods like bagels and knishes also became icons of a new Jewish American culinary identity as migrants from geographically different areas taught their descendants to embrace these foods as markers of a distinct identity. Bagels, rolls made with wheat flour that are traditionally boiled and then baked, may have originated in Poland. Immigrant bagel bakers in the Lower East Side could carry their products, which are ring shaped and have a hole in the middle, on long sticks. The most typical accompaniment to these bagels soon became cream cheese and smoked fish. These breads, which have become a symbolically significant Jewish food, are associated primarily with New York, where they became far more popular than they had been in eastern Europe.

Yonah Shimmel Knish Bakery. This iconic Jewish food business began as a
pushcart in the late nineteenth century and has been selling knishes on East
Houston Street in New York City continuously since 1910. *Source*: Photo by
Charles Bittner.

Another important food in Jewish American cuisine is the knish, which originated in Ukraine as a way to utilize leftovers. Pastry would be wrapped around leftover food, which would be transformed into a portable snack after the pastry shell was solidified by frying or baking. When the food was transplanted to the United States, the most common variety was made with mashed potatoes and chicken fat. These cheap and filling snacks were soon sold from pushcarts and shops throughout the Lower East Side and were so ubiquitous that Houston Street surrounding the iconic knishery Yonah Schimmel, which has been operating for more than a hundred years, was once referred to as "knish alley."

Jewish eaters in regions outside the population center of New York also manifested a dual desire to use food to celebrate a unique Jewish American identity and as a means to assimilate. Jewish women were some of the most enthusiastic students to enroll in cooking classes in the early twentieth century. Cooking schools during the era were designed both to impart the latest scientific knowledge about nutrition and to encourage their students to literalize the metaphor of the American melting pot by learning how to cook broadly interpreted "American" dishes. Lizzie Black Hander created a fundraising cookbook using recipes given to her by both the Jewish and non-Jewish women who had enrolled in her Milwaukee cooking school or who lived in the surrounding area. The resulting *The Settlement Cookbook* first appeared in 1910 and proved to be so popular that it was reprinted several times in the following years. The contents of the book reveal a wide variety of culinary influences. Contributors provided instructions for making traditional Jewish foods alongside a variety of less ethnically identifiable dishes. It provides these instructions for making "Noodle Kugel," a traditional Jewish pudding often eaten on the Sabbath:

3 cups noodles, ½ inch wide, 4 eggs, salt and pepper
(¾ cup fat, chicken, goose, or butter)

Cook Noodles (page 118) in salted, boiling water, 10 minutes. Drain and add the fat and the eggs, well beaten. Place in a well greased pudding dish and bake in a hot oven until top of the Kugel is well browned. Serve hot with Raspberry Jelly.

Cooks who wished to expand their repertoire beyond Jewish specialties could also use *The Settlement Cookbook* to learn how to make "Spaghetti Italienne," a simple recipe of tomatoes, garlic, bay leaves, salt, pepper, olive oil, and parmesan cheese or the decidedly not kosher dish of "Oyster Stew," which consisted of oysters, milk, butter, and salt and pepper.

Jewish migrants to New York and other places in the United States may have escaped pogroms, but they were not able to find freedom from anti-Semitism, which increased proportionately with the Jewish population. Observing this phenomenon, Abraham Cahan remarked, "When there are only a few Jews, gentiles go slumming to inspect the novelty. When the Jews fill up the streetcars and parks, we are resented." Indeed the first and much smaller wave of German Jewish immigrants were more widely accepted than the larger migration that followed. *The Cook* magazine published a number of articles in the 1880s that expressed admiration and curiosity about Jewish food habits. The editors declared, "Jewish communities enjoy a remarkable immunity, comparatively speaking, from many of the direst scourges of people outside their pale," a development that they attribute to dietary practices, claiming this was because "by the Jews the most rigorous safety precautions are taken against the sale of infected meat." Other issues of the magazine supplied their readers with various recipes under the headline of "Jewish Cookery." The editors were far more complimentary of their descriptions of "How the Jews Fry Fish" or "Purim Fritters" than they had been when describing the "overwhelming" recipe for Italian meat sauce and pasta.

However, as the Jewish population increased, many white Americans began to view the food habits of their neighbors with a greater measure of suspicion. Domestic scientists in the early twentieth century believed that poor diets were responsible for many social ills, and they believed that most recent immigrants should abandon their traditional foodways in favor of generally blander diets informed by the latest scientific knowledge. The New York Association for Improving Conditions of the Poor advised against eating delicatessen foods popular in Jewish neighborhoods, such as salami and pickles, claiming that these items were bad for the digestive system. These ideas were so pervasive that many educated Jewish women adopted them and began to criticize the cuisine they had been raised on. Nutritionist S. Etta Saddow harshly judged the Jewish diet to be "over rich and poorly balanced" and urged her community to make significant changes.

Italian Americans and Jewish Americans were hardly the only immigrants from Europe who had to find ways to balance their desires to maintain their food traditions with pressure to assimilate in their new country or to leave their culinary imprint on the nation. German Americans taught other Americans how to appreciate lager-style beer and adapted sausage-making traditions to create the uniquely American frankfurter. Polish Americans preserved the tradition of making pierogi, dumplings filled with ingredients such as mashed potatoes, sauerkraut, and cheese. Immigrants from Asia brought entirely new culinary paradigms with them to the United States. Each cuisine was greeted by a mixture of xenophobia and curiosity. Over time, however, the trend has been toward cultural fusions more than exclusion. At no moment is this more true than in the twenty-first century, when diners can partake of dishes as varied and as chaotic in culinary terms as "sushi" made from beef, bulgogi hot dogs, or pizza bagels. Nowhere has culinary melding been more visible than in

New York City, the place where so many newcomers first touched American soil. Cara De Silva has argued that the cuisine that has emerged from culinary fusion is one that is necessarily in flux and that American food traditions are not fixed. She writes:

> [T]his current infusion of fusions, this diffusion of fusions, this effusion of fusions, and this confusion of fusions are as much a matter of fission, of blowing apart, as they are of bringing together. And soon enough, they, too, will change.

Indeed, change has been one of the most constant attributes of food habits in the United States. Although cross-cultural encounters were one of the primary forces shaping and transforming the American diet over time, the next chapter will demonstrate that technological advancements also played a prominent role in creating the various recipes that have filled the American stomach.

4

⚜

Technology and Taste

Modifications in American eating habits were brought about not only by geographic expansion across the continent but also due to technological innovations that accelerated decade by decade. The late nineteenth and early twentieth centuries were a period of rapid industrial growth in the young nation. This economic transformation was fueled by abundant natural resources, expanding markets created by westward expansion, and a growing labor force supplied by millions of immigrants. Until the decades following the Civil War, most Americans supplied their desire for manufactured goods with imports, with items produced at home, or with products created by skilled artisans who worked for small businesses. During the closing years of the decade, economic transformation took place at an astonishingly rapid pace. Factories employing dozens or even hundreds of workers soon replaced many small businesses. The United States soon surpassed all other industrialized nations in the pace of its growth and manufacturing output. By 1913, the country produced more manufactured goods than Germany, France, and the once indomitable Great Britain combined.

This economic revolution changed nearly every aspect of American life. It transformed the population of the United States into one that was more than 50 percent urban by 1920. Between 1870 and 1920, more than eleven million Americans moved from rural areas to cities to seek work in urban factories. Many of these migrants had been displaced by innovations in agriculture, which had made growing crops less labor intensive. Others were African Americans who fled the southern countryside for urban centers in the North looking both for more lucrative industrial jobs and for a less virulent form of racism than they had known in the South. These internal migrants were joined by more than twenty-five million overseas immigrants who arrived between 1860 and 1920, the vast majority settling in urban areas. The size of cities swelled during this time period. In 1860, nine American cities had populations of one hundred thousand or more. By 1900, the number of cities had increased to thirty-eight. By 1920, it had reached sixty-eight. By the turn of the twentieth century, the metropolises of New York and Chicago boasted populations of 3.4 and 2.7 million, respectively.

The new class of city dwellers who found homes in urban centers developed a much different relationship to their food than that of previous generations of Americans. Displaced from the farm, most went from being producers of the food they ate to mere consumers who purchased foods grown, harvested, and butchered by someone else. Due to the technological innovations of the time period, many who had once primarily eaten foods that were raised locally now had greater access to food items from around the nation and the world. Although spices, wines, oils, and other luxury items that were not highly perishable had been imported into the country since the colonial period, new, more rapid forms of transportation made possible by steamships and railroads meant that less hardy foodstuffs could now reach consumers before they spoiled.

Speed in transportation was soon combined with technological innovations in the field of refrigeration, which meant that eventually even highly perishable foods could be sent to markets far from the point of production. Improvements in food preservation led to the creation of canned goods, which were easy to transport and which could be preserved for long periods of time. Many Americans took pride in their nation's industrial prowess and delighted in eating the foods associated with the new era. One of the ways that the Second Industrial Revolution influenced the nation was that it gave Americans with the financial means to purchase whatever they wished to eat more influence over how they stocked their pantries and sought to please their palates than ever before.

ABUNDANT WHEAT

One of the first innovations in the American diet to come from industrialization was that at long last residents of the United States could fulfill the dream that had been inherited from the English and nourished by the colonists of having the means to eat large quantities of white bread made from wheat flour. In early America, techniques of milling flour were laborious. Although millstones were turned by water power, the rest of the process of grinding wheat was done by human hands. Millers had to roll the grain through a screen designed to remove its chaff, a hard material surrounding the grain; place it between millstones to grind; spread it out onto a large surface to dry;

and carefully separate fine white flour from the coarser bran and germ. Inventor Oliver Evans observed this arduous process and gave himself the challenge of designing something more efficient. In 1784 he began work on a new mill, designing an intricate system of belts, buckets, and elevators that transported the grain throughout the mill without any human intervention.

Evans's mill efficiently produced much cleaner and finer flour than that made with older methods. Because his process was more successful at removing the germ, which contained oil that fermented quickly, flour produced in one of his mills also had a longer shelf life than flour made with traditional methods. The resulting product was also lighter in color, allowing customers to produce coveted whiter breads. Although this new technology held obvious appeal to consumers, most mills served local communities of farmers and could not afford to make costly capital improvements to their small operations.

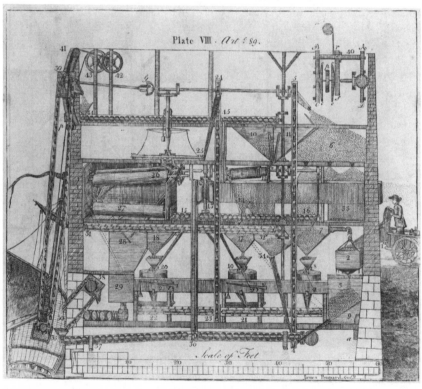

Automated Mill Designed by Oliver Evans, 1795. This invention made grinding wheat into flour easier and less expensive, making the coveted grain more accessible to American eaters. *Source: The Young Mill-wright & Miller's Guide* by Oliver Evans, Library of Congress, Prints & Photographs Division, LC-USZ62-110379.

The larger mills that began employing Evans's method quickly found that after the initial investment they were able to produce less expensive flour using his system. Soon smaller mills could no longer compete with larger operations. While Americans happily began consuming much cheaper wheat flour, many old-fashioned mills were driven out of business. The production of flour, which once happened at the neighborhood level, was soon controlled by fewer and fewer large processing facilities. The consolidation of American food production into fewer hands and the transformation of food processing from local communities to distant conglomerations soon became a trend that impacted almost every facet of the American food supply. The automated mill had such a large influence on American food history that food historian Andrew F. Smith has labeled its invention as a major "turning point."

The ability to grind wheat into flour more efficiently was accompanied by an increase of wheat production in the United States. Although early European settlers, particularly those who lived in New England, had difficulty growing wheat, as Americans of European descent began migrating westward they soon found conditions more suitable for the cultivation of the crop. Technological innovations in the first decades of the nineteenth century such as more efficient plows, the McCormick reaper, and the Pitts mechanical thresher enabled farmers to plant and harvest bigger plots of land more quickly. Farmers in New York State and in Pennsylvania successfully grew wheat and were quickly joined by producers in the upper Midwest and the Great Plains who grew enough of the grain to supply not only their region but to export to other parts of the country as well as abroad.

In the late nineteenth century, American millers began adopting the European technology of steam-powered iron and porcelain rollers. Flour produced using this new equipment contained even less bran and germ than that made in older facilities. Millers further exploited the consumer's desire for white flour by adding bleaching agents to the final product. Most nineteenth-century eaters did not yet know that most of the nutrients were stored in the darker portions of the grain, and they were delighted by the white, fluffy bread this highly processed flour produced.

These newly designed mills were even more efficient than the Evans model, and the price of wheat flour plummeted. Geographer Richard Pillsbury calculates that the relative cost of wheat flour in 1900 was less than 20 percent of its cost in 1800. As the price of wheat dropped, demand for the once rare and coveted grain grew. By 1900, Americans were consuming two hundred pounds of wheat per person per year and only fifty pounds of cornmeal, the most widely consumed grain during the early colonial period. Americans were able to satisfy their tenacious appetite for more wheat bread not only because of technological innovations in the field of milling flour but also because new modes of transportation enabled growers to more easily transport their goods to mills and to distant markets. The development of a network of roads, canals, and railroads led to lower freight rates and the greater availability of wheat and other food products in areas far distant from where they were produced.

INNOVATIONS IN TRANSPORTATION

During the first two decades of the nineteenth century, major innovations in transportation took the form of ambitious road-building campaigns. Municipalities, private investors, and states all began commissioning the building of toll roads known as "turnpikes," which dramatically improved both the quantity and the quality of roads in the United States. For example, Pennsylvania's first major toll road was completed in 1794, and by 1821 the state was crisscrossed by 1,800 miles of roads. In 1806 Congress authorized the first federally financed road project. The resulting National Road stretched from Cumberland, Maryland, to Wheeling in what is now West Virginia by 1818. The expanding network of reliable roadways greatly increased the speed of travel in some areas. In 1800 a stagecoach trip from Boston to New York took four days. By 1832, the travel time for the trip had been cut in half, as had the price for the journey.

Despite these improvements, overland travel was still slow and costly and thus impractical for transporting large quantities of foodstuffs such as coveted but bulky wheat. The dirt roads became rutted with use, making travel by coach jarring both for passengers and delicate goods. During inclement weather, firm road surfaces could be transformed quickly into rivers of mud that could not be traversed. So although new and improved roadways enhanced the possibilities for trading food items between different regions of the country, this development alone did not dramatically alter American eating habits.

Travel became even more efficient after Robert Fulton developed the first commercially successful steamboat. Fulton's *Clermont* demonstrated the potential of steam travel when it made the journey up the Hudson River from New York City to Albany in 1807. The vessel could move upstream against the current, a capability that dramatically speeded up travel times and enhanced the possibility of trade among port cities. As steamboat technology improved, travel times continually decreased. The time it took to travel from New Orleans to Louisville by river was reduced from three or four months to slightly more than a week by 1826.

Innovations in water travel resulted not only in more efficient movement upstream in rivers but also in the ability to travel more rapidly at sea. Newly developed faster sailing ships known as "clippers" or steamships traveling up the Atlantic coast could bring fruits and vegetables from Central America, the Caribbean, and ports in the southern United States to the northernmost part of the country more rapidly than ever before. One of the food items that made this journey with increasing frequency in the nineteenth century was the banana. Historian Joe Gray Taylor claims that southerners living in Charleston and New Orleans were able to enjoy imported tropical bananas before the Civil War. Due to the increased speed of travel, by the 1880s the once rare luxury item also became a common cargo in northern ports, including Boston, Philadelphia, and New York.

However, even after imported bananas became a common sight in Atlantic port cities, they were still less well known in the interior of the country until refrigerated railroad cars were available. Climate control was necessary in order to slow the fruit's rapid ripening process, enabling it to survive the inland journey without rotting. Thanks to further technological advancements in this area, by the turn of the twentieth century bananas were widely known throughout the country. Summarizing the fruit's rise in popularity, in 1916 *Current Opinion* magazine proclaimed, "Forty years ago it was a rarity; thirty years ago a luxury. . . . Today it is a food eaten by the humblest and the highest."

Although successful attempts were made to grow the fruit in Florida, homegrown bananas could not compete with fruits produced farther south in climates better suited for its cultivation. Thus, most bananas came from the Caribbean or Central America. However, their foreign origination did not stop Americans from rapidly adopting them into their diets or in inventing uniquely American uses for the fruit. Eventually the banana became primarily considered a raw snack food or as the basis for a variety of cooked desserts, but some cookbook authors, including the famed Fannie Merrit Farmer, initially experimented with more savory uses for the fruit. In the 1916 version of her *The Boston Cooking-School Cook Book*, she included the following recipe for "Banana Salad":

> Remove one section of skin from each of four bananas. Take out fruit, scrape, and cut fruit from one banana into thin slices, fruit from other three bananas into one-half inch cubes. Marinate cubes with French Dressing. Refill skins and garnish each with slices of banana. Stack around a mound of lettuce leaves.

The "French Dressing" that Farmer instructs home cooks to use to marinate the banana pieces is not the same as the sweet, orange dressing that consumers find bottled on supermarket shelves today. Instead she was referring to a simple vinaigrette of olive oil, vinegar, salt, and pepper. Although Farmer's recipe for stuffed bananas served alongside lettuce has disappeared from the collective American cookbook, other early uses for the fruit have proved to be more enduring.

Recipes from the southern United States claimed the banana as primarily a dessert item early on. Estelle Woods Wilcox's 1885 *The Dixie Cook-book* contains a recipe for "Banana Pie," which calls for combining the fruit with butter, vinegar, allspice, sugar, and cider and baking it between two crusts. In the ensuing decades, many regional cooks began preparing a dish that became known as "banana pudding," which has since come to be identified as a southern specialty. According to Stephen Criswell, this dessert has "delighted generations of southerners across racial, economic, and social lines." Mrs. F. A. Smith's recipe, which appeared in the 1921 *Atlanta Woman's Club Cook Book*, contains the same ingredients generally used to create the dish today: bananas, flour, milk, butter, eggs, vanilla, and packaged vanilla wafers.

Ironically, the cooks who created this recipe and who passed it down to future generations of southerners created a regional specialty using ingredients not native to the South. Technological innovations in the area of transportation gave American cooks more numerous opportunities to create new "American" and regional dishes from items imported from distant places. Americans living in the technological age of the Second Industrial Revolution generally did not share the reluctance of some of the first English settlers to try new and exotic food items. Bananas and other foods imported from far-off places were interpreted as a symbol of modernity and progress that patriotic eaters could label as distinctly American.

For members of the middle and upper classes who could afford luxury items, imported foods became a way to demonstrate sophistication and show off social status when hosting dinner parties. In the 1870s, hostess Elizabeth F. Ellet said, "In the dessert, I generally introduce some new importation such as bananas, sugar-cane, American Lady apples, prickly pears, etc.; these also give a subject for the gentlemen to talk about when the ladies have left, as freetrade, colonial policy, etc." Status-conscious diners would often serve imported food using specially designed table accessories such as the banana boat or would eat newly available items with special cutlery, such as specially designed orange spoons with pointed tips to help eaters neatly extract bits of fruit from the peel.

As the advent of steam travel began to help Americans develop larger trading networks, it also inspired a craze of canal building as investors began to grasp the commercial potential of water travel. In 1817, the country had less than a hundred miles of canals, but by 1840, the mileage had increased to an astonishing three thousand. Most of the barges that traveled down these canals were not powered by steam but by draft animals that traveled on well-worn paths on the bank and could transport much larger cargoes on water than by land. The most ambitious building project of the era was the 363-mile-long Erie Canal, which linked the Great Lakes and New York City by water. New York governor De Witt Clinton wanted the canal to serve "as a bond of union between the Atlantic and Western states." He emphatically believed that building a convenient and rapid transportation network between coastal and inland settlements would "prevent the dismemberment of the American Empire," which he thought had the potential to become disconnected as it grew geographically. He was certainly correct in his prediction that the Erie Canal would "create the greatest inland trade ever witnessed."

When Clinton first revealed his lofty scheme, the longest canal in the country spanned a mere thirty miles. Naysayers doubted that the project could be completed due to its enormous manpower requirements and the fact that the nation had a scarcity of trained engineers. When ground was broken on the project in 1817, detractors referred to the worksite derisively as "Clinton's Ditch." Ultimately, the project offered many aspiring engineers on-the-job training as they devised successful techniques for clearing the landscape and digging the forty-foot-wide and four-foot-deep trench. The project was completed in 1825 at a cost of seven million dollars, and the governor's vision became reality.

For the first time, farmers in western New York had the ability to market their wheat economically to other parts of the United States and overseas. The price of shipping a ton of wheat by wagon had been approximately one hundred dollars. The cost of transporting the same load by canal boat quickly plummeted to ten dollars a ton. By 1841 more than a million bushels of wheat were being transported from upstate New York to wider markets each year. The promise of being able to make a living growing or marketing wheat and servicing and provisioning the constant traffic of boats moving along the canal encouraged a wave of westward migration. Profit-minded entrepreneurs quickly realized that lighter flour was even less expensive to ship than the bulky unprocessed grain. Investors opened flour mills in places like Rochester, which quickly became a commercial center, connected as it was to New York City, which was now the busiest port in the United States. Affordable and abundant wheat soon became the backbone of the American diet.

Not only did the Erie Canal allow upstate New Yorkers to transport their wheat to eastern markets, but westerners also gained access to products that were imported from distant ports into New York City and to food items produced in coastal areas. In 1828, an editor in Rochester marveled over the ease with which goods were exchanged throughout the length of the canal, remarking, "The artificial river is thronged with vessels bearing to market the products of our highly favored country & returning to us the luxuries and comforts of other climes." Recent immigrants from the Eastern Seaboard were particularly delighted to receive shipments of fresh oysters, which provided them with a taste of the sea in their new inland homes. Historian Carol Sheriff remarks that the canal "reduced distance and time in ways that had previously seemed impossible." When a shipment of fresh oysters packed in ice reached Batavia, New York, in 1824, residents marveled at the technological innovation that had reduced the travel time for the precious food item from weeks to days, enabling them to enjoy the perishable delicacy so far from its point of origin. The upstate New Yorkers who relished this bounty had in a sense outsmarted nature as they indulged themselves on a food item not native to their environment. When the local newspaper proudly advertised, "Oysters! Beautiful Oysters," it was also marking a decline of strictly regional diets in the United States. Food from far-flung places became cheaper and easier to procure year by year.

The practice of eating locally was transformed further by the development of the railroad. The first railroad began operating in England the same year that the Erie Canal was completed, and Americans quickly embraced the technology as a way to transport people and goods across the expanding nation. Within fifteen years, there were more miles of railroad track than canals. Unlike the Erie Canal, the railroad tracks were not in danger of freezing and thus of travel delays during winter months. Travel by rail was also not dependent upon proximity to networks of rivers. Most importantly, rail travel was much faster, making it easier than ever before to transport perishable goods over vast inland distances. After the completion of the transcontinental railroad in 1869, it became possible to travel from coast to coast in days rather than months.

Soon railroads were being used to transport food items between different regions of the United States, leading to a transformation not only in eating locally but also in eating strictly seasonally. Fruits and vegetables grown in warmer regions of the country could be shipped to regions with cooler climates and a shorter growing season, enabling people to taste spring and summer produce ahead of their own growing cycles. Just as Americans learned about the pleasures of eating exotic foods when they began importing large numbers of bananas in the late nineteenth century, they soon learned how to overcome the limitations of seasonal eating as well. Shortly after the transcontinental railroad was completed, agricultural items such as tomatoes, pears, plums, and assorted vegetables were being transported from California to the East Coast. It was not long before area farmers recognized the lucrative potential of transcontinental trade networks, and new farms growing a wide variety of food items, including coveted citrus products, were created precisely to take advantage of the trade possibilities.

A CARNIVOROUS NATION

As thrilling as it must have been for northeasterners to enjoy a tomato months before local crops were due to be harvested, the food item that was the most dramatically impacted by rail travel was meat. Since colonial days, Americans had been known as a nation of enthusiastic carnivores. For many descendants of the original European colonists as well as new arrivals, success in the United

States came to be measured by how much meat you could afford to have on your table. By the late colonial period, Americans were consuming 150 pounds of meat per capita per year, a figure that remained relatively constant until the middle of the twentieth century.

Due to the limited ability to preserve fresh meat, most early European settlers ate it only rarely, right after the slaughter. Most of the meat that found its way onto colonial tables had been salted or smoked as a way to preserve it for long-term storage. Most of the salted or smoked meat eaten in the United States was pork, which was considered to be tastier than cured beef. Although corned beef or pastrami eventually became common fare at American deli counters, they did not become widely consumed until the nineteenth century. Traditionally, Americans favored eating fresh rather than preserved beef. As cities sprang up, residents of urban areas with fresh meat markets could eat this delicacy as frequently as they could afford to purchase it. Rural Americans could enjoy it only occasionally.

As the population of the country urbanized, more and more residents of the United States bought their meat at market rather than butchering it at home. Initially cattle were delivered to local slaughterhouses on the hoof. The development of railroads soon meant that animals could be transported vast distances before being slaughtered. In the two decades following the end of the Civil War, Texas cowboys drove large herds of cattle from points south to railheads in Kansas. From Kansas the animals were shipped via railcar to Chicago and to points farther east. By the 1880s railroad networks were extensive enough that it was no longer necessary to drive animals long distances on foot, and greater and greater numbers of Americans had access to desirable fresh beef.

Entrepreneurs soon set about finding ways to make the shipment and processing of meat more efficient. Beginning in the early nineteenth century, attempts were made to consolidate various local meat-processing facilities into larger operations. The river city of Cincinnati, which was linked to a network of canals, became an important center of pork packing beginning in the 1820s but was superseded by Chicago, the "hog butcher of the world," within a few decades as rail travel made canal networks obsolete. The pork products that were processed in Chicago and shipped throughout the nation were cured products of varieties similar to those eaten during the colonial era. Meat processors could not solve the problem of transporting butchered, fresh meat to distant markets until the invention of refrigerated railcars in the 1880s.

Because 45 percent of the weight of a cow could not be processed as meat, meat packers soon realized that shipping slaughtered animals would be far less expensive than transporting bulkier livestock. Because American consumers were not fond of salted, smoked, or pickled beef, packers needed to find another way to preserve the fresh meat, such as chilling it, a process that could, in the memorable words of Sue Shepard, render potentially harmful microorganisms "sluggish, unable to reproduce and less keen on their putrefy-ing activities." During the coldest winter months it was possible to safely ship processed beef between some destinations, but packers were frustrated by their inability to continue this practice throughout the entire year after tempera-tures began to increase. During the 1860s and 1870s experiments were made shipping both produce and meat in boxcars cooled with ice, but this solution was far from ideal. Ice acquired from lakes often contained bacteria that con-taminated food as it melted. Furthermore, because of melting, the ice had to be periodically replenished along the way. Even after ice-making machines were invented in the 1870s, these cumbersome devices were deemed too large to install inside railcars.

Despite these limitations, entrepreneur Gustavus Swift became convinced that shipping processed meat from a central destination to far-off markets could be profitable. When he could not convince any rail companies to invest in refrigerated railcars, he purchased his own and built his own re-icing facili-ties alongside frequently traveled rail routes. Through his determination and careful attention to detail, he soon proved that shipping meat from Chicago to eastern markets was possible all year round. His railcars used technology designed by Andrew J. Chase, who realized that blocks of ice and circulating air could keep food cool without direct contact. His Cold-Blast refrigerator, patented in 1881, was based on the principle that air that came into contact with ice would become heavier and flow to the bottom of his refrigerator be-fore gaining moisture and rising. As the air flowed, it cooled the items inside. The railcar that Chase designed for Swift took advantage of the natural pro-cess of circulation. Ice containers, which could be filled from the roof of the boxcar, were placed on each end, and air circulated between them, keeping the meat in the railcar cool.

Refrigeration technology became increasingly more effective decade by decade, but the necessary equipment and infrastructure remained expen-sive. Just as improvements in wheat milling were too costly for small millers to install, refrigeration equipment too was affordable only to major meat packers. By 1890, four companies packed 89 percent of the country's beef. Year by year, the American food supply was controlled by fewer and fewer corporations.

Local butchers tried to fight back against the ascendency of the central-ization of meat processing. They spread rumors that beef slaughtered in Chi-cago and shipped to eastern cities was covered with mold and inedible once it reached its final destination. They hoped in vain that consumers would prefer their truly fresh products and localized customer service over beef that was processed by unknown hands and carried over vast distances. However, local butchers were unable to compete with the large processors, who could take advantage of economies of scale and offer lower prices. The price of beef tenderloin processed by Swift and other large meatpackers decreased by 40 percent between 1883 and 1889. Americans enthusiastically chose eating cheaply and fulfilling the colonial dream of eating large quantities of fresh beef over eating locally.

THE ASCENDANCY OF INDUSTRIAL FOODS

While refrigeration technology was useful in transporting meat and other perishable items to distant markets in the nineteenth century, consumers who purchased foods like chilled beef had to consume it quickly because most lacked cold storage in their homes. However, other developments in food technology allowed buyers to purchase canned items, which remained edible for months or even years. Food preservation had traditionally been one of the American housewife's chief concerns. The initial colonists marveled at the fact that many of the Native American groups they encountered had reconciled themselves to periods of food scarcity and accepted seasonal hunger as part of the natural order of things. In contrast, European migrants were not prepared to accept periods of doing without and went to great lengths to stockpile enough food to fill their stomachs throughout the calendar year.

In addition to smoking or salting meat, early American settlers stockpiled grain and legumes and dried, pickled, and preserved fruits and vegetables. Both sugar and vinegar were used to help preserve food items during the period of winter scarcity. In sufficient quantities, both substances create an environment where bacteria are unable to grow. Fruit jams could be sealed with paper or with wax, and pickled cucumbers, onions, green beans, and other vegetables could be kept for some time in stoppered jars.

Preserving fruit required large quantities of sugar. Cookbook author Eliza Leslie admonished her readers in 1844, "If too small a portion of sugar is allowed to the fruit, it will *certainly* not keep well." For early colonists, sugar was expensive and thus had to be used sparingly. Preserved food of this kind could not be used as a universal solution to keeping fruit out of season, and drying was often turned to as a more economical alternative. As plantation slavery grew in the Caribbean throughout the seventeenth century, the price of sugar decreased, making preserving fruits in the form of jams and jellies increasingly common. Although some may not have been consciously aware of this fact, American housewives were able to feed their families fruit out of season due to the coerced labor of African slaves. This connection was not lost on British abolitionists who began promoting a sugar boycott in the late eighteenth century.

The largest boon to home canning was, however, not increased access to sugar, but the 1858 invention of the Mason jar. This glass container had a zinc lid that could be screwed on and sealed tightly thanks to a rubber seal that kept out potentially contaminating outside air. These jars had the additional benefit of being reusable, an attribute that inspired many home canners to keep more summer produce than ever before. In her instructional manual *Canning and Preserving*, which was published in 1887 and reprinted in 1912, Sarah Tyson Hester Rorer exalted about the new process, saying, "Canning is an improvement upon the old-fashioned method of preserving fruits pound for pound in sugar. It retains more of their fresh and natural flavor, is far less troublesome to do, and more economical." As she was writing, many Americans were making the even less labor intensive decision to stop relying on home canning and to buy newly available commercially produced canned goods.

In 1809, French chef Nicholas Appert invented the technique of hermetically sealing containers of food and then heating the containers, a process that kept the food from spoiling. He perfected his technique after more than a decade of trial and error and was rewarded for his efforts by Napoleon, who gave him twelve thousand francs in recognition of his invention. Napoleon was impressed with the technology primarily because it provided the means for safely provisioning armies who had to travel great distances during military campaigns. In 1810, Appert published a cookbook that explained the process of canning, *L'Art de conserver les substances animales et végétales* (or *The Art of Preserving Animal and Vegetable Substances*). His technique was so simple and effective that it was widely adopted not only by home cooks but also by culinary entrepreneurs.

English immigrant William Underwood was the first businessperson in the United States to attempt to can and bottle foods for the consumer market. He founded the William Underwood Company in Boston in 1821 and was soon not only preserving fruit but also bottling ketchup and other sauces. In 1825, Thomas Kensett, a recent immigrant to New York, filed a patent for tin cans, which quickly replaced glass in commercial operations.

Initially tin cans were constructed by hand, and the lids had to be soldered in place. A hole in the top allowed steam to escape during the can's water bath. The opening had to be filled by hand when the process was completed. Because it was such a laborious procedure, canned items were initially expensive luxury goods. Lobster and salmon were the first items to be canned in tin, and like all early canned goods they were most often used to provision ships or purchased as novelty items by those who could afford to eat them. Many consumers were initially reluctant to purchase commercially canned and bottled items not only because of their expense but also because they were sometimes unsafe to eat. Imperfect knowledge about how to seal cans and how long items should be heated sometimes led to contaminated products that sickened or even killed those who ate them.

The American Civil War was enormously beneficial to the nascent canning industry after the federal government began purchasing canned goods to feed the Union army. Government contracts inspired others to open canneries, and in the coming decades new developments in producing and sealing cans made them less expensive and far safer than they had once been. Many soldiers consumed canned milk, meats, vegetables, and fruits for the first time in their lives during the war, and they returned from the conflict with an appetite for both the convenience and apparently also the taste of canned foods. Canned fruits and vegetables no doubt seemed luxurious in comparison to rations of hardtack, the notoriously hard bread that was the subject of countless jokes intended to raise the spirits of those forced to survive on it. The substance was often infected with insects and stale by the time it reached soldiers, who were sometimes forced to contend with worms for their portion and who often had to soak the reviled hardtack in liquid before eating it to avoid damaging their teeth.

Both the demands of the military and the changed appetites of the servicemen at the end of the conflict caused the demand for canned foods to soar. In 1860, five million canned goods were produced; a decade later the figure had reached around thirty million. The proliferation of canned products gave Americans access to a more healthful diet as it became increasingly easier to eat fruits and vegetables out of season. Canned products also contributed to the trend against regional foodways as Americans throughout the nation gained access to identical products. Their widespread adoption freed many housewives from the arduous task of preserving food at home as these goods created an even greater division between consumers and producers of foods. As was the case with wheat milling and meat packing, canneries required costly equipment, a reality that eventually led to the consolidation of the canning business into the hands of a few large businesses.

In their pioneering history of American food, Waverly Root and Richard de Rochemont remark that the widespread adoption of canned goods in the United States reduced "the pleasure of eating." Their assertion is based in part on the fact that canned goods are generally considered to be inferior in taste to fresh products or to the frozen ones that would became widely available after a series of new innovations in refrigeration. Because they are manipulated to fit into cans and heated, canned meats and vegetables certainly cannot approximate the taste, texture, or appearance of the fresh item they replace.

Gail Borden, one of the pioneers of canning in the United States, ultimately made a fortune by providing canned milk to the military during the Civil War. Portability was of the utmost importance to Borden rather than taste. Before he began manufacturing milk, he developed a meat biscuit that he hoped would provide nourishing and convenient food. He declared, "I meant to put a potato into a pillbox, a pumpkin into a tablespoon." In his mind, technological innovation, ease, and convenience should be prioritized over the experience of cooking and eating. Due to the work of innovators like Borden, Americans living in urban areas had the ability to purchase and consume food that was not only grown and slaughtered by someone else but also cooked by unseen hands. Canned foods were often packaged in bite-sized pieces, saving consumers the trouble of even cutting their food before ingesting it. If these food items were not quite as appetizing as fresh foods or items preserved at home, many decided that what they lacked in taste was compensated for by their convenience.

As the twentieth century dawned, many Americans had grown to crave factory-processed foods. One of the most successful companies at capitalizing on American infatuation with the new convenience foods was the Campbell Soup Company. Beginning in 1869, Joseph A. Campbell began canning vegetables, including peas and tomatoes. From this tentative beginning, he eventually expanded his company until it produced more than two hundred products, including soup. In 1896, John T. Dorrance, a chemist for the company, developed something he called "condensed" soup. Consumers were instructed to dilute these dense, flavorful products with a full can of water. By enlisting consumers to add liquid at home, Campbell could pack more soup into a smaller container, making it an economical food item that retailed at ten cents a can. Within a few years, the company's first condensed soup offerings of tomato, vegetable, chicken, oxtail, and consommé proved to be so popular that Campbell stopped producing most of its other food products and began concentrating on soup. By 1904, it had added sixteen more flavors to its menu and was selling more than sixteen million cans a year.

Campbell was one of the first canning companies to fully exploit the power of advertising to convince consumers to buy its products. The company provided free samples in areas where grocers did not stock the soups in an attempt to generate popular demand. It also took pains to create a red and white label that consumers would quickly recognize. The design has since become so iconic that in 1962 pop artist Andy Warhol created a work of art that consists of thirty-two canvases, each containing the image of one variety of Campbell's soup. He regarded the cans with the now familiar red and white label as an enduring symbol of contemporary American culture.

In addition to painstakingly crafting a visually striking label, the company also sought to convince consumers that the contents inside the can were healthy. In 1905, it introduced the rosy-cheeked "Campbell's Kids," whose images soon adorned streetcars and the pages of popular magazines selling consumers on the idea that condensed soup was a convenient and nutritious food for children. The Campbell Soup Company not only tried to convince Americans to feed more soup to the younger generations, but it also set out to create additional uses for its products. In 1916, Campbell published the first of many product cookbooks, *Helps for the Hostess*. The company advised home cooks that condensed soup could help them better utilize leftovers. It advised using the soup as a tasty sauce for meats and fish, which could transform an "unattractive 'left-over'" into "an attractive, appetizing dish." Among other uses, the recipe developers also recommended using tomato soup as a convenient base for a pasta sauce:

SPAGHETTI À LA CAMPBELL

1 can CAMPBELL'S TOMATO SOUP.
¼ pound smallest tube spaghetti.
½ pound sliced smoked ham.
1 can button mushrooms (or one half pound fresh).
2 small onions, thickly sliced.
3 small peppers, thinly sliced.
½ teaspoonful thyme.
Clove of garlic.
2 tablespoonfuls olive oil.
Grated cheese (American or Parmesan).

Boil spaghetti in rapidly boiling salted water, with clove of garlic, until tubes are soft and all water absorbed. To a heated skillet, add oil, onions, pepper, and mushrooms, reserving a few whole mushrooms and pepper rings for garnish, and cook slowly until tender. Add to drained spaghetti. Fry slice of ham, cutting into three or four narrow strips when cooked. Pour CAMPBELL'S TOMATO SOUP into skillet containing ham dripping, add spaghetti, onions, pepper, and thyme. Mix thoroughly, and mound on round chop dish or platter. Lay ham strips crosswise on top, sprinkling with grated cheese. Garnish base with whole mushrooms and pepper strips.

Inspired by its initial success at convincing homemakers to use its soups as the base for more elaborate meals, the company has since produced dozens of similar cookbooks and pamphlets. The heyday of cooking with Campbell's soup came in the 1950s when Americans learned how to create a number of now familiar dishes like tuna noodle casserole using a soup base. Home economists at the company also taught Americans to combine canned cream of mushroom soup with crispy fried onions and green beans to create a "Green Bean Bake," which has since become a standard potluck item for many.

In urging home cooks to take shortcuts, Campbell made working in the kitchen less laborious, but it also led to a further transformation of the relationship between Americans and their food. Before the advent of canned soups, a cook wishing to make a dish similar to "Green Bean Bake" would have started the process working with fresh ingredients like mushrooms and flour. She would have been able to modify the recipe, making the sauce thicker or thinner or more or less salty, to suit her own particular taste. By beginning with a canned base, the cook gave up a measure of creativity and control. If she precisely followed the recipe, she would create a final product nearly identical in flavor and composition to that made by anyone else who followed the same instructions. This trend led to a greater homogenization of American foods not only across broad regional lines but within individual households.

UNSANITARY AND ADULTERATED FOODS

Many Americans willingly and trustingly ceded the responsibility of growing food, slaughtering animals, and even cooking to the food-processing corporations that sprang up during this era. Many did not initially realize that food manufacturers sometimes operated in unsanitary facilities or adulterated some of the items they purported to sell in a pure form. Many Americans first realized that in giving up control over the production of the food they ate they were at risk of compromising the quality of what they consumed during the "embalmed beef scandal" of the Spanish-American War.

Major Nelson A. Miles shocked the public when he openly alleged that much of the 337 tons of refrigerated beef and 198,508 tons of canned beef that were sent to Cuba and Puerto Rico as provisions to American troops during the 1898 conflict were tainted. He suspected that canned meat had been adulterated with waste from processing plants and that the inferior products could cause the illness or even death of those who consumed it. Miles told the *New York Times* that at best, the canned meats served to soldiers were the remnants left over from making other products, claiming, "There was no life or nourishment in the meat. It has been used to make beef extract, and after the juice was squeezed out of it the pulp was put back into cans and labeled 'roast beef.'" Furthermore, Miles and his supporters also believed that the refrigerated beef fed to the soldiers was also inedible because it had been doused with harmful chemical preservatives. Miles suspected that not only did these additives give the meat a strange and unappetizing appearance and an "embalmed" taste, but that it was harmful to the health of anyone who ate it as well.

A number of officers, including no less than future U.S. president Theodore Roosevelt, gave testimony supporting Miles's allegations of foul-smelling, sickness-inducing beef. The military responded to these claims by conducting an official investigation that revealed that the canned meat was of low quality but that neither it nor the refrigerated meat was tainted. Not only did the investigation conclude that nothing was wrong with the meat, officials also censored Miles for raising the issue in a public forum. American newspapers had capitalized on the drama by writing dramatic stories designed to humiliate not only the meat packers but also the officials charged with provisioning U.S. troops. William Randolph Hearst's *New York Journal* enthusiastically reported that soldiers were fed "ancient" beef, horse meat, diseased meat, and chemically treated beef. Despite the military's attempts to squash the scandal, the authorities did not manage to convince the men who believed they had been poisoned by the food otherwise. The investigation could not undo the public's negative perception, which had been fueled by sensationalist stories about the incident. When Teddy Roosevelt entered the White House in 1901, he did so harboring deep suspicions about the safety of industrial beef production.

If the embalmed beef scandal raised the question in the public mind about the safety of industrial food, Upton Sinclair's 1906 novel, *The Jungle*, provided an unappetizing answer. In 1904 the novelist and devoted socialist took a job in a meat-packing plant in Chicago for nearly two months to learn about the working conditions there. Sinclair translated his insider's perspective into a novel about a family of Lithuanian immigrants whose meager livelihood came from working in meat-processing factories. His intention in writing the novel was to expose the poor working conditions and crippling social problems experienced by industrial laborers. His descriptions of the meat-packing facilities were designed to serve as generalized indictments of capitalist abuse of workers, not as a criticism of that industry alone.

The novel was initially published in a serialized form in the socialist magazine *Appeal to Reason* in 1905, so the initial readers had to receive Sinclair's literary indictment in a piecemeal fashion. Nonetheless, he attracted immediate attention as word of his exposé soon reached audiences beyond the subscribers to the magazine. His novel was deemed notable not, as he hoped, because it exposed the dismal living and working conditions of Chicago's impoverished industrial workers, but because of his descriptions of the poor quality of the food produced in the factory setting. Sinclair despaired that he had failed in his goal of winning his readers' sympathy for the workers. He claimed, "I aimed at the public's heart and I hit its stomach."

The protagonist in the novel's first glimpse inside the meat-processing facility where he is to work is of the hog-processing assembly line. He is immediately assaulted by the sounds of the unfortunate animals meeting their fate. He hears "high squeals and low squeals, grunts, and wails of agony; there would come a momentary lull, and then a fresh outburst, louder than ever, surging up to a deafening climax." Sinclair's character cannot help but feel sympathy for the doomed beasts, whom he sees as "so innocent." He sadly notes that "they came so very trustingly; and they were so very human in their protests." Most of Sinclair's readers apparently felt as little sympathy for the animals brought to the slaughter as for the human beings who were enlisted to work on the killing and processing assembly line, for despite his gruesome description of their transformation from living creature to packaged product, Sinclair's writings inspired relatively few Americans to contemplate vegetarianism. Instead, what most struck his readers were his descriptions of the final meat products that made their way from Chicago slaughterhouses to homes throughout the nation.

According to Sinclair's descriptions, many of the products that emerged from Chicago's meat-processing plants had been soaked in chemicals, picked off of the floor or drudged from the factory pipes and then canned, or made with the flesh of dead or diseased animals. Sometimes, he told his horrified

Workers Labeling Cans in Chicago Meat Packing Plant, 1909.
Historically Americans have been enthusiastic in their adoption of
industrially produced foods, but periodically alarms have been raised
about unsanitary conditions in processing plants such as this one. *Source*:
Library of Congress, Prints & Photographs Division, Stereograph Cards
Collection, LC-USZ62-97322.

readers, human body parts found their way into processed meat products after
workers injured themselves on the job or accidentally fell into huge vats of
boiling animal flesh. His most famous description of unsanitary and adulterated meat production was his account of how sausage was made:

> There was never the least attention paid to what was cut up for sausage;
> there would come all the way back from Europe old sausage that had
> been rejected, and that was moldy and white—it would be dosed with

borax and glycerine, and dumped into the hoppers, and made over again for home consumption. There would be meat that had tumbled out on the floor, in the dirt and sawdust, where the workers had tramped and spit uncounted billions of consumption germs. There would be meat stored in great piles in rooms; and the water from leaky roofs would drip over it, and thousands of rats would race about on it. . . . These rats were nuisances, and the packers would put poisoned bread out for them; they would die, and then rats, bread, and meat would go into the hoppers together. . . . Under the system of rigid economy which the packers enforced, there were some jobs that it only paid to do once in a long time, and among these was the cleaning out of the waste barrels. Every spring they did it; and in the barrels would be dirt and rust and old nails and stale water—and cartload after cartload of it would be taken up and dumped into the hoppers with fresh meat, and sent out to the public's breakfast.

Sinclair's horrifying descriptions of the conditions in meat-packing plants reached even more readers in 1906 when Doubleday agreed to republish the serialized tale in the form of a single novel, *The Jungle*, which immediately became a bestseller. Unsurprisingly, meat packers vehemently denied Sinclair's allegations, and many embarked on an aggressive campaign of damage control. However, vehement denials and denunciations of Sinclair's political leanings could not undo the damage *The Jungle* had done.

The public outcry inspired by Sinclair's allegations was the most intense demand yet to be made by American consumers for oversight of the food supply. For many, it was the first time they had contemplated the full implications of eating foods processed and packaged in a distant factory. However, the 1906 uproar was not the beginning of agitation for what supporters labeled "pure food." Many local laws prohibiting the adulteration of various food items, particularly milk, were passed in the late nineteenth century. A grassroots movement asking for greater federal oversight of food production emerged in the 1870s and had as one of its greatest supporters Harvey Wiley, a medical doctor who taught chemistry at Purdue University and who later became head of the Division of Chemistry at the U.S. Department of Agriculture. He made his campaign against food preservatives, which he deemed harmful, famous after he enlisted a group of volunteers who became labeled the "Poison Squad" to eat items laced with borax, sodium benzoate, formaldehyde, and other items commonly used in industrial food preservation. Unsurprisingly, the study was discontinued after the volunteers became sick from their chemical diet. Although Wiley's study gained some notoriety, the pure foods movement was not able to achieve a national legislative victory until after the publication of *The Jungle*.

For President Roosevelt, who had been caught up in the embalmed beef scandal, Sinclair's findings were worth taking seriously. However, because of the power of what critics labeled the "beef trust" of powerful meat packers, his allegations could not be accepted uncritically. Furthermore, Sinclair's radical political leanings and his polemical purpose in writing the novel made his findings suspect to mainstream political figures. Roosevelt sent out two trusted investigators to survey the conditions in meat-packing plants in Chicago. Even though the facilities had begun cleaning up their operations in the face of increased public scrutiny, Roosevelt's team found a great deal of evidence to corroborate Sinclair's claims. They easily convinced the president to become a strong proponent of increased federal oversight.

Despite lackluster support for previous attempts to clean up the national food supply, in 1906 the Senate easily passed the Pure Food and Drug Act with only four dissenting votes. The new law made it illegal to adulterate or falsely label foods that were shipped over state lines. However, foods processed and consumed within a city or state were still subject only to local laws. The Meat Inspection Act granted the secretary of agriculture the right to inspect all factory-processed meat and decide whether or not it was fit for human consumption. The legislation established the premise that the federal government had the right and the obligation to make sure that industrial foods were safe.

The laws also had the effect of restoring and even bolstering American confidence in meat packing and other processed foods. Consumption of industrially produced foods continued to grow in the aftermath of *The Jungle*. Ironically, because of increased government oversight, some consumers had more faith in factory-produced foods than in locally made items. Sheet music for the 1914 popular song "Pretty Puppy" displays a drawing of an independent sausage maker, whose caricatured representation was likely designed to signify a German immigrant in the popular imagination, shoving a small dog into his sausage-grinding machine. Another song from the same time period, "The Original Frankfurter Song," brazenly announces, "Fido Is a Hot Dog Now." If these songs are any indication of the popular mindset in the years following the passage of pure food legislation, it seems that lack of food purity had become associated with immigrants and small businesses rather than with corporate food processors who were ostensibly under federal supervision.

In 1956, Walter Goodman assessed the fifty-year legacy of the Pure Food Act for the *Nation* magazine and determined that the federal government had not allotted enough funding or human resources to enforce food safety legislation. He informed his readers that despite "a commemorative resolution by Congress and a postage stamp honoring Dr. Harvey W. Wiley . . . the returns of the day are not entirely happy." He blamed American complacency on the issue for the fact that there had been no scandal in the past half century on the same scale as that surrounding the publication of *The Jungle*, and he urged consumers not to let their guard down. However, his warnings fell on more or less deaf ears as most Americans believed that the problem had been solved.

The Second Industrial Revolution had wrought such an enormous change in the way Americans ate that most American cooks and eaters could not contemplate a diet that did not include industrially produced items. Many Americans took pride in living in a technologically advanced country, and they had no problem eating foods that they thought reflected the modern age they were living in. Artisan food practices were no match for inexpensive, convenient, and technologically sophisticated industrial foods for the increasingly urban population, who did not have the time or the resources to produce their own foods. Despite the changes brought about to American eating habits due to technological innovation, one characteristic remained constant. Women have continually played a larger role than men in cooking and in maintaining food traditions. No examination of American food habits would be complete without asking how ideas about food relate to ideas about gender roles.

5

⚜

Gender and the American Appetite

A merican ideas about food are inextricable from American attitudes about gender difference. Although all Americans have collectively created ideas about what should constitute the national cuisine, historically women have always been at the front lines of adjusting to the realities of the shifting availability of ingredients, the expanding influence of industrial foods, and the culinary questions posed by migration. Women have used their unique position as the nation's predominant cooks not only to help create an American style of cooking but also to establish culinary attitudes about issues such as immigration and technology. Meanwhile, they have also used their dominance over the collective kitchen to respond to and help create changing ideas about gender roles.

During the colonial era and early national period, women were the nation's primary cooks, but, as Ruth Schwartz Cowan has pointed out, most worked in close conjunction with men. When the vast majority of Americans were subsistence farmers who grew or made most of the items they consumed or used in their household, men played an active and highly visible role in the preparations necessary before cooking could begin. They grew the wheat that was transformed into bread. They gathered fuel necessary to keep the hearth heated. Although cooking pots and fireplace implements would have been purchased, the men in the family crafted many of the items used in the kitchen, such as the wooden trenchers that held the prepared food. They cared for and slaughtered the animals that found their way into the family's cooking pots. Men and women worked in close proximity and in collaborative ways to make sure that the members of the household would have enough to eat. Although most tasks were segregated by sex, in times of hardship, such as death or illness, the lines of designated sex-specific tasks could be and were crossed. The issue of survival was far more important than societal rules for who should perform which household function.

This collaboration around the tasks of food procurement and preparation, however, began to fade in the nineteenth century due to changes brought about by the market revolution. In the first half of the nineteenth century, improvements in transportation brought about by better road construction, an expanding network of canals, and the technological innovations of the steamboat and the railroad began connecting family farms to expanding urban marketplaces. These changes made it easier for farmers to sell their surplus agricultural products and to purchase goods that out of necessity would have once been done without or produced at home. These trends ended the economic isolation of individual families and shifted their orientation from collectively ensuring the family's subsistence toward also producing goods for the market. These developments soon led to a great increase in urban centers, which contained not only agricultural trading hubs but increasingly also workshops and factories that began to produce items for sale that had once been made at home or by small local artisans. Soon the economic center of family life began to shift from the home to the arena of commerce. For example, cloth, which once would have been woven at home or imported at great expense, could now be easily purchased due to the expansion of the American textile industry.

The ability to buy many of the items that had once been produced by women's labor led to the degradation of the status of women as workers. Significantly, however, the expanding marketplace also enabled households to purchase items that once would have been produced by men. As men were freed from their traditional chores, society did not correspondingly deem the labor power of men less important than it had been before. Instead the significance assigned to women's work in the home was further downgraded as many men abandoned their former roles as farmers and collaborators in the household economy and took jobs in a proliferating network of factories or in other new occupations.

Decade by decade the country became more industrialized and more urban. By the late nineteenth century, the economy was no longer focused on small farms and artisan-produced goods, but it became centered on industry. By 1880, the majority of the workforce was employed in nonfarm jobs. Most American workers had become paid employees rather than the owners of a farm or small business.

The growing dependence on wages and on the ability to become a consumer in the contemporary marketplace suddenly made the unpaid labor of women who worked in the home seem less significant than the work of men who were remunerated for their efforts. Although many economically disadvantaged women joined men in the search for industrial jobs, those with the financial means to do so were under the strict social injunction to continue to work at home, as had their colonial forebearers. An ideology soon arose to explain and to justify the new working relationships where women stayed at home while the men worked elsewhere. By 1825, the idea of "separate spheres" had emerged, and the dominant belief was that women belonged in the home, while men were better suited for the wider world of commerce. This doctrine was accompanied by various gender stereotypes, which supported the idea that men and women were innately suited for different kinds of work. Women were deemed to be more emotional than men and thus unfit for the rational responsibilities of conducting business. While men were competitive and domineering, the ideal woman was meek and submissive. No longer was her role that of economic partner in a household economy; woman was now in a more obviously subservient position as she was given the task of creating a serene, loving, virtuous home environment for her husband to return to. Men were given the unique advantage of the societal blessing to travel freely between the spheres and to sample the benefits of both worlds. The ideal woman was commanded to stay peacefully at home and under her husband's control.

Under this division of labor, one of the chief responsibilities of women remained that of feeding their families. Instead of working with her husband as a partner, a woman increasingly became a partner of the marketplace and a consumer of items that she could no longer make at home. Although some thrived under the challenge and found ways to be both creative and satisfied with their role, others began to chafe at the burdens and restrictions of domestic life. Some early proponents of greater social and political freedom for women believed that the position of women in society would not be improved until they were freed from their domestic responsibilities, particularly the often burdensome task of cooking.

OUTSOURCING THE SEPARATE SPHERE

Melusina Faye Peirce, the wife of Harvard philosophy professor Charles Sanders Peirce, described a bold plan for a reorganization of household tasks in the pages of the *Atlantic Monthly* in a series of articles that appeared in 1868–1869. Living during the period of rapid industrialization, Peirce viewed the changes that had been made to women's daily working lives with dismay. She believed that in the past women had served a more important economic role in the household as producers of a variety of goods, while in the modern era they were now merely customers of the burgeoning marketplaces that were controlled by men. She suggested that the degradation of women's work was particularly acute in the case of middle-class women like herself who could afford servants to aid them in running the household. She mourned the fact that women like her had "sunk from [their] former rank of manufacturing producers to that of unproductive consumers."

Peirce realized that the market revolution could not be undone and that manufacturing would never return to the individual household level. Given this fact, she proposed that women regain their economic status of the past by assuming control of the retail trade for items related to the household. She disparaged the idea of men working, for example, selling cloth to female customers, arguing that they were forsaking their natural role as agricultural laborers. She urged, "Give us the yard-stick, O heroes, and let us relieve you behind the counter, that you may go behind the plough and be off to those fields. . . . Thus, each in a fitting sphere, shall we make a good fight for the world."

Her recommendations, however, went beyond giving women control of the existing retail trade. She envisioned transforming the way that the marketplace and the household functioned. She imagined forming cooperative associations where middle-class women would supervise working-class women who would perform domestic chores such as sewing, doing laundry, and cooking in a centralized location outside of the home. All women would be paid for their labor at a wage equal to that given to male workers, and they would sell their services and prepared foods at a reasonable price. Surplus earnings would be divided among the members of the cooperative, who would use their new financial power to fund a variety of institutions that would benefit women, ranging from newspapers to educational facilities. Their dependence on men for financial support would be over, and both sexes would be equal economic partners. Because the most arduous household chores would be done outside of the home, houses would be redesigned and would no longer contain laundry or kitchen facilities.

Peirce believed that the professionalization of housework and the control by women of the related retail trade would not only restore the former dignity of the labor of women but would lead to an enhanced quality of life for everyone. Individual women would be able to concentrate on the tasks that best suited their individual abilities rather than being forced to dabble in all aspects of housekeeping. Although Peirce had some empathy for working-class women and envisioned a system where they would be paid a fair wage and would work moderate eight-hour days at their labor, she believed that privileged women like herself should serve in supervisory capacities. "Educated women," she advised, "should seek to produce, not with their hands, but with their heads." She proposed that other less formally educated women who were talented cooks would be given the job of cooking, while those less skilled in that area would take on other tasks. Under her system, no one would be forced to eat meals produced by a reluctant or indifferent cook. "What feasts fit for the immortals might grace every table if we only knew how to turn our treasures to the best advantage—and to think that millions of us live on salt pork, sour or saleratus bread, and horrible heavy pies!"

Because Peirce lived in the rarefied intellectual world of Cambridge, Massachusetts, where she associated with the families of a number of intellectual luminaries affiliated with Harvard University, she was able to convince many in her unusual circle to take her ideas seriously and even to experiment with implementing them. In 1869, she established the Cambridge Cooperative Housekeeping Society. The group established a cooperative laundry, a bakery, and later a store that sold household supplies at wholesale rates. They planned eventually to open a kitchen, which would deliver prepared food to individual homes. Although the laundry was moderately successful, the store was a failure because few members of the cooperative actually shopped there. The kitchen was never established because, due to financial difficulties, the organization shut its doors after operating for little more than a year. They failed in part because they faced opposition or lackluster support from some of the husbands of the women involved, but financial concerns proved to be even more pressing.

Although the experiment would never have taken place without the backing of well-off supporters, Peirce later speculated that their efforts were also undermined due to the privileged class position of the members:

> They were all people of means and position, and they only looked upon co-operative housekeeping, even if successful, as a convenience. Its economical side did not attract them in the least. Still less did they look upon it as a duty to do all they could to make the attempt succeed. Most of them subscribed their money as to a charity, and there, for them, the matter ended.

Women of the cooperative could, and did, fall back on their servants to manage their households when the scheme failed. Never in danger of being forced to perform the most arduous household tasks themselves, they could regard their experiments in alternative forms of household management as something of a hobby. However, for Peirce, it was a deep disappointment that they were unable to gain the respect they craved as businesspeople and professionals. In her utopian dreams, society could be reinvented in a more equitable way where men and women would perform different but equally respected and remunerated tasks. In reality, however, these pioneers found it impossible to completely escape from their unpaid roles in the separate and stubbornly subservient sphere of the household.

The idea that domestic tasks were the responsibility of women was so deeply entrenched in society that even a visionary like Peirce considered the general division of labor according to sex roles to be natural and inevitable. If a woman were to assume a larger role in society, the assumption was that she would first have to figure out how to make sure her domestic obligations were met. Not incidentally, in Peirce's scenario, although a woman could aspire to be paid for her labors and could even hope to attain a managerial job as opposed to that of hands-on domestic drudgery, she could never escape from the fundamental obligation of being the one to make sure that her family was fed and clothed.

Twenty-seven years after the Cambridge Cooperative Housekeeping Society closed its doors, another reformer articulated an even more radical vision for women's liberation from domestic drudgery. In her 1898 book *Women and Economics*, Charlotte Perkins Gilman complained that "the woman in marrying becomes the house-servant, or at least the housekeeper, of the man." She chafed against the limitations imposed by the expectation that women should work in the service of their husbands and families as unpaid laborers. She believed that women had the right to pursue any profession that best suited their abilities. Although she accepted marriage as a valuable social institution, she questioned its wisdom as an economic relationship, believing that both partners should be wage earners. In order to achieve the freedom to pursue a career outside the home, she knew that the issues of cooking and housekeeping would have to be settled. She envisioned a system somewhat similar to that devised by Peirce, where homes would be designed without kitchens and laundry facilities and businesses would supply food and laundry services to their paying customers. She did not go so far as to imagine a world where men would be employed in these tasks, but she also did not, like Peirce, relegate all women to working in the arena of housework.

The different system of organizing household chores that Gilman embraced not only was a means of freeing women for other pursuits, but it was also economically pragmatic. She argued that it was inefficient for each household to have an elaborately equipped kitchen, arguing that stoves and cooking implements should be jointly shared. She emphatically declared that "there is nothing private or special in the preparation of food. . . . There must be freedom of personal choice in the food prepared, but it no more has to be cooked for you than the books you love best have to be written for you."

Gilman also argued that the ability to cook was not an innate gender characteristic and that in fact the task was done indifferently by women across the country who lacked proper training. Gilman decried what she regarded as the poor state of American cooking as it existed under the separate spheres arrangement:

> The art and science of cooking involve a large and thorough knowledge of nutritive value and of the laws of physiology and hygiene. As a science, it verges on preventive medicine. As an art, it is capable of noble expression within its natural bounds. As it stands among us to-day, it is so far from being a science and akin to preventive medicine, that it is the lowest of amateur handicrafts and a prolific source of disease.

The idea that cooking was not something that required training and skill was, in Gilman's mind, a dangerous one. Women who had not received specialized education in the field could cause illness to the very families that society had charged them with serving. She argued, "The development of any human labor requires specialization, and specialization is forbidden to our cook-by-nature system." Just as men worked at a variety of occupations, Gilman longed for a society where women would have equal options. Those who worked at traditionally defined female tasks required training and should be regarded as professionals.

Gilman received a great deal of criticism and notoriety for her personal life. Although she married in 1885 and had a child a year later, she was not well suited for the conventional lifestyle society demanded of her. She tried to be content in a separate, female sphere, but finding herself unable to do so she fell into severe depression. Her condition was made worse after a doctor prescribed a lengthy "rest cure," where she was to stay in bed near her child and to avoid extended intellectual activity. Gilman gamely tried to obey these instructions for more than three months, but she found herself, in her words, "on the borderline of utter mental ruin." She then reversed her doctor's orders, seeking her own cure by throwing herself into her writing, noting that without work "one is a pauper and a parasite." After reaching the conclusion that her intellectual pursuits were her cure, rather than, as her doctor seemed to believe, a problem, she also realized that she could no longer stay in her marriage and attempt to fulfill the societal expectations of being a traditional wife and mother. She divorced, and her former husband married Gilman's close friend. Gilman's daughter lived with her father and his new wife rather than with her mother. Understandably, her example was unsettling to those who subscribed to nineteenth-century ideas about proper female behavior.

Gilman radically lived out her ideology and flouted social conventions. Despite the disapproval she garnered from many quarters, her personal example and her eloquent and bold writings also proved inspirational to many. After leaving her marriage and resuming her writing, Gilman soon became a popular public lecturer. Her ideas resonated with a certain group of women, particularly those who had the leisure time and the means to begin experimenting with new social arrangements.

Between 1870 and 1920, some middle-class and upper-class people began to try living in what were known as "apartment hotels," which sprang up in New York, Boston, Hartford, and Kansas City among other places. These nicely appointed and often expensive apartments were generally spacious and nicely furnished, but they contained only minimal kitchens. Residents of the building could eat as many meals as they wished in the centralized dining room or sometimes even have prepared food delivered to their apartments via dumbwaiters. Inhabitants of the apartment hotels also had access to housekeepers who kept their dwellings tidy and to a laundry service that eliminated that chore as well. Women living in those apartments were freed from house-work and could indeed live Gilman's dream of pursuing their own economic and intellectual interests. However, only a few women had the luxury of living in such accommodations.

Residents of apartment hotels and reformers like Gilman and Peirce had difficulty imagining the domestic problems they hoped to solve from the point of view of lower-class women, those who were charged with performing the most arduous domestic tasks both under the current system as well as un-der the various proposed reform schemes. Peirce attempted to elicit empathy for the plight of working women, telling her middle-class followers, "I say, let any educated house-mistress who thinks she has the physical strength, try 'doing her own work' for six months, or if she will not try it, let her cease her unreasonable wonderings at the shortcomings of her servants." However, her admonition was still colored with a large degree of class condescension. She adds, "On the contrary, the wonder is that with their uneducated brains, servants contrive to keep the hundred details of their work so well in mind as they do." Gilman similarly held disdainful views about working-class women and sought to outsource housekeeping in part to remove maids from the homes of the middle and upper classes, regarding them as "Strangers by birth, by class, by race, by education—as utterly alien as it is possible to conceive." Literary critic Ann Mattis points out that in Gilman's poem "Two Callings" she uses a napping woman in luxurious surroundings who is rudely wakened by domestic duty to embody "the global and historical suffering of all women," indicating a lack of understanding about how her own class privi-leges impacted her understanding of the problems of domestic life.

Apparently untroubled by the implications of freeing themselves from their domestic burdens by hiring working-class women to perform their chores for them, many with the financial means to employ servants bus-ied themselves with the task of solving what they regarded as the "servant problem." They were concerned with the difficulty of finding and keeping reliable household help that would save the mistresses both the drudgery of housework and the burden of continually training new servants. These efforts did not challenge the primary assumption that housework was the woman's domain, but instead these reformers strove to make life in the domestic arena more pleasant for those who had the luxury of hiring help.

Although working as a servant was the most frequently recorded occupation for a woman in every census until 1940, relatively few families had the financial ability to hire full-time help. In most regions of the country, servants were the most common in substantial cities, which had large populations of immigrants in need of jobs and numerous families with the means to hire them. In the South, however, even white women of relatively moderate incomes could afford domestic help because of the depressed wages paid to black women. The eco-nomic situation of black families was such that few African American women had the luxury of deciding whether or not to stay in the "separate sphere" of the home. Due to rampant discrimination, few employment opportunities besides domestic servitude were available to this group of women.

Because the ideology of racism was deeply entrenched in the hearts and minds of white southerners and was also sanctioned by the state, black women in the South had few avenues open to them to resist poor treatment by their employers, who often demanded twelve- or thirteen-hour work days and infrequent days off. Many whites believed that African Americans had inferior intellects but superior physical strength and thus could be worked relentlessly. An 1865 South Carolina law stated that servants "in all domestic duties of the family shall at all hours of the day and night and on all days of the week promptly answer on all calls and obey and execute all lawful orders."

African American female servants were also treated as social inferiors who had to enter the house through the back door and otherwise maintain a subservient demeanor. Although one of the primary tasks of black women in southern households was that of cooking, an intimate activity where food is handled and tasted, black employees were frequently prohibited from using the same restroom facilities or eating off of the same dishes as their white employers. These hard-working women were also widely subjected to sexual abuse by white men who had close access to them in the privacy of their home.

Even in the midst of these oppressive circumstances, African American women had a measure of power due to the fact that white families became utterly dependent on their labor. The presence of black servants was so ubiquitous in middle-class households that some white women did not even know how to cook. Given the societal and familial pressure that women felt to fulfill their wifely and motherly duties of caring for the home and for the well-being of their families, an inability to prepare meals made these women vulnerable and unusually dependent on their beleaguered servants. African American domestics could capitalize on this and could extract concessions from employers by threatening to quit, particularly before a significant event such as a holiday or a dinner party, when their skills were more in demand than ever. They could also exact revenge on unfair employers by contaminating their food, abusing kitchen utensils and appliances, or refusing to perform their duties cheerfully. Thus, even in the constrained environment of the South, where black women had few other options, the job of employing servants was a source of great worry.

These pressures were multiplied for white northern women who did not live in a social world free of prejudice but who nonetheless also did not live, like their southern counterparts, in a rigid caste system that had created a perpetual class of servants. For those northerners privileged enough to be able to afford to hire a servant, the chore of finding and keeping good employees created ongoing anxiety. The issue was considered so pressing that many would-be employers of domestic servants gathered together in the late nineteenth and early twentieth centuries to attempt to collectively solve the "servant problem."

THE RISE OF THE KITCHEN TY

The Rise of the Kitchen Tyrant and How She May Fall, 1901. This illustration shows middle-class women desperately begging for the services of a maid, which many considered to be in short supply at the turn of the twentieth century. The

V.
While her evenings at home are on a scale of magnificence that she would once have considered royal.

FAMILY APARTMENT HOUSE.
MORE COMFORTS THAN AT HOME.
NO MORE WRANGLING WITH SERVANTS.
MEALS, LAUNDRY WORK, VALETS, CHAMBERMAIDS, AND ALL DOMESTIC SERVICE PROVIDED BY THE MANAGEMENT.

THIS ROW OF DWELLINGS TO LET CHEAP NO REASONABLE OFFER REFUSED

VII.
And this shows a ready and delightful solution of the whole problem; — one that we are all coming to.

J.OTTMANN LITH.CO.PUCK BLDG.N.Y.

RANT; — AND HOW SHE MAY FALL.

drawing features an "apartment hotel," where housekeeping services are provided as a potential solution to the "servant problem." *Source*: *Puck*, March 6, 1901, Library of Congress, Prints & Photographs Division, LC-DIG-ppmsca-25505.

These women organized to try to find a solution to the fact that there was a shortage of women willing to be employed as live-in servants as well as a high turnover rate among those already employed. Northern domestic servants were overwhelmingly recent immigrants who were desperate for immediate employment but who were primed to seek better job opportunities as soon as they appeared. In large households, servants would serve specialized tasks, but in smaller ones a maid was expected to cook, to clean, and to be constantly available at the whims of her employer. Servants often worked excruciatingly long hours and had little privacy. They were generally not allowed to entertain visitors, particularly those of the opposite sex, and they were forced to wear uniforms that advertised their subservient status at first glance. For these reasons, domestic work was an unpopular profession, one that was considered less preferable than even factory jobs, which in the early twentieth century offered grueling, dangerous, and low-paying work.

The popular discourse around the issue of the "servant problem" did little to make the job seem respectable or appealing to potential employees. Due to hardships imposed by British colonialism coupled with a devastating blight on the nation's staple food of the potato, many Irish—particularly young, single women—immigrated to the United States in the late nineteenth century seeking better opportunities. Many initially found themselves working as domestic servants. Because of the preponderance of Irish servants, domestics were often generically and snidely referred to as "Bridgets." Irish immigrants had come from a society where food had been scarce; many had subsisted primarily on potatoes. Therefore, few came to the United States already possessing the elaborate catalog of recipes and cooking skills required by middle-class American housewives. For that reason, jokes about cooks who lacked the basic skills of their professions abounded. A stereopticon slide from the era showed a picture of a maid derogatorily referred to as "Biddy" clad only in her undergarments doing her best to oblige her employer's request that she serve "tomatoes undressed."

One of the most elaborate attempts to solve the "servant problem" was undertaken in Boston by the members of the Women's Educational and Industrial Union (WEIU), who formed a "Domestic Reform League" in 1897. The organization opened a public dialogue about the responsibilities of servants and recommended the creation of contracts that would specify hours and other terms of employment. They also collected extensive hiring data and established an employment bureau that would match up employers and employees. They were, from the beginning, beset by the problem of a shortage of willing workers. Between January 1, 1903, and January 1, 1904, they had 2,852 requests from employers but only 606 applications from employees looking for work. Given these odds, many would-be employers had to settle for having occasional, part-time help rather than the full-time live-in servants they hoped would lift the burden of housekeeping from them.

Even though the Domestic Reform League could not solve the problem of a growing shortage of servants, its efforts anticipated another way that women would respond to the societal burden of being relegated to a "separate sphere" dominated by duties of housework. The Domestic Reform League developed its "School of Housekeeping," designed to train not only potential domestic employees but also would-be employers and young, future housewives in the art of homemaking. Peirce and Gilman's dreams of houses without kitchens and of greater gender equality in the area of wage earning had not come true. Thus, many women began to accept this reality and to redefine their relationship to household tasks. If they could not outsource their cooking and laundry chores or, in the case of middle-class women, find a reliable supply of servants to perform the tasks for them, it behooved them to learn the most modern and efficient methods for performing these labors.

The School of Housekeeping's rationale was that "Housework is a trade." Its founders argue that "women on whom the care of a household falls, whether she be employer or employee, should have special training for her work." The eight-month-long course could be taken free of charge by would-be domestic servants who would eventually pay for their instruction by working as servants. Better off young women could sign up for a course at their own expense designed specifically for college women to prepare them for their future work as wives and mothers or potentially as workers in newly developing female occupations in the social services. The curriculum was to consist of "all branches of Housework" along with courses in "House Sanitation," "Personal Hygiene," and "Economy of Foods."

Interestingly, at the same time that the Women's Educational and Industrial Union was training its middle-class members and the women they wished to employ in how best to perform household chores, it was concurrently exploring the possibility of creating a professional kitchen that would supply families with ready-made meals and thereby reduce the pressure on the women in a household that was unable to employ servants. An 1898 study jointly prepared by the School of Housekeeping and the Boston branch of the Association of Collegiate Alumni declared, "The tendency to buy wholly or partially prepared food is in harmony with . . . the principles governing the industrial world."

Not only did the WEIU look for ways to liberate women from the responsibilities of cooking and other housework by training servants, providing education in the best methods of housework, and exploring options for outsourcing tasks like cooking, it also saw potential for women's unique skills in the kitchen to improve their lives and their economic outlook. One of the organization's projects was a retail store, opened in 1877, which sold items made by women, including a variety of food items. In exchange for a small percentage of their sales, women who needed extra income were allowed to sell food items in the organization's attractive and often-frequented store. The organization carefully monitored the quality of the products it consigned as well as the sanitary conditions under which they were created. Minutes from a WEIU food committee meeting gravely note that the executive committee had voted that "Miss Caldwell be told that unless the quality of her chocolate cake improved by November 1 . . . it will be dropped." Food quality and food preparation were a serious business.

The variety of ways that the WEIU imagined and attempted to reinvent women's relationship to housework, particularly food preparation, is representative of the contradictory relationship women have always had between food and gender roles. Cooking could be a burden that many wanted to cast off, or it could be a valuable skill that if finely honed could be used for one's economic advancement. The WEIU was among a number of women's organizations that had begun to depict cooking as an expertise that needed to be cultivated and that required a great deal of specialized knowledge.

THE INVENTION OF THE DOMESTIC SCIENTIST

Beginning in the late nineteenth century a number of intellectual women began to respond to the fact that housework, whether it was done as an unpaid job by a family member or by a maid regarded as a social inferior, was not accorded the respect of other forms of labor. One of the earlier champions of this cause was Catherine Beecher, the sister of the famed author of *Uncle Tom's Cabin*, Harriet Beecher Stowe, who was determined to "redeem woman's profession from dishonor." In her 1841 *Treatise on Domestic Economy*, Beecher warmly embraced the idea of separate and complementary spheres for men and women. She accepted the prevailing belief that women belonged at home rather than in the realm of politics or commerce. Because it was women's God-given duty to fill this role, she maintained that even women who had the means to employ servants were obligated to be familiar with all aspects of housekeeping so that they could be self-sufficient in the case of an economic misfortune or of a shortage of help. Although women were, from her point of view, uniquely suited to perform domestic tasks, she also represented homemaking as a complicated undertaking that required practice and study rather than the outgrowth of mere womanly instinct. She declared, "There is no housekeeper so expert but she may learn something from others whose experience has been different, and particularly from those who have made the art of housekeeping a scientific study."

In her formulation, homemaking was depicted as both an art, which woman was well matched for due to her inherent characteristics, as well as a science that required intellectual heft and necessitated constant experimentation. In 1869, in collaboration with her famous sister, she wrote *The American Woman's Home*, which contained the sisters' elaborate designs for optimally efficient kitchens. Her version of what constituted women's work went far beyond unthinkingly repeating familiar chores. Women were to use their minds to learn existing best practices and to imagine new and better ways of doing things. They bemoaned that fact that "women are not trained for these duties as men are trained for their trades and professions, and that as the consequence, family labor is poorly done, poorly paid, and regarded as menial and disgraceful."

Ironically, given Beecher's strong admonition that women should embrace their natural roles as wives and mothers, Beecher never married but instead maintained her financial independence and a busy professional life. In addition to writing domestic advice manuals, Beecher worked as an educator, founding the Hartford Female Seminary in 1823. She also wrote a cookbook, *Domestic Receipt Book*, in 1846, which, given her interest in training women in the newest techniques, included instructions on how to use new technologies, including the iron cook stove and ice cream maker. Peculiarly, she made her living training women to embrace a much different lifestyle from her own. The knowledgeable, contented housewives she hoped to inspire were apparently not to follow every aspect of her example. Although she may have firmly taught her pupils that their place was in the home, Beecher did not adhere to her own advice and stay there.

Beecher was hardly the only woman to make a career of teaching other women how to fulfill their gender-specified roles as cook and housekeeper. Juliet Corson opened the New York Cooking School in 1876. She offered classes to both the wealthy, who paid for their courses, and the poor, who were able to attend for free. Although Corson came from a privileged background, as a young woman she was thrown out of her house by her stepmother, who insisted that she earn her own living. She did so by working briefly in a library, by selling her writings about cookery, and by fund-raising for her cooking school and other related endeavors. However, despite becoming a well-known cooking instructor whose accomplishments were written about in a variety of publications, including the *New York Tribune* and the *Nation* magazine, she was seldom financially secure.

In 1892, she humbly wrote to her friend, New York society woman Julia Keese Colles, asking for a "few dollars for bread and fruit." In her letter she disparaged a "social system . . . which leaves free to face with actual daily fight for food anyone who has lived so for her kind, and worked as I have." Despite having an active professional life, she never enjoyed a worry-free financial existence. Shortly before her death, her friends put together a fund for the medical care needed during her final illness.

Her inability to adequately support herself as a cooking teacher and author is indicative of the problems that many women faced as they tried to find a way to earn wages in a society that expected them to stay at home. Since housework was done either as unpaid or as poorly paid labor, it is unsurprising that professionals like Corson would have difficulty transforming their skills into an adequate living. Her experiences trying to live frugally gave Corson both insight and empathy into the experiences of the working poor, and in 1877 she wrote a pamphlet titled *Fifteen Cent Dinners for Workingmen's Families*, which she published and distributed at her own expense in an attempt to help those even less fortunate than herself learn how to prepare meals on a tight budget. Although Corson taught cooking skills to wealthy New Yorkers, her primary interest was in helping the disadvantaged, believing that proper eating habits were of enormous social significance.

Many late nineteenth-century reformers, including Corson, believed that poor diets contributed to alcoholism among the poor. Famed reformer and urban photographer Joseph Riis agreed, claiming that substance abuse in tenement neighborhoods in New York City could best be cured by the establishment of "a cooking school slapped right down in the middle of the block." Riis blamed their wives for the behavior of working men who spent some of their hard earned wages on social drinking. His belief that properly prepared food would quench the craving for drink and would encourage men to stay at home with their families had been articulated decades earlier by Mrs. M. H. Cornelius, whose *The Young Housekeeper's Friend* (1868) had contained the warning that "many a day-laborer, on his return at evening from his hard toil is repelled by the sight of a disorderly house and a comfortless supper . . . and he makes his escape to the grogshop." In 1885 the *Cook* magazine quoted Professor Williams's claim that as ways to fight alcoholism, "speech-making, and pledge-signing, and blue-ribbon missions can only effect temporary results, unless supplemented by satisfying the natural appetite of hungry people by supplies of food that are not only nutritious, but savory and varied."

Much of the anxiety about the alleged drinking habits of some members of the poorer classes stemmed from the fact that drinking was most closely associated with recent immigrants, particularly the despised Irish, who came from a culture of male social drinking, and the Germans, who brought their beer-making traditions and the social space of the beer garden to the United States with them. When reformers wanted to teach cooking as a means of curing alcoholism, they were also engaged in the mission of assimilation through food habits. These middle-class reformers sought to change the eating habits of the poor and the newly arrived both because they believed that these changes would make them more temperate and healthy as a group and also because they hoped to help them become better integrated into mainstream American culture.

Women were at the forefront of teaching Americanization through eating habits not only by teaching cooking classes to recent immigrants but also as teachers in the public school system. They capitalized on the fact that the children of immigrant families could be made to feel ashamed of appearing different from their classmates and thus could be convinced to abandon family food traditions in the name of fitting in. These children had varying degrees of success in convincing their parents to modify what was eaten at home. When Leonard Covello brought home oatmeal and presented it to his father as a proper breakfast food, the father was outraged, asking, "What kind of a school is this? They give us the food of animals and send it home with the children!" Undaunted by failures such as this one, Jane Addams, the famous founder of the Hull settlement house in Chicago, remained optimistic, hoping that "an Italian girl who has had lessons in cooking at the public school, will help her mother to connect the entire family with American food and household habits."

The People's Institute in New York City adopted a number of programs designed to educate both children and their harder-to-convince parents about the culinary ideas of their adopted country through an experimental program at the city's Public School 40 in 1918. A group of volunteers known as the "Food Scouts" were selected from the student body, which comprised mostly Italian and Jewish students, to participate. Those who were selected were fed hearty school lunches and given lessons on eating habits that were supposed to guide them as they consumed breakfast and dinner. The students who were

Breakfast Lesson, Carlisle Indian School, 1901. In the early twentieth century, cooking classes were often used as a tool of assimilation into American culture. *Source*: Library of Congress, Prints & Photographs Division, Frances Benjamin Johnston Collection, LC-USZ62-55456.

chosen had been identified as being malnourished, and the organizers of the program believed that if they abandoned their traditional eating practices they would become healthier and gain weight.

Although many children were initially reluctant to eat unfamiliar foods or disavow their parents' ideas about proper diets, over time they became increasingly amendable. The Food Scouts coordinators were appalled to discover that many of the Italian children in the group drank coffee and ate bread for breakfast, a combination that they deemed to be an exceedingly unhealthful way to start the day. They required the children to keep journals where they recorded their diets and to keep each other accountable for eating in accordance with their newly learned principles. They adopted as the group's slogan: "Round and rosy,—Round and rosy. Tea and coffee are bad,—milk and oatmeal are good." The organizers of the Summer Health School, another child nutrition program sponsored by the People's Institute, claimed that it was "not in the least difficult" to get the children to eat food "to which they were unaccustomed at home." In order to accomplish the goal of getting children to change their palates, the instructors practiced the timeless technique of forbidding the children to eat dessert before they had finished the other portion of the meal.

To reinforce the message that they were carefully delivering to the students, the People's Institute offered both English and cooking classes to their parents as well. In an era when assimilation was generally considered to be more desirable than ethnic pride, the parents who enrolled in these courses could not fail but to note the conflation of the language and the foodways of the United States as being equally important aspects they must adapt to in this new culture.

Sarah Tyson Rorer, a Philadelphia cooking school instructor, author, and early dietician, argued that not only could a well-rounded diet cure alcoholism and assimilate recent arrivals, it could also influence other aspects of human behavior. She claimed that "a well-fed man was never behind bars." In her mind, the issue of good cooking far exceeded the limited sphere of the private, domestic world that Beecher sought to improve. According to the arguments of Corson, Riis, the staff of the People's Institute, and Rorer, proper eating behavior could reform a wide variety of social ills. The modification of undesirable kitchen habits was necessary to ensure the well-being of the entire social order. Given their close association with the task of cooking, women were to be at the forefront of cleaning up America by concentrating on its collective stomach. Food reformers found ways to straddle both spheres by taking the private concerns of individual families over what and how to eat and making them public.

Women culinary reformers seized on the spirit of the Progressive movement, which began in the late nineteenth century and ended, or at least diminished in importance, with the United States' entry into World War I. This broad-based reform movement was inspired by many of the various problems that accompanied industrialization, ranging from unhealthful and crowded urban living conditions, to environmental degradation, to unsafe working conditions. The movement was fueled by the increasing number of middle-class Americans who had both the leisure and the impulse to donate their efforts toward making social improvements. Many of the most enthusiastic Progressives were women. Some worked in paid capacities in newly created professions such as social work or public health nursing. Others worked as enthusiastic volunteers. Whatever their status, the increase of women's participation in the public sphere during this era provided a partial challenge to the separate spheres ideology. However, most women had at best only one foot outside of the kitchen, for most participated in the reform movement of the era in a capacity that reinforced stereotypes about innate female talents and characteristics. Most found themselves working in some capacity as caregivers, whether directly aiding the poor, working in issues of public health, working to assimilate immigrants, or giving cooking instruction as a means to accomplish a variety of their other goals.

Women who became professional cooking or nutrition experts often capitalized on the belief that their interest in such topics was natural and thus acceptable. In order to have the societal blessing to have a career outside the home, they couched their choices in the language of what were then considered proper womanly pursuits. One such woman was Ellen Swallow Richards, who, after graduating from Vassar, became the first woman to be admitted to the Massachusetts Institute of Technology, where she pursued an advanced degree in chemistry.

Her first book, *The Chemistry of Cooking and Cleaning* (1881), was indicative of the approach she was to take throughout her career as she combined her scientific interests with topics deemed most suitable for a woman to explore. In the book, she tutored her readers in some basic principles of chemistry, using this knowledge as a basis to make recommendations about selecting and preparing the healthiest foods. She justified the need for her study by claiming, "In this age of applied science, every opportunity of benefiting the household should be seized upon. The family is the heart of the country's life, and every philanthropist or social scientist must begin at that point." Not only would science improve life for the family, it would also elevate the significance of female work. Richards proclaimed, "The woman who boils potatoes year after year, with no thought as to how or why, is a drudge, but the cook who can compute the calories of heat which the potato of given weight will yield, is no drudge."

After being admitted to MIT, Richards trod carefully on what had been the all-male enclave of the research laboratory. She won over much of the faculty by performing feminized tasks such as sewing buttons on the shirts of her professors in an attempt to make them less leery of what might have been perceived as an unwomanly interest in science. While still a student she teamed up with the local Women's Education Association and MIT to equip a laboratory so that she would have a space to teach a chemistry class to local women. Her efforts helped pave the way for MIT's decision to regularly admit female students beginning in 1884. At that point, she was remarkably offered a position on the MIT faculty. She went on to become a mentor to many other women who aspired to combine an interest in science with the domestic arts that most still felt they were compelled by society if not by nature to master. By bringing together the kitchen and the laboratory, Richards helped create the new role of the "domestic scientist."

Richards, too, was inspired by the idea that proper eating habits could cure a variety of social ills and aid the assimilation process for immigrants. She was one of the key organizers of Boston's New England Kitchen, which provided inexpensive, plain American fare at a low cost to area residents. The kitchen was run on the principles of a laboratory. It was kept impeccably clean, and the domestic scientists who labored there strove to make consistent and replicable dishes so that each batch of soup or loaf of bread would taste and look identical to the others. Her closest partner in this pursuit was Mary Hinman Abel, whose prize-winning manuscript, *Practical Sanitary and Economic Cooking Adapted for Persons of Moderate and Small Means*, was strongly rooted in the chemistry of cooking. Abel used the latest scientific research to create her suggestions for how the working poor could meet their minimum food requirements in the most economical fashion.

Abel and Richards teamed up to create the menu at the New England Kitchen that each deemed healthful, inexpensive, and thoroughly American. They offered many New England regional dishes such as baked beans, Indian pudding, chowders, oatmeal, and succotash. This last attribute made their efforts unappealing to the immigrant population whom they hoped to feed with their efforts. Richards complained that their target clientele "have very decided preferences for the looks and flavors of food to which they have been accustomed. They will not try new things, and are exceedingly suspicious of any attempt to help them." Although they did have some loyal customers, including working women who sometimes stopped by on their lunch break or single people who resided in local boarding houses, they were unable to transform the eating habits of the neighborhood.

For the most part, local families proved to be unwilling to stop cooking at home in favor of already prepared meals. They were even less inclined to trade in the tastes of their home countries for the bland foods prepared in the New England Kitchen. Creamed chicken, rice pudding, lettuce sandwiches, and applesauce were insufficiently alluring to many potential customers, no matter how hygienic an environment they were prepared in. Records kept by the Women's Educational and Industrial Union, which eventually took over management of the kitchen, acknowledge their inability to gain a large lower-class customer base, dryly noting, "Working men were not interested in being scientifically fed."

Although the scientific cooking did not seem to be a palate pleaser to the New England Kitchen's potential customer base, the principles that the kitchen was organized on proved to be immensely appealing to many women who wished to follow in Ellen Swallow Richards's footsteps and learn a style of cooking that provided the intellectual satisfaction that was often missing from household chores. In 1899 Richards called together a meeting of like-minded individuals who wished to work "for the betterment of the home" to be held in Lake Placid, New York. This meeting led to the founding of the discipline of "home economics," the scientific study of nutrition, cooking, sanitation, and general housekeeping. In 1908 the American Home Economics Association was founded with Richards as its first president. The founding of a professional organization helped inspire and validate an expanding group of high schools and universities who offered classes in the new discipline. Many female scientists who were unwelcome in the more traditional scientific disciplines found themselves relegated to using their training in chemistry or biology to teach home economics students.

The new curriculum in scientific housekeeping was the most popular at land grant colleges, whose students were more oriented toward the expectation that college would teach them some practical skills. It was less popular at elite women's colleges, which favored a liberal arts curriculum comparable to that taught to male students. M. Carey Thomas, the president of Bryn Mawr, concluded that "nothing more disastrous for women, or for men, can be conceived than this plan for the specialized education of women as a sex." A female member of the faculty at Sophie Newcomb College bitterly noted that the women leading the charge for the new discipline of home economics had themselves been trained in the traditional liberal arts curriculum of the kind these new ideas about educating women seemed to threaten.

Thus the burgeoning field of domestic science, as it was sometimes called, was interpreted by some to be a detrimental development in the emancipation of women and by others as a chance to improve the status of women by finally elevating traditional women's work to the esteem given to male-dominated fields. One of the women who relished the challenge of bringing the precision of science to the kitchen was Fannie Farmer, a graduate of the Boston Cooking School who went on to become principal of the school and founder of her own Miss Farmer's School of Cookery. In 1896, Farmer revised a series of recipes created by Mary Lincoln, the first principal of the Boston Cooking School, and published *The Boston Cooking-School Cook Book*, which was so widely read that Farmer became the most beloved cooking expert of her day. She became known as the "Mother of Level Measurement" for her insistence that ingredients be measured precisely, with no guesswork necessary, for novice cooks. She instructed her readers to level the contents of measuring cups and spoons with a knife to make sure that only the proper amount was used.

On the surface, her cookbook was written in the trademark style of the domestic scientists. Taking nothing for granted, she begins with the straightforward definition that "FOOD is anything which nourishes the body" and goes on to provide explanations of the constituent parts of food, such as proteins and carbohydrates. But despite this pedantic beginning, much of the book is infused with a love of cooking and a whimsical interest in making food presentations creative and visually appealing. Unlike many of her sisters in the field of domestic science, Farmer was not content merely to make healthful food with scientific precision in a sanitary environment; she wanted to make food that was fun to prepare and that tasted good. She proclaimed that cooking would never be elevated beyond "mere drudgery" unless one put "heart and soul" into the effort. Food historian Laura Shapiro notes that "Miss Farmer was uniquely talented at putting her education toward the service of delight." One variation of her recipe for lobster salad demonstrates her interest in food that transcends the functional cuisine of the New England Kitchen:

LOBSTER SALAD III

Remove large claws and split a lobster in two lengthwise by beginning the cut on inside of tail end and cutting through entire length of tail and body. Open lobster, remove tail meat, liver, and coral, and set aside. Discard intestinal vein, stomach, and fat, and wipe inside thoroughly with cloth wrung out of cold water. Body meat and small claws are left on shell. Remove meat from upper parts of large claws and cut off (using scissors or can opener) one-half the shell from lower parts, taking out meat and leaving the parts in suitable condition to refill. Cut lobster meat in one-half inch cubes and mix with an equal quantity of finely cut celery. Season with salt, pepper, and vinegar, and moisten with Mayonnaise Dressing. Refill tail, body, and under half of large claw shells. Mix liver and coral, rub through a sieve, add one tablespoon Mayonnaise Dressing and a few drops anchovy sauce with enough more Mayonnaise Dressing to cover lobster already in shell. Arrange on a bed of lettuce leaves.

The domestic scientists and the women who attended their cooking classes and read their publications had to contend not only with the still persistent belief that women belonged in the home but also with a number of beliefs about the eating habits of women that drew on equally essentialist ideas about the innate characteristics of the female sex. Although Farmer wanted to create food that both looked appealing and tasted good, many domestic scientists concentrated on the first attribute without any regard for the other. Although Progressive food reformers were irked when working-class people disregarded their suggestions for low-cost, simply prepared, plain food, they were more accommodating to the idea that middle-class women might turn their noses up at the same things. They were operating under the widely held belief that women, particularly middle- and upper-class women, were creatures of very slight appetite. Food had to be made to look appealing in order to please this finicky group of eaters.

THE FEMALE APPETITE

In her important study of domestic scientists, *Perfection Salad: Women and Cooking at the Turn of the Century*, Laura Shapiro uses the various salads that were popular around the turn of the century to sum up prevailing ideas about women's palates. Because an appetite for food was associated too closely with having sexual desires, the ideal chaste, late nineteenth-century woman was trained not to show any kinds of hunger. As historian Harvey Levenstein notes, the prevailing belief was that "to have lusty tastes in foods seemed to betray a weakness for other pleasures of the flesh as well." Instead women were to favor foods that could be described—in the parlance of the day—as "dainty" and feminine. Salads met these guidelines, and Shapiro shows that these dishes soon evolved beyond simple green or chicken salads into more elaborate concoctions, such as various fruit and vegetable mixtures served inside carefully carved-out tomatoes or banana skins. Fruits and vegetables were also frequently artfully suspended in gelatin. Foods of these kinds were designed to be attractive rather than filling or even necessarily tasty.

Women allegedly had a taste for light and sweet foods, like candy. Candy makers around the turn of the century both capitalized on and helped perpetuate the stereotype of women as having a much greater sweet tooth than men by using images of gorgeously attired, joyous young women in their advertising campaigns. Not only were these women enjoying the luscious bonbons or fudge, but they were supposed to in some respects resemble the candy themselves. Jane Dusselier observes that at the time, "Women were expected to be sweet, delicate, pure and perhaps even luscious, just like a winning bonbon."

In contrast, society expected men to prefer heartier food, particularly meat, and to disdain more "feminine" food such as salads. Meat was considered such a "manly" food that many adolescent girls of the time period went to great lengths to avoid eating it, even though it was the most common source of protein of the day. Choosing "dainty" foods instead, many became iron deficient. Feminist social critic Carol J. Adams observes that these ideas are not new. Since the beginning of human civilization, societies have reserved meat for men rather than for women or children, during times of scarcity. This was true even in instances when pregnant or nursing women had greater nutritional needs than men. Meat was associated with male virility and with the belief that meat eaters would actually imbibe some of the physical strength of the animal they consumed. The assumption was that men needed meat in order to fulfill their role in the family. For women, it was perceived as being a luxury. In turn-of-the-twentieth-century America, the middle-class eaters who were schooled by domestic scientists generally were not faced with the kind of food scarcities that plagued early man, but nonetheless they willingly perpetuated these gendered ideas about proper food consumption.

The scientific cooks during this era not only perpetuated ancient ideas about proper eating habits for men and women, they also made significant culinary decisions that would change the future of American eating habits. Far more concerned with being "scientific" than with producing food that was soulful and tasty, the culinary reformers from this era enthusiastically embraced processed foods. Ironically, given the unsanitary conditions at many food-processing plants during this time period, many domestic scientists applauded canned and later frozen foods as "pure" because they were often made with little direct contact from human hands. The domestic scientists applauded processed ingredients because not only were factory-produced goods allegedly cleaner than items that came into more intimate contact with people, but they were also uniform in packaging and in taste, a value that domestic reformers admired. They were also, to many, desirable as a symbol of modernity. They were more directly a product of science and technology than even the most carefully composed-from-scratch recipe created by a home economist.

Reformers' interest in these items was also reflected in the fact that many domestic scientists became spokespersons or even employees of industrial food companies. The makers of processed foods needed domestic scientists' endorsements to confer legitimacy on their products, and the domestic scientists needed to find a sphere where they could find jobs beyond that of education. Sarah Tyson Rorer, for example, wrote promotional materials for a number of companies, including Wesson oil and Tabasco sauce, among others. Ultimately, home economists taught American women how to become good consumers and eagerly to embrace their number one role in the still largely sex-segregated market economy. Historian Susan Strasser points out that the label these women gave themselves as "home economists" pointedly signals the role they saw for themselves as instructors in the art of how to become good consumers.

Although the invention of the field of home economics created a number of jobs for female professionals, domestic scientists did not succeed in transforming housekeeping into a profession that was regarded as intellectually rigorous as male-dominated scientific fields. Even as the most prominent ambassadors for the new creed of scientific cookery created careers for themselves, they did so because most other middle-class women stayed at home, registering for their cooking classes and buying their publications and the products that they endorsed. Although the domestic scientists did little to change the overall status of women, their embrace of technology profoundly influenced the way future generations of American women would cook. After slowly making inroads into the American kitchen beginning in the late nineteenth century, industrial foods assumed a newfound place of prominence in American kitchens beginning in the 1950s.

THE IDEALIZED HOUSEWIFE CONFRONTS
CONVENIENCE FOODS

The idealized white, middle-class American housewife that was portrayed in the popular culture of the 1950s was not a scientist. She did not wear a severe bun or the starched white attire of the cooking school student. Instead she glided around her kitchen carefully coiffed and wearing high heels. Her apron, color coordinated to match her outfit, seemed superfluous, for she never seemed to engage in particularly arduous or messy kitchen chores. Her gleaming suburban kitchen symbolized a modern triumph over drudgery. Due to labor-saving devices and an ever increasing plethora of processed foods to choose from, she could fulfill the duties of her still separate sphere without ever breaking a sweat. At least this is the silent claim made in advertisements in glossy magazines and on the smiling faces of actresses in sitcoms such as *Leave It to Beaver* and *The Adventures of Ozzie and Harriet.*

These images of prosperous, contented nuclear families whose stomachs were filled and minor troubles soothed by an elegant and serene wife and mother figure were enormously influential. They provided many American families with a template for how they should live. Families learned not only about gender roles but also about a variety of consumer products—the kinds of clothing, foods, cars, and appliances they should purchase. For those whose lives did not resemble these fictional television families, their smiling examples could be oppressive. Popular culture's ideas about family life could be particularly burdensome to those whose real lives deviated the most from those images: members of ethnic and racial minorities, gays and lesbians, unmarried people, and the working poor. The model housewife could also be a specter in the minds of white middle-class women who did not find all of the satisfaction that society promised them in their gendered role.

Despite women like Peirce and Gilman and a whole host of domestic scientists who had struggled either to free women from the burdens of the kitchen or to elevate the stature of household labors, women in the 1950s were still expected to cook and clean for their families, and these tasks were not widely regarded as difficult or significant. Historian Megan Elias observes that by the 1950s many found the discipline of home economics to be "adorably silly." The purposeful, scientifically minded domestic scientists had not succeeded in convincing the culture at large that home economics was a serious discipline. Although the giant food processors that fed more and more Americans decade by decade and at an accelerating pace in the 1950s all hired home economists to help test and develop new products, most people's understanding of the field did not encompass that level of sophistication. Most assumed that home economics classes merely taught women how to sew on buttons or flip pancakes, tasks that many still believed were innate to woman's nature, abilities that were coded into her DNA.

At the same moment that ideas about women's proper roles reached a new apex, ironically more and more women were entering the workforce. Economically disadvantaged and unmarried women had long worked for wages, and during World War II many previously unemployed women temporarily took paying positions to help meet the wartime labor shortages. So the idea of women working outside the home was hardly new; however, in the 1950s many married women began working part-time jobs even when economic necessity did not compel them to do so. Millions of women, even more than had done so during World War II, entered the labor force in the 1950s. In 1957, 32 percent of the full-time labor force was female, and many were married with children. One half of all working mothers were middle class. In keeping with the ethos of the era, these middle-class women took jobs in order to be able to purchase more consumer goods. For this group, the message of 1950s television and of the advertisers who targeted "Mrs. Consumer" had worked. Women's incomes helped families maintain their middle-class lifestyles and purchase late-model cars, washing machines, televisions, and other items that were associated with a prosperous lifestyle.

These new working women now had to juggle maintaining their wifely and motherly responsibilities with the demands of the workplace. The modern gas or electric stove made cooking easier than in the days when fuel had to be purchased or gathered and fires continually stoked. Refrigerators and, increasingly, freezers made food preservation simpler and trips to purchase supplies less frequent. Frozen dinners and cake mixes could shorten meal preparation time considerably. The new supermarkets that sprang up to replace individual greengrocers and butchers streamlined the shopping process.

However, in spite of these advances, historian Ruth Schwartz Cowan claims that the work week for middle-class women actually increased after the introduction of these conveniences into the home. In most sections of the country, by the 1950s only the very richest families could afford servants. Those who had once worked as domestics now enjoyed enough postwar affluence to be able to become freed from that undesirable role. In spite of the promises of modern conveniences, those who took on part-time jobs quickly discovered "that they were working even longer hours than *their* mothers had worked" as they struggled to juggle both paid and unpaid responsibilities.

Even when their hours were longer, the tasks that homemakers performed in the 1950s were still different from those of previous generations. They were subjected to an unprecedented onslaught of messages from food producers about how adopting their products would make the task of cooking easier.

Campbell's soup, relentless in its marketing since the company had been founded, succeeded in convincing record numbers of home cooks that its condensed soups were a kitchen necessity. Cream of mushroom soup could be quickly mixed with tuna, egg noodles, and canned or frozen peas to make a tuna casserole or combined with green beans and French-fried onions to create a green bean casserole popular enough to make inroads onto the traditional Thanksgiving table in many homes. Hungry children could be fed almost instantaneous meals of fish sticks or complete frozen meals. Frozen orange juice could be stockpiled in the family freezer and made far more quickly than oranges could be squeezed by hand. Cake mixes, which yielded far more predictable results than cakes made from raw ingredients, could be assembled quickly to round out a meal.

Peg Bracken's 1960 *The I Hate to Cook Book* capitalized on the mood of women who saw convenience foods as a way to minimize their time spent in the kitchen. It was aimed at "those of us who want to fold our big dishwater hands around a dry Martini instead of a wet flounder, come the end of a long day." Her "Ragtime Tuna Casserole" recipe could be prepared with only minutes of hands-on time in the kitchen:

2 cans macaroni and cheese
2 cans chunk tuna
grated cheese

Alternate layers of macaroni and tuna in a greased casserole dish till you run out of material.
  Sprinkle the grated cheese lavishly on top and bake, uncovered, at 300° for thirty minutes.

However, the American kitchen was not overtaken by modern convenience foods overnight, and it was never taken over completely. Women who had long been trained to see cooking as one of their primary purposes in life initially viewed labor-saving items like cake or muffin mixes with suspicion. Not only did these items often have an inferior, or at least different, taste to their homemade counterparts, but the ease of preparation made some women feel like they were somehow shirking their responsibilities. In 1947, Charlotte Cramer, an early entrepreneur who made dry mixes for cakes, popovers, and muffins that needed only to be mixed with water and baked, sent out free boxes of her Joy cake mix along with surveys to a number of women. The responses she received give clues about early reactions to new processed food products. One woman deemed the mix a "wonderful time saver." Another admitted, "My family enjoyed your prepared cake better than my own homemade." Others were less enthusiastic about giving over such a large measure of control to Joy cake mixes, complaining that the resulting cake was too sweet or too small or too fattening to suit their tastes. One respondent declared that the mix was "unusually good" but that she still preferred to bake from scratch.

Even after the introduction of products like Joy cakes, many home cooks continued baking as they had always had from family recipes, favorite cookbooks, or hints traded among friends. Over time, however, women became increasingly willing to stock their pantries with premade products to be used when time was short. By 1957, ten years after Cramer sent out her survey about Joy cake mixes, half of all cakes baked at home were made from a mix.

Similarly, frozen foods were adopted only gradually, and only after persistent marketing by the producers of both frozen food products and freezers. By 1952, most American families, except for the most impoverished, owned a refrigerator. There were thirty-three million home refrigerators in operation that year. However, only four million families owned freezers. Most refrigerators made before 1946 had freezing compartments only large enough to hold ice cubes; therefore, many families simply did not have the space available to store the frozen food products that were flooding the market that decade. Initially, frozen foods were something that consumers purchased only occasionally. Of the 190 pounds of vegetables eaten per capita in 1954, the vast majority were eaten fresh. Forty pounds were consumed out of cans, and only six pounds were from frozen products.

These figures began to multiply due to the unprecedented affluence many families enjoyed in the postwar period. More and more people had the means to purchase refrigerators with larger freezer compartments, and the owners of suburban homes increasingly had the floor space for freestanding units. Homeowners were inspired to invest in these appliances due in large part to effective marketing. The Ben Hur Home and Farm Freezer Company promised housewives that a home freezer would save them shopping trips because they could stockpile food. A full freezer would also ensure that they would be well supplied in case unexpected guests arrived. Like canned goods, frozen vegetables could free families from the culinary limitations of eating only seasonably available fruits and vegetables. Advertisers told women that if they could convince their husbands to go hunting or fishing and to fill the freezer with the results of their trip, the freezer could even save them money. Overall, producers of frozen foods emphasized ease of preparation, promising Mrs. Homemaker that a freezer full of food of frozen meats, fruits, and vegetables would translate into far less time spent in the kitchen.

No early product seemed to fulfill the promise of rapid food preparation as obviously as the Swanson TV dinner. Swanson and Sons, a wholesale grocer that had begun producing canned and frozen turkey products during World War II, found itself with 520,000 pounds of surplus turkey in 1953. An ingenious executive for the company produced a sketch of an aluminum tray with three separate compartments that would hold a portion of turkey with cornbread dressing, sweet potatoes, and peas. The meal would be sold frozen, and consumers would reheat the already cooked food in their home ovens. Shortly thereafter, Swanson introduced fried chicken and Salisbury steak dinners. In the coming decades, the variety of prepared food available would multiply into seemingly endless variations, ranging from ethnic foods to meals designed for individuals on limited or restricted diets. The relentless marketing and the infinitely expanding product line worked together to convince Americans to stock their new freezers with frozen products. In 1940, consumers spent 150 million dollars on frozen foods. By 1970, the number had climbed to a staggering seven billion dollars.

Even after frozen, fully prepared meals were available, the 1950s homemaker was far more reluctant than food processors had predicted to cede the entire responsibility of cooking to them. Although many must have relished the thought of what food studies scholar Sherrie Inness labels the "subversive message" that they should aspire to spend less time in the kitchen, they also remained reluctant to abandon their socially created role of the family cook. Many enjoyed being in control of meal preparations because they liked cooking or because they were accustomed to tangibly caring for their family members by feeding them. Others who were less attached by inclination or affection to the role of cook also found it hard to free themselves of the burden of a lifetime of indoctrination about their proper role. Reheating an already cooked meal in the family oven hardly seemed like "cooking." Women of the era were more likely to feed a Swanson TV dinner to their children as a special "treat" when they went out for an evening than they were to present every member of the family with a foil tray on a regular basis.

Food manufacturers responded to this reality by encouraging home cooks to cook *with* processed foods. Instead of serving premade products in the state they arrived in from the manufacturer, Mrs. Consumer could be creative and add her own personal touch to the items. A writer for *Better Homes and Gardens* proclaimed, "Canned, frozen, and packaged foods are the major ingredients—they fairly jump off the shelf to partner with each other in new and exciting dishes." Frozen vegetables or fish could be livened up with sauces made from canned soup. Frozen French-fried potatoes could be spruced up by topping them with ham, cheese, or nuts. Prepared soups could be enlivened with the addition of sherry or cream or canned crabmeat. Cake mixes posed endless opportunities to be creative. They could be enhanced with fruits, nuts, and liqueurs. Dried soup mixes could be used to season ground meat or combined with dairy products to be made into a vegetable dip. Refrigerated biscuits could be baked on top of canned stews to create a nearly instantaneous pot pie. All of these foods could be produced more quickly and with less mess than their made-from-scratch equivalents, but by combining various ingredients the illusion of cooking just as previous generations had done could still be preserved.

Creative cooking with processed foods sometimes resulted in disastrous combinations. Betty MacDonald, the author of *The Egg and I* (1945), complained that unsavory concoctions were frequently served at women's club meetings, where women became the primary victims of the creativity of other women run amuck. At a garden club meeting, MacDonald was served "creamed tuna fish and peanuts over canned asparagus." At another gathering she was accosted by a "salad of elbow macaroni, pineapple chunks, Spanish peanuts, chopped cabbage, chopped marshmallows, ripe olives and salad dressing." She emphatically proclaimed that cooking of this kind "ought to be stopped." Other Americans apparently agreed. In spite of the fact that talented female home cooks continued to make appetizing meals and managed to avoid the pitfall of overreliance on processed foods, Americans in the 1950s associated haute cuisine primarily with men.

This association of simple home cooking with women and of fine cooking with men was hardly an American phenomenon. It was an inherited attitude from the French, whose top chefs and exclusive gourmet societies were exclusively male. In spite of American ambivalence about "fancy" French cooking, that nation's cuisine remained the benchmark for gourmet delights. Although the United States in the postwar years was known far more for the abundance of rather than the quality of its cuisine, the stereotypical epicure was a man. Even in the most feminized of social roles, that of cook, women discovered that there was a glass ceiling and that the most prestigious culinary roles were reserved for men.

Paradoxically, although men were the nation's most prestigious cooks and allegedly most discriminating eaters, they were generally not considered fit to give advice to home cooks. Marshall Adams, a food writer and editor for *McCall's* magazine, was forced to write under the pseudonym of "Marsha Roberts" in order to be taken seriously by the female readers of the magazine, who had grown long accustomed to taking advice from female domestic scientists.

This all began to change, however, when cooking celebrity Julia Child arrived on the culinary scene after her best-selling *Mastering the Art of French Cooking* was published in 1961. She reached even wider audiences as the host of the wildly popular cooking television show *The French Chef* between 1963 and 1973. She had already defied the French culinary establishment by registering for and completing the professional class at the Cordon Bleu in Paris. As a television celebrity she challenged gendered ideas about gourmet tastes and about who should be doing the cooking at home. Through her passion, lack of culinary snobbery, and legendarily warm sense of humor, she broadcast the message that French cooking was a skill that anyone could learn and enjoy. She urged home cooks—both male and female—to reconsider their romance with premade meals and to enjoy both the triumphs and the failures to be had while experimenting in the kitchen with raw ingredients.

Thanks to the gains made by second-wave feminists in the 1970s, more and more women entered the paid workforce. By 1982, a majority of married women were employed outside of the home. Although women have yet to stop doing the majority of the cooking and cleaning in American households, men have increasingly shouldered greater parts of these burdens. Historian Harvey Levenstein has noted the paradoxical fact that "as more males mastered home cooking, its status rose; as its status rose, it became more acceptable for males to do." Beginning in the 1970s and increasingly decade by decade, home cooking was no longer exclusively woman's domain. Furthermore, the task has finally gained the prestige that the domestic scientist had dreamed of more than a century earlier. When Julia Child broadcast her first cooking show, it was an experimental novelty. In the twenty-first century, television shows related to home cooking can be viewed on television every hour of the day. These programs are hosted and watched by both men and women.

Although home cooking has become a socially acceptable hobby for men to enjoy, men are still less likely than women to be the primary cooks at home. According to United States Bureau of Labor statistics from 2010, in an average day 41 percent of men reported doing some household work related to food preparation or cleanup, while 68 percent of women did some work in the kitchen. Despite the gender disparities reported in the sphere of home life, the differential in work performed by men and women in the professional kitchen remains even greater. In 1972, when the second-wave feminist movement was in full swing, only 5 percent of the students at the prestigious Culinary Institute of America were women. Apparently still uncomfortable with the idea of women assuming the traditionally male role of professional chef, instructors at the CIA attempted to make Lyde Butchenkirch, one of the first female students, wear a blue dress rather than the white chefs' uniform that she insisted upon and ultimately received. Staggeringly, a quarter of a century later, while there were 2,134 executive chefs working who were certified as such by the American Culinary Federation, only 92 were women.

Although women have historically been the most central figures in feeding generations of Americans, their contributions have often been forgotten or dismissed as less significant than the developments in the male-dominated professional kitchen. However, many prominent male chefs are the culinary godchildren of Julia Child or of local and seasonal foods advocate Alice Waters, who has consistently been cited as one of the country's most admired chefs. Furthermore, in 2011, the enrollment at the Culinary Institute of America was 55 percent male and 45 percent female. Thus, a new generation of professional women is in the process of redefining yet again the relationship between women and American foodways. While doing so, they are participating in the long-standing American trend to use eating and cooking practices as ways to express beliefs and attitudes as well as appetites. As the next chapter will demonstrate, throughout the nineteenth and twentieth centuries, American eaters also intermingled ideas about food with a variety of thoughts about what it meant to be pious or patriotic.

6

✦✦✦✦

The Pious or Patriotic Stomach

This chapter is sweeping in its chronological scope and touches upon events taking place over more than a century of United States history. It seeks to examine briefly a variety of the different ways that Americans have struggled—sometimes more successfully than others—to use food habits as a way to express different value systems. The examples presented here are meant to be illustrative but are far from exhaustive. For Americans who have not had to worry about food insecurity, of simply having enough to eat, eating habits have sometimes been a way to exemplify their spiritual beliefs or their feelings of patriotism. In fact, for some, eschewing certain kinds of food in the name of God or country has been partially a response to shame over overindulgence. The usage of food choices to make statements about piety or patriotism has been most common among those who have had the means—both in financial terms and in terms of the leisure time to weigh such considerations—to make dramatic changes to their diets.

Poor Americans have historically been far less likely to find satisfaction in giving up the sensual pleasure of food, which had been too often denied to them, than those who had the means to pile their plates high with hearty portions. Nonetheless, less fortunate Americans, too, have had to respond to the idea that food and virtue are somehow linked, but they often have had to do so in response to the dictates of more powerful people—often agents of the federal government—who have frequently attempted to determine what they should eat. The pressure to make food choices deemed desirable by various authorities was particularly intense during U.S. involvement in World War I and World War II, and much of the burden of implementing government mandates fell to women of all social classes. The issue of clashing ideas about

143

the nature of moral eating practices was also evident during World War II when Japanese American residents of internment camps had to struggle to be fed adequately during their period of detention.

Clashing cultural values about the significance of kitchen practices continued to be evident during the Cold War when Richard Nixon and Nikita Khrushchev sparred over competing ideals. Although many nineteenth- and twentieth-century Americans flirted with deprivation in the name of improving their bodies or souls or in the hope of serving the military goals of their country, the overarching American food ethos has been a sense of entitlement to modernity and abundance, standards that Khrushchev found alienating. Strung together, the various examples provided in this chapter demonstrate that much more than human survival is always at stake when dinner is served.

SYLVESTER GRAHAM'S CRITIQUE OF THE AMERICAN DIET

In the early nineteenth century, "dyspepsia," the preferred contemporary term for indigestion, became a common complaint among eaters whose bodies rebelled against diets comprising greasy meats and gravies, ample carbohydrates and alcohol, and few fresh fruits and vegetables. The physical complaints of those who had the resources and inclination to overconsume were also augmented by other anxieties. Burgeoning American industrialization was changing the demographics of the country as Americans moved from farm to city in search of new kinds of employment. This trend continued decade by decade throughout the nineteenth century as American migrants were joined by immigrants from overseas in expanding urban centers. Not designed to rapidly absorb large numbers of people, many cities became overcrowded. Slums bred tension and disease. These new conditions created anxiety among the middle classes who feared the social problems that accompanied this influx of the less fortunate.

This population growth added to the unease of better-off urban dwellers who feared the changes being brought to their comfortable existence. However, the changes also brought culinary excitement, which inspired what was initially a timid intermingling of diverse recipes. Improvements in transportation such as better roads, canals, and eventually railroads also added to the food selection of the prosperous, who were no longer limited to eating locally or indulging only in preserved imported foods that could survive arduous journeys. Furthermore, the proliferation of commercial bakeries and the ready availability of increasingly less expensive canned goods transferred much of the work of food production out of the home and into the marketplace, a transition that rattled the sensibilities of many a traditionalist. As more and more eaters became consumers rather than producers of food products, their concern about who was preparing their food and with what ingredients steadily mounted. Fear of contamination and adulteration, much of which was founded at least in part by genuine fraud and unsanitary conditions on the part of unscrupulous industrial food outlets, grew.

Many nineteenth-century Americans were now faced with more food options and culinary abundance than ever before, a development that brought both excitement and trepidation. While some responded by eating too much, others sought to monitor their eating habits in an attempt to exercise a measure of control, at least over their own bodies, in a rapidly changing world.

Sylvester Graham, a Presbyterian minister who began his interest in American consumption while working as the general agent for the Pennsylvania Temperance Society, had an enormous influence on American eating patterns. While urging Americans to consume less alcohol, a substance that many believed contributed to some of the problems arising from urbanization and industrialization, Graham came to believe that gluttony was an even greater health problem than overindulgence in alcohol.

Although his religious beliefs likely pushed him in the direction of the temperance movement, his interest in diet was also influenced by his growing awareness of the latest scientific information about nutrition. He was persuaded by François J. V. Brouissais's contention in his 1826 *Treaty on Physiology* that most illness was caused by gastrointestinal distress. Armed with this idea, Graham spent the rest of his life developing theories about how to ease digestion. He believed that the best way to soothe the American stomach was to avoid "stimulating" foods. These included alcohol, tea, coffee, spices, condiments, and meat, especially pork. Graham believed that food should be simple and should be served in a state as close to nature as possible. He argued that the human body was designed to eat a vegetarian, largely raw-foods diet. Although his ideas about healthful eating resemble many modern theories, they were startling at the time. Many Americans, following the advice of medical practitioners, avoided eating fresh fruits and vegetables, which some believed carried disease. Furthermore, the admonition to avoid eating animal protein was anathema to many in the general population who maintained the historical American association with meat and prosperity.

Graham's concern about the pedestals of the contemporary diet was heightened by his belief that many processed foods were adulterated by their manufacturers. He publicly condemned bakers for using inferior flour, which he argued was often infused with harmful substances. Indeed, some bakers infused their loaves with fillers like alum, which disguised an inferior product and helped give the bread a whiter appearance, which consumers ironically associated with quality and purity. Graham also chastised farmers who grew wheat for using fertilizer on the soil, a practice that he claimed contaminated it and ruined the taste. He also spoke out against modern milling practices, where the bran was removed from the grain, making the resulting flour whiter but removing much of the nutritional value of the product.

Sylvester Graham. Nineteenth-century food reformer Sylvester Graham encouraged Americans to eat a vegetarian diet and whole grains. *Source*: *Harper's New Monthly Magazine*, vol. 60 (1880), p. 190, Library of Congress, Prints & Photographs Division, LC-USZ62-123830.

Instead Graham recommended baking bread with whole-wheat flour. Revealing his lingering, though perhaps subconscious, fear of modernity, Graham argued that bread should ideally be baked at home. He chastised mothers for failing to "comprehend the importance of good bread, in relation to all the bodily and intellectual and moral interests of their husbands and children." Homemade bread was also, Graham claimed, vital to "domestic and social and civil welfare" and to "religious prosperity." In Graham's mind, no decision was as important as those made at mealtime, and for women—who still bore the largest share of responsibility for purchasing and preparing food—the decision of what they fed their families was a reflection on their own moral virtue.

Unsurprisingly, many found Graham's advice literally hard to swallow. His advocacy of a vegetarian diet was considered faddish and extreme in an exceedingly carnivorous culture, and many were reluctant to forgo the new convenience of commercially available bread. For their part, the producers of the substances that Graham condemned were terrified that his message would take root. In 1837, a group of butchers and bakers threatened to violently disrupt a lecture that Graham planned to give in Boston. The owners of the venue bowed to the pressure of the food producers and cancelled the engagement, but an undaunted Graham found another platform. The bakers made good on their promise to attempt to disrupt his speech, but Graham's admirers responded by dispersing the crowd by throwing lime into it, making sure that the lecture could continue.

Graham also made others uncomfortable by his frank and public discussions of human sexuality at a time when such subjects were not seen as fit for conversation, particularly in audiences consisting of both men and women. In 1834, an incensed crowd stopped Graham from delivering a planned lecture on chastity to an all-female audience in Portland, Maine. When Graham spoke of avoiding "stimulating" foods, one of the chief forms of stimulation he hoped to help eaters avoid was of the sexual variety. Unlike most contemporary reformers of the era who sought to encourage Americans to keep sexual behavior confined to the bonds of matrimony, Graham believed that sex even within marriage was harmful to the health. He suggested that healthy people restrict themselves to engaging in sexual intercourse no more frequently than once a month. Taking care to avoid stimulating foods would, he argued, limit potentially destructive sexual appetites. Unsurprisingly, Graham argued that the organ that could be most damaged by excess sexual behavior was the stomach. Too much sex could lead not only to pain and dyspepsia but also to an "indescribable sensation of sinking, death-like faintness . . . without intermission."

Despite how extreme his dietary views were in the context of the time and in spite of the fact that he violated strong cultural taboos by talking so frankly and openly about sexual behavior, Graham's philosophies gained a number of adherents who wished to gain control over their unruly hungers, both for food and for sex. One convert spoke of his decision to follow the Graham regimen in religious terms, claiming that when he heard the dietary authority speak, "*I heard and trembled.* The torrent of truth poured upon me and made me a thorough convert." For this Graham follower, the biggest sticking point was the prohibition on coffee, which after a struggle, he eventually managed to forgo.

Graham boarding houses became popular after the first one was established in New York in 1833. Male disciples could stay temporarily at these hotels to learn Grahamite principles and begin the process of curing their ailments through healthful living. Those staying at the hotels kept to a rigid and precise routine and ate bland vegetarian meals. Even many Americans who did not turn over their entire lives to Graham's principles slowly absorbed many of his ideas. As the century progressed, Americans ate more and more fresh fruits and vegetables. And whole-wheat "Graham" flour began to appear in a greater number of recipes. Although many of these recipes combined the flour with white flour or with stimulating ingredients that Graham would have disapproved of, they are a testimony to the widespread influence of his ideas.

CONTROVERSY AND THE SHAKER DIET

Graham's principles trickled into many social arenas, even impacting the Shakers, a religious group with avowed intentions to separate themselves from the values of the wider world. "Mother" Ann Lee, an Englishwoman, was the leader of this offshoot sect of Quakerism, which was known for its expressive worship style characterized by dancing and what appeared as "shaking" to many observers. In 1774, Mother Ann received a divine revelation that directed her to move to America and establish the sect there. Although the Shakers were never a large group, they enjoyed a period of relative prominence in the 1820s and 1830s, when they attracted most of their converts. They established settlements in eight different states and could claim at their height about six thousand members.

The group believed in celibacy, and members referred to themselves platonically as "brothers" and "sisters." The converts lived together communally and followed a rigid schedule, rising, working, eating, and worshiping at fixed hours. Their unusual physical proximity combined with their preference for structure and order that the group had to strive to find consensus on various issues related to daily living. As Graham's ideas about an ideal diet spread to the group, they had a divisive impact. In light of this new information, members could not agree on whether or not they should be allowed to continue to eat meat and to drink tea and coffee as they had always done.

From their founding, Shakers were expected to eat plain diets, a practice that reflected their belief that functionality and lack of ornamentation should characterize their personal attire, their homes, and their furnishings as well. Some specific communities had a few somewhat random dietary rules, such as a ban in some places against eating raw or unripe fruit. These particular dictates were, however, applicable only to the local residents in certain areas and not to all Shakers. Beginning in 1821, the entire group was ordered by a church document known as the "Millennial Laws" to subject itself to certain restrictions on the drinking of alcohol. For example, alcohol was not to be consumed before breakfast. Drinking the substance was, however, not banned or even severely restricted. For the most part, there were few rules beyond the expectation that the brothers and sisters graciously and unselfishly eat the food that the community cooks prepared. They ate hearty but plain diets dictated by the availability of ingredients in their locality. The issue of what constituted ethical eating practices did not become a particularly contentious one until Graham's ideas began to spread.

Historian Priscilla J. Brewer documents that beginning in the mid-1830s many members of the sect began following Graham's dietary principles—giving up meat, coffee, and tea; using Graham flour to bake with; and forgoing highly flavored foods and condiments. Given Graham's belief that these kinds of "stimulating" foods heightened sexual appetites, it is perhaps unsurprising that his theories would be appealing to many Shakers because of the fact that their creed demanded celibacy.

According to Brewer, dietary concerns increasingly impacted the internal dynamics of the group. Although the Shakers generally strove for communal uniformity of behavior, the lead ministry of the group initially refused to issue a binding mandate on the issue of diet, allowing individual members to let their own consciences dictate their eating practices. Because there was no universally applicable directive nor uniformity of opinion on the subject, the issue of dietary practices caused many conflicts among members. Opponents of Graham's philosophies did not believe that their diet was a reflection of their religious sincerity, and adherents of the new food program often caricatured those who were not taken in by the new ideas as gluttonous hedonists. Many of the members who experimented with the new diet were later seduced by the ready availability of familiar and beloved foods still being eaten by those who had refused to abstain. Others remained fanatical adherents to Graham's laws.

Brother Ephraim Prentiss, a boys' caretaker in one of the communities, claimed that by forcing his charges to change their eating practices, he had also managed to cure many health and behavioral problems. He reported, "Their sores have healed up . . . their headaches have ceased, their fevers gone . . . that ferocious fighting spirit . . . seems to have entirely vanished away. . . . In short, they are the most peaceable and happy little company of boys I ever saw." Understandably, given his zealous belief that dietary matters were linked closely to spiritual ones, Prentiss was enraged when he could not convince all of his fellow believers to adhere to his regime. These disagreements led to disunion and fighting for years to come. Tensions were so severe that one member believed that "the Devil" intended to use Graham's diet to destroy "the union of God's people."

In 1841, the lead ministry surprised the local communities when it claimed that divine inspiration now demanded that members give up the consumption of tea, coffee, and pork. A church newspaper that year reported that pork was now considered "unclean and positively unfit for the children of Zion." In the aftermath of this, the war between Grahamites and carnivores only intensified. Many who opposed the dietary rules begrudgingly removed pork, tea, and coffee from their diet, but this did not mean that they abstained from eating all meat or embraced Graham's ideas about other kinds of stimulating foods. Zealous Grahamites wished now to obey all of his mandates and felt cheated by their partial victory. Some seem to have ignored the new rules altogether.

In 1855, perhaps in response to a decline in membership, the lead ministry decided to relax many rules. Once again members were allowed to openly drink tea and coffee. However, the leadership had no need to issue a specific mandate on the consumption of pork, which had already crept back into use. Although the Shakers were willing to give up many liberties, including that of sexual intercourse, many were ultimately unwilling to alter their traditional eating practices. In keeping with the American tradition of enthusiastic meat consumption, it seems fitting that even members of this utopian order fought for their right to consume animal flesh.

THE SEARCH FOR TRANSCENDENT FOODWAYS AT FRUITLANDS

The Shakers were hardly the only idealists to struggle with the issue of whether or not dietary choices impacted one's spiritual health. Bronson Alcott, an educator, writer, reformer, and father of the famed novelist Louisa May Alcott, enlisted his family to embark on an experiment of dietary reform and communal living in 1834. Alcott was associated with the transcendentalists, an early nineteenth-century American philosophical movement most closely associated with Ralph Waldo Emerson. The transcendentalists emphasized individualism, personal intuition, and the belief that all humans had divinity within them. Many transcendentalists, including Alcott, were strong social critics of a variety of aspects of American society ranging from slavery to the treatment of Native Americans to the inequalities arising from the expanding market economy.

Alcott's search for enlightenment and his dismay at many aspects of life in the United States led him on a mission to find a more ideal way of living. He convinced Charles Lane, an English admirer of Alcott's work, to embark on the social experiment with him. At Alcott's behest, Lane purchased a farm in Harvard, Massachusetts, for $1,800 in 1834. The Alcott family and Lane and his son William became the founding members of a commune founded on the property. They were joined by a handful of other unconventional people, including a nudist, a local eccentric who refused to shave his unruly beard, and an individual who reversed the order of his given and surnames in order to show his disdain for social conventions. At the commune's height, twelve adults resided together there. They labeled their community "Fruitlands" to demonstrate their hope that they could live off of the fruit of the land and bow out of the market economy.

The group was bound together both by their belief that American society was corrupt and by a vow to abstain from the use of animal products. Members of the group promised not only to avoid consuming meat but also to forgo all food items that came from animals, including eggs, milk, and even honey. They hoped to subsist on whole-wheat bread, fruit, and vegetables. They also wished to consume only items that they grew themselves. Alcott, who visited a nearby Shaker village before establishing Fruitlands, was critical of the fact that Shakers traded their homemade crafts and produce in exchange for items like meat. His community would, he hoped, be economically independent.

The belief that animals were not intended to be food was related not only to Grahamite ideas about health and stimulating foods but also to the conviction that animals had rights because all things in the world were interconnected. In her diary written during the Fruitlands experiment, Alcott's daughter Anna articulated their beliefs on the issue of eating animals, writing, "Life was given to the animals not to be destroyed by men, but to make them happy, and that they might enjoy life. But men are not satisfied with slaying the innocent creatures, they eat them and so make their bodies of flesh meat. O how many happy lives have been destroyed and happy families have been separated to please an unclean appetite of men!" Her sister Louisa made the group's connection between dietary practices and moral issues explicit in a short verse written during her time at Fruitland:

Without flesh diet
there could be no
blood-shedding war.

The utopians also refused to wear clothing made from animals like wool or leather and were reluctant to use animal labor in farming. Although they eventually utilized one yoke of oxen, they did as much farm work as possible by hand. They also refused to use manure for fertilizer, finding the substance filthy, a prejudice shared by Graham. Their belief in their principles was so strong that one member of the group, Anna Page, was expelled for eating a bite of fish.

The residents of Fruitlands quickly found that it was difficult to sustain themselves and their high ideals. Most members of the group had little experience with farming, and they found it impossible to produce enough food to meet their needs. By some accounts, Alcott and Lane's intellectual and spiritual concerns triumphed over practical ones, and they lacked the needed organizational skills to effectively lead the group. Joseph J. Thorndike notes that when planning for the experiment, "Alcott and Lane had brought almost a thousand books, mostly dealing with mystical philosophy, but not a single pamphlet on agriculture. They did have ideas on the subject, but many of those ideas were at war with practicalities." Fruitlands had a chronic shortage of labor, and Alcott's wife, Abby, had to eventually resort to selling some of her meager personal possessions to feed her children. She also expressed frustration at the fact that the women in the male-dominated household seemed to be expected to shoulder a disproportionate share of the work.

The group was also beleaguered by other personality conflicts. Charles Lane felt the Alcott family was too exclusive, privileging their biological bonds over the development of spiritual connections among members of the larger group. Lane shared the Shakers' belief that celibacy was a superior spiritual choice and seems to have put pressure on the Alcotts to abstain from marital relations. The Alcott children found Lane's influence on their family life to be a negative one, and Louisa bluntly recorded in her journal that she was happy when he was away from home. Bronson Alcott's ascetic vision was not appealing to many, and the group had little hope of attracting new members and resources to help prop up the failing endeavor. The Fruitlands experiment lasted a mere seven difficult months.

KELLOGG AND THE CEREAL REVOLUTION

Another group that linked what people ate to the health of their souls and who made a much more lasting impact, albeit somewhat indirectly, on the contemporary American diet were the Seventh-day Adventists. The group originated in the 1840s when the Shakers were still thriving and Alcott was still coming to terms with the failure of his vision of communal vegetarian living. One of its founders, Ellen G. White, was considered to be a prophet by the group, and she received many visions that influenced its religious doctrines, including one in 1863 that showed White that health issues and spiritual issues were closely linked. An angel commanded her to eat two meals a day; to avoid meat, coffee, tea, and alcohol; and to consume primarily whole-grain bread, fruits, and vegetables. From then on, eating properly became a spiritual duty of church members.

White inadvertently impacted American culinary history forever when she met young John Harvey Kellogg in the 1870s. Kellogg had suffered from a series of childhood illnesses and had developed a strong interest in contemporary wisdom about healthful eating and had, of his own accord, adopted a vegetarian lifestyle. White encouraged him to pursue medical studies and even loaned him money to aid him in his pursuits. He studied at the Hygeio-Therapeutic College, the University of Michigan, and Bellevue Hospital. After earning these credentials, he went to work for the Western Health Reform Institute, which had strong ties to White and to the Seventh-day Adventist Church. A visionary with a tireless work ethic, Kellogg rose through the ranks, eventually becoming chief physician of the institute. He used his influence to expand the once small clinic and in the process changed its name to the Battle Creek Sanitarium and formally separated the health organization from the church, a move that assured that his version of healthful eating and living practices would remain unchallenged for the more than sixty years he presided over the institution.

Kellogg believed that dietary reform and social reform were connected. In addition to running the Battle Creek Sanitarium, in the 1890s he donated his services to an Adventist mission for the disadvantaged in Chicago. He helped establish a clinic staffed by nurses trained in Battle Creek who provided medical care for indigent Chicagoans who were eligible to receive, free of charge, special foods that were considered to be part of their medical care. He also opened a lunch counter where the hungry could buy lunches of bean soup and zwieback crackers for a penny. He hoped that by providing free or affordable physical nourishment he was also saving souls, claiming, "The intimate relation of mind and body, of health and morals, is recognized as an important factor requiring careful attention and consideration."

Problems with financing and conflicts between Kellogg, White, and other members of the Adventist Church eventually led Kellogg to close the mission, but his activities there reveal his ongoing belief that food practices had important physical and spiritual implications. He put his altruistic ideas into practice in an even more personal way when he adopted the son of a prostitute who was found foraging in a garbage can, named him George, and took him home. To Kellogg's disappointment, his adopted son did not enthusiastically embrace his father's ideas and was a constant source of frustration. He had been unable to save this particular soul through his regimen.

Despite Kellogg's piety, the religious roots of the organization quickly became obscured in the minds of many who flocked to Battle Creek. As a physician Kellogg was, however, happy to treat those who were more interested in the health of their bodies than in religious pursuits. Although many of the employees of the institution had church ties, patients at the sanitarium were not limited to members of the church and included notable Americans such as J. C. Penney, President William Howard Taft, Thomas Edison, and Henry Ford, who became convinced that Kellogg's dietary regimen, even if followed for only the short term, would benefit their health. Kellogg persuaded many with his claim that "the causes of indigestion are responsible for more deaths than all other causes combined." Buoyed by that belief, his patients cheerfully paid for the privilege of following a regimented schedule that included cold baths and workouts in the gymnasium and meals that consisted of items such as yogurt, stewed prunes, and unseasoned grains served in various guises.

In addition to advocating a diet along the lines of that prescribed by Graham, Kellogg was a proponent of mastication, the process of repetitively chewing food until it largely dissolved in the mouth, allegedly making digestion easier for the stomach. He soon discovered, however, that due to the sorry state of nineteenth-century dental care, many of his patients had teeth problems and were unable to chew the hard zwieback bread he gave them. He attempted to solve the problem by grinding up biscuits, creating an early form of granola similar to one that had been invented by James Jackson in the 1860s. He also began looking for other ways to soften the grain he served to his patients. While pressing grain and nuts through a set of rollers, he created peanut butter, which quickly became a popular vegetarian food. He also ultimately created cornflakes, which were destined to become a popular breakfast cereal even among those with no interest in Kellogg's entire dietary program.

Kellogg sold his products from his sanitarium, but his brother Will had a larger vision and created the Kellogg Company to make and distribute the cereal, which he successfully proved in court he had a proprietary right to produce and market. Will Kellogg poured money into advertising his product, using catchy slogans such as "It won its favor through its flavor" coupled with pictures of beautiful women purchasing his cereal. He convinced many Americans who were not interested in following a vegetarian diet that a bowl of cereal was a more healthful and appealing breakfast than a plate full of greasy meat products, potatoes, syrup, and bread. Will Kellogg took the tactic that cereal manufacturers would take in their advertising campaigns from then on with his argument that eating grains for breakfast was not only good for you but that these products tasted good as well. Cereal was no longer being promoted exclusively as a kind of medicine but also as a pleasing food to eat.

The popularity of the cereal products served at the sanitarium and later marketed to the broader world by Will Kellogg inspired many imitators. One of the most successful was Charles Post, a onetime patient at Battle Creek Sanitarium, who claimed that his stay there did not improve his health. However, it did inspire an interest in creating his own versions of the foods served there as well as in founding a rival therapeutic institute across town that he called La Vita Inn. Although he shared Kellogg's distrust for products containing caffeine, his facility did not prohibit the serving of meat. His treatment program consisted largely of encouraging his patients to think positively about their health, claiming that "there is a power within you that can and will work miracles." He created a product called Postum Cereal Coffee, which he succeeded in marketing beyond Battle Creek with the aid of a Chicago advertising agency. He quickly developed his own breakfast cereal, too, which he called Grape-Nuts. He was rewarded for his efforts by becoming a millionaire and by making a place for himself in history for the role he played in helping to transform what Americans ate for breakfast, for although breakfast cereal began as an obscure health food, it steadily gained in popularity decade by decade. By the twentieth century it was being consumed by more than eighty million Americans each day.

EATING AS WARFARE DURING WORLD WAR I

As the twentieth century unfolded, Americans began to have the unique opportunity to use their food practices not only as a way to actively perform their religious, spiritual, and moral beliefs but also as a way to demonstrate their patriotism. This opportunity presented itself the most clearly when the nation entered World War I and the government asked citizens to voluntarily conserve certain foods in order to aid the war effort. Congress passed the Food and Fuel Control Act in 1917, which gave the president the power to regulate the distribution of the nation's food and fuel supply if deemed necessary for the war effort. To coordinate food production, conservation, and distribution, President Woodrow Wilson created the U.S. Food Administration and appointed Herbert Hoover, who had established a good reputation for his work running a war relief effort in Belgium, to head the new organization.

The legislation that led to the creation of the Food Administration granted the president, and by extension Hoover, substantial authority to regulate the country's food supply. Among other powers, Hoover was authorized to fix prices and impose rationing if he deemed those actions necessary to make sure that sufficient food could be sent to hungry allies in war-torn Europe and to feed American troops. Hoover took advantage of his power to set prices and did so for the key commodities of sugar and wheat. However, he was reluctant to impose formal rationing. The Food Administration made timid experiments in this direction by limiting sugar purchases to wholesalers and retailers and suggesting they impose their own restrictions on how much individual consumers could purchase. However, demonstrating the piecemeal nature of government policy, the administration also encouraged consumers to purchase large quantities of sugar—up to twenty-five pounds at a time—to use for home canning, another conservation measure. Hoover also asked Americans to make and consume "Victory Bread" made with equal portions of wheat and another grain. Retailers were in fact required to sell wheat only along with an equal weight of another grain product such as oatmeal, buckwheat flour, corn meal, potato flour, or soybean flour.

In spite of these timid gestures in controlling American consumption, for the most part Hoover preferred to appeal to American patriotism and volunteerism rather than government-mandated restrictions, hoping that his fellow citizens would change their eating patterns out of love for the country. Hoover was reluctant to exert too much direct control over American purchasing decisions in part because he feared that an organization with strong regulatory powers such as the Food Administration could pose a "danger to democracy." It was imperative, he told Congress, that such an organization be "absolutely emergency in character" and "disappear instantly with peace." In keeping with his anxiety about heavy-handed government intervention, he employed more subtle means to encourage Americans to modify their eating habits as a way to support the war effort—a propaganda campaign.

In a wide variety of Food Administration advertisements, Americans were asked to make the following weekly modifications to their diet:

Sunday—One meal Wheatless; one meal Meatless.
Monday—All meals Wheatless; one meal Meatless.
Tuesday—All meals Meatless; one meal Wheatless.
Wednesday—All meals Wheatless; one meal Meatless.
Thursday—One meal Wheatless; one meal Meatless.
Friday—One meal Wheatless; one meal Meatless.
Saturday—All meals Porkless; one meal Wheatless; one meal Meatless.

In order to encourage participation in the program, the government produced a steady stream of printed material ranging from visually striking posters designed to appeal to the emotions to dry informational pamphlets about nutrition. It also asked citizens to display prominently on their homes Food Administration cards to visually demonstrate their commitment to the cause and to encourage their neighbors to also comply.

Posters with anatomically detailed images of fish encouraged Americans to eat fish instead of beef or pork. Drawings of Uncle Sam and Lady Liberty begged fellow citizens to grow, can, and conserve food. Others employed more violent, warlike images. A poster advocating canning food at home in order to save commercially produced canned food for American troops urged, "Can vegetables, fruit and the Kaiser too" and showed an image of a dejected-looking Kaiser trapped inside of a Mason jar alongside jars of tomatoes and peas. A government-sponsored exhibit urging the consumption of potatoes proclaimed that "Potatriots" who followed the suggestion were also helping to "Spud the Kaiser." Other posters equated food with weaponry, declaring "Beans are Bullets—Potatoes are Powder." Another declared, "Food is ammunition. Don't waste it." Americans were promised repeatedly in Food Administration publications that their efforts would be rewarded and that "Food will win the war."

World War I Food Administration Poster in Yiddish. The poster reads, "Food will win the war—You came here seeking freedom, now you must help to preserve it— Wheat is needed for the allies—waste nothing." *Source*: Library of Congress, Prints & Photographs Division, World War I Poster Collection, LC-DIG-ppmsca-0565.

The government also utilized the newest information about nutrition as a way to encourage Americans to think critically about their eating habits and to support the conservation effort. In the mid-nineteenth century German scientist Justus van Liebig led groundbreaking studies that revealed that food could be classified as carbohydrate, fat, or protein. It soon came to be understood that the body needed each of these components, and scientists set about looking for ways to figure out what quantities of each were needed. In the 1890s, Wilbur O. Atwater, a chemist who worked for the U.S. Department of Agriculture, made important advances in measuring how many calories (a unit used to measure energy) were contained in various foods. Based on his research, he made recommendations for how many calories an individual should consume each day.

In Atwater's mind, different carbohydrates, fats, and proteins were interchangeable. During the era of World War I, other important research about vitamins was being conducted that explained why people with adequate caloric intake who did not get enough vitamins could still contract diseases related to malnutrition. However, these ideas were not fully developed and incorporated into the scientific community or the public consciousness until the 1920s. The Food Administration's appeal to get people to show dietary flexibility was based upon Atwater's simpler understanding of the body's nutritional requirements.

Because Atwater thought that all calories were created equal, he was a strong proponent of substituting foods in the same category for each other. Initially his efforts were aimed at educating the poor, whom he accused of carelessly spending far too much money on food. He urged the needy to forgo concerns about maintaining traditional foodways or about taste and to purchase the cheapest proteins available to them. This kind of reasoning translated well to the Food Administration's desire to get Americans to conserve red meat for consumption by the troops and by allies in Europe. Much of its propaganda campaign highlighted the concept of substituting allegedly equivalent foods for each other. For example, a poster encouraging the use of cottage cheese declared that one pound of the substance had more protein than a pound of beef, pork, lamb, or fowl. Consumers viewing the poster could write to request a recipe card with suggestions for how to incorporate this "meat substitute" into their diets. In the book *Food Guide for War Service at Home*, written by Florence Powdermaker at the request of the Food Administration, the author makes a similar point about grains, proclaiming in bold print, "Remember that as far as nutritional value is concerned, it makes practically no difference whether we eat wheat, or oats, rye, or barley."

In their 1918 cookbook *Foods That Will Win the War and How to Cook Them*, C. Houston Goudiss and Alberta M. Goudiss give a number of tips on how to bake bread using a variety of grains and how to make sugarless desserts in order to conserve wheat and sugar. They also offer a number of suggestions for how to make vegetarian dishes. These meal suggestions may have sounded appealing to those who had been open to Graham's message, but they were not necessarily appetizing to Americans used to consuming large quantities of meat. Goudiss and Goudiss make the case for using meat substitutes by providing elaborate and comparative nutritional information for meat and a variety of substitutes ranging from cheese to eggs, to fish (which was not considered "meat"), to lentils, to peanuts in an attempt to demonstrate nutritionally sound alternatives to red meat. Some of the meat substitute dishes are meant to resemble the meat they replaced, including the "Boston Roast," which seems designed to approximate a meatloaf:

> 1 teaspoon onion juice
> 1 cup grated cheese
> 1 teaspoon salt
> ⅛ teaspoon cayenne
> 1 cup beans (kidney)
> About 1 cup breadcrumbs

> Soak and cook beans. Mix all ingredients into loaf. Baste with fat and water. Bake 30 minutes. Serve with tomato sauce.

Americans were encouraged to demonstrate their commitment to reducing their consumption and looking for substitutes for foods such as red meat, wheat, and sugar by signing a pledge card. Fourteen million Americans signed cards promising that their families would adhere to the program. After signing the card, those who made the pledge would receive an emblem that they could place in the window of their family home to show they were members of the Food Administration. These decals gave those who displayed them the opportunity both to demonstrate their own patriotic feelings and to implicitly pressure their neighbors to support the government's initiatives out of the same motivations. In this heightened atmosphere, what a family chose to eat for dinner could be interpreted as a reflection of their degree of loyalty to the United States.

Women in particular were targeted by the propaganda machine of the Food Administration as they were still the primary cooks in most American homes. By depicting food as a weapon that could win the war, Hoover's agency attempted to transform women into domestic soldiers who could combat the enemy from the safety of their own kitchens. Children, too, were encouraged to see themselves as part of the military apparatus on the home front. The Bureau of Education and Department of Agriculture created a "School Garden Army" where young people could learn the skills of gardening and get an opportunity to help build up the nation's food supply by putting their skills into practice. Thus all segments of the population were encouraged to see themselves as combatants, and many Americans eagerly seized upon this identity.

Historian Helen Zoe Veit claims that many Americans participated voluntarily and proudly in the food conservation program not only because they wanted to see themselves as playing a role in the conflict that paralleled that of the men doing the actual fighting, but also because they saw denial as a way to exemplify their moral virtue. She argues that in the mind of many, "Overeating, luxury, greed and waste" had characterized American eating practices before the war, and the "austerity and self-discipline" advocated by the Food Administration could be morally cleansing for a nation whose values had been obscured by too much abundance.

Self-denial, however, could only be practiced by those with the means necessary to make the choice to forgo certain luxuries. Those who could not afford to eat expensive foods such as large quantities of red meat found the Food Administration's admonitions to cut down superfluous and irksome. The principles of economy and substitution that the Food Administration taught to middle-class Americans through their propaganda campaign were not new ones to the nation's poor, who were all too familiar with doing without preferred foods. Railroad worker John Donahue laughed at the Food Administration's idea of economy, claiming, "If I could follow your directions and give my family what you direct, I would consider myself a millionaire."

The same propaganda campaign that inspired middle-class Americans to feelings of patriotism and virtue alienated many working-class Americans, who were unimpressed by their fellow citizens' definitions of sacrifice. Not only did the Food Administration demonstrate ignorance about the food realities of poorer people and the possibility that its campaign could inflame class antagonisms, it also demonstrated ethnic insensitivities by asking Jewish Americans to sign pledge cards promising to eat more shellfish, a food that violated the rules of kosher.

Thus, buy-in to the Food Administration's program was hardly universal. The sacrifices of prosperous Americans combined with programs designed to increase agricultural production did allow the nation to dramatically increase its food exports during the war years. For example, before the war, the United States exported an average of 645,000 metric tons of meats and fats annually. In 1918, this number soared to 2,369,630 metric tons. However, this was not due to a change in eating habits among the American poor, who ironically began eating more red meat than ever during the war years. Higher wages provided by jobs in war-related industry allowed many the newfound opportunity to purchase expensive foods. The ability to improve their diets and to purchase high-status foods, such as meat, that they had infrequently enjoyed before the war proved to be more compelling than the opportunity to use their diet as a way to demonstrate abstract virtues. That was a luxury enjoyed primarily by the middle class. For this reason, historian Amy Bentley deems the Food Administration a failure. During World War II, the federal government would continue to appeal to Americans to use the dinner table as a space to demonstrate their patriotic fervor, but this time it bolstered its propaganda campaign with a mandatory rationing program.

GOVERNMENT-MANDATED PATRIOTIC EATING DURING WORLD WAR II

During World War II, the government no longer intended to rely solely on a spirit of volunteerism and patriotism to convince Americans to conserve food. Although government propaganda once again encouraged these virtues, these abstractions were reinforced by an elaborate program of rationing. For some scarce items such as sugar and coffee, each individual was allowed to purchase a set amount. Other items were rationed according to a point system, and consumers were given the opportunity to make choices—something that was important psychologically to Americans—about how they would spend their points and what they would eat. The program was sold to consumers as the most fair way to handle the issue of food distribution.

Government literature appealed to the consciences of those who read or viewed it, framing the recipients of the message as patriotic citizens. Rationing, it was implied, was necessary in part because other, less scrupulous people might take more than their share without federal restraints. The government made films and pamphlets exposing the crimes of fictional characters such as Mrs. George Grabwell who was labeled a "helpmate" of Hitler for hoarding food and Miss Miranda Glucose who stockpiled sugar before rationing went into effect but did not notify the government about her supply. Compliant Americans were encouraged to feel morally superior to these fictional deviants.

The system was initially one of trial and error. As had happened during World War I, the middle-class administrators of the rationing program often did not understand the dietary realities of poorer Americans. For example, officials initially assigned a point-rationing system for chitterlings, or pig intestines, which were often eaten by African Americans and poorer white southerners, that was deemed too high by those who would normally have purchased them. Those assigning the point values likely had never eaten chitterlings and thus did not realize that when cooked they shrank considerably, meaning that large portions of the raw food were needed to make an adequate meal.

Despite the mandatory nature of the program, patriotism was an important motivator in discouraging consumers from buying goods on the black market or hoarding certain food items and thus creating artificial scarcities. Once again, much of the government propaganda about food behavior was aimed at women, who were to think of their aprons as military uniforms and their kitchens as theaters of conflict. The war years were a time of enormous social change as many women entered the labor force to take jobs vacated by men fighting overseas as well as newly created defense industry positions. Many women worked in traditionally masculine vocations and performed physical tasks like hammering and welding that were foreign to those who had spent their previous working lives tied to the domestic realm. These new roles were liberating to many but caused uncertainty for some as these newly feminized vocations implicitly called into question set ideas about gender roles.

For those uncomfortable with the kind of gender role–bending patriotism exemplified by Rosie the Riveter, the prorationing propaganda published by the Office of Price Administration (OPA) was a comfort because women were depicted primarily in domestic capacities. The female figures on OPA posters were white, middle class, nicely attired, and presented as being concerned primarily with domestic responsibilities. For example, a perfectly coiffed blonde woman wearing a striped dress and ruffled apron appeared on numerous posters with her right hand raised, somberly taking the "Home Front Pledge" to support the rationing program and not to buy black-market goods. For this woman, the job of feeding her family, not building munitions, was assumed to be her primary role in the war effort.

Women could display their patriotism not only by cooperating with the rationing program but also by canning goods at home to save industrially processed foods for troops and allies overseas. Again this was depicted as a properly feminine way to aid in the war effort. In one propaganda poster, a mother and daughter with identical swept-up curly blonde hair, red dresses, and frilly aprons are shown working side by side canning produce. The child beams, and a caption reads, "We'll have plenty to eat this winter, won't we Mother?" Although the woman and girl depicted on the poster were not representative of the racial, ethnic, and economic diversity of the American public, they were probably a reasonable representation of the profile of women who took up canning to support the war effort.

Although many rural women had long canned as a way to preserve the bounty of their gardens for winter, by the 1940s the practice was far less common among urban women. Historian Amy Bentley points out that those who wished to experiment with canning had to have the leisure time to learn a new skill, something that many working-class women did not possess, and even more importantly money to spend on the necessary equipment. For this reason, canning became a middle-class means for demonstrating food piety and patriotism.

Those who had the resources to can their own produce did so enthusiastically, and 40 percent of all of the vegetables consumed by Americans during the war years were canned at home or in community canning centers. Virginia Raymond Ott cheerfully recalled having plenty to eat during the war years because the family canned the produce from their garden. She also proudly remembered other economizing measures such as the year when the family celebrated six birthdays simultaneously with one cake in order to conserve sugar. Mild deprivations of this kind enabled her and her family to feel that they were making a concrete sacrifice and were directly aiding the war effort.

The federal government also encouraged Americans to produce as much of their own food supply as possible by growing "victory gardens," which again required the availability of leisure time and the ability to purchase gardening supplies. Women who did not have their own gardens were still urged to help in the production of the nation's food supply in appeals to join the Women's Land Army. The Department of Agriculture placed more than two million women in agricultural jobs between 1943 and 1945. Workers were given a uniform to wear and an insignia denoting their membership in what was depicted almost as a branch of the military. These women were not described as "farmers" or as "field hands" but as soldiers. Children fourteen years of age or older could also aid the war effort as "Victory Farm Volunteers." A particular emphasis was made on recruiting children who lived in towns and cities to spend time in rural areas working on farms. Their labor was depicted as vital in "the tremendous job that must be done on the farm to achieve victory."

By making food behavior military behavior, the entire population could be depicted as being directly a part of the war effort. However, for some, feelings of patriotism had their limits, and for many, traditional ideas about what constituted an adequate diet proved to be as emotionally important as the desire to feel that personal food actions were a vital part of achieving military victory. For the most part, Americans did not suffer from a shortage of food during World War II. Three quarters of Americans reported that their serving sizes at meals did not diminish at all. However, the limited availability of certain items, particularly meat, was trying to many. Meat, particularly red meat, always an important symbol of wealth and abundance to American eaters, became an even more powerful sign to many as it became harder to obtain. Although sources of protein like soybeans and peanut butter were easier to come by during the war years, most considered eating a main dish made out of these proteins to be a hardship and a sacrifice. Atwater's theory of substituting one protein for another did not take into account the psychological importance of certain foods.

One college girl saved ration coupons to have a steak dinner on a visit home to see her family. Her sister reported that the "steaks" her father brought home were cod steaks, a situation that created "some unhappy campers at dinner." Catherine "Renee" Young wrote to her husband, who was fighting overseas, about the food shortages at home. She complained, "Yesterday I didn't take any meat not because we didn't have any but because I am sick of the same thing." She was tired of eating sausages made from scraps and craved a better cut. She was certain that a shortage of steak was responsible for the fact that "there is so much sickness and colds this winter." Another mother wrote to her son overseas about the shortage of turkeys available for Thanksgiving but proudly proclaimed that she had won a bird in a raffle, ensuring that their family could eat what she obviously considered to be the only proper Thanksgiving fare. Another woman who was less fortunate in her quest to secure a familiar protein for a holiday meal tried to make the best of things, cheerfully remarking to her soldier son that Spam made a surprisingly "tasty Easter Dinner." Another woman recalled that shrimp and fish were plentiful during the war years, but this did not sate her family's appetite. She recalled, "There was no meat. If you found any it looked so bad that its source was questionable and you were afraid to buy it." For these eaters, consuming particular foods was an important part of their identity as Americans. They felt entitled to eat large quantities of red meat and to enjoy special holiday meals. The satisfactions brought by patriotic denial did not completely dull their appetites for these foods. As soon as the war and rationing ended, Americans began eating more red meat than ever before, indicating that wartime scarcity did nothing to alter the American concept of an ideal meal.

Although many got satisfaction from making culinary wartime sacrifices, denial never became a long-lasting marker of American identity. Americans saw themselves as living in a land of abundance, and neither the war nor economic depression could shake the shared middle-class certainty that American tables should be overflowing. One food item that became synonymous with Americans during the war years was Coca-Cola. Executives at Coca-Cola consciously tried to frame their product as being patriotic and distinctly American. In 1942, the company produced a short film titled *The Free American Way*, which contrasted life in the United States with life in the nations of the Axis powers, making the greater material wealth of Americans the primary basis of comparison. The company also distributed marketing materials disguised as games and other items to American soldiers and made sure that its product was cheaply available on military bases. Company advertisements often depicted American GIs drinking Coke.

Soldiers got the company's message and learned to embrace Coca-Cola as a reminder of home, as did the rest of the world, which learned to see the beverage as a symbol of the United States and thus of prosperity. The United States did not suffer from the same crippling shortages of food and other supplies after the war as the countries where the fighting actually took place. In the postwar years, middle-class Americans were once again able to eat as much red meat as they desired and to fill their larders with coffee, sugar, and Coca-Cola.

For some American eaters, postwar abundance could not displace the memories of hard times during the war years. Many of the 120,000 people of Japanese descent who were imprisoned in internment camps during the conflict suffered from food shortages and poor nutrition, making their situation a far more serious one than that faced by the general population who had enough to eat and merely lacked a prewar diversity of options. Their inadequate care at the hands of the U.S. government highlighted the extent to which many viewed Japanese Americans as less entitled to the same rights as other Americans, particularly white Americans. Sonoka Iwata recalled one of the first meals she ate at the Colorado River Relocation Camp:

> We had to stand in line under the hot sun and when inside we had to again stand in line with our plates and cutlery. Honestly, it made me think of what might be in a cheap restaurant. It was like survival of the fittest, too, as small babies and grown ups had the same chance. On top of all that, there would be just sauerkraut and wienies and rice.

Louis A. Ferguson, a white woman, and her husband worked as teachers at the Manzanar camp. She was startled at the inequality between the food served to Japanese prisoners and to white employees:

> A large mess hall is set up in each block. The people have to line up outside and stand in the sun for 15–20 minutes until cafeteria-style serving progresses sufficiently so they get into the hall. They get as much as they want to eat. The food is pretty heavy—rice and many other starchy foods three times per day. Only very young children get milk with each meal. Other children and adults get milk only once in awhile. More fresh fruits and vegetables should be served. . . .
>
> There is a special mess hall for the Caucasian personnel. The meals here are well-balanced, more than you can possibly eat, all the milk you can drink and only 35 cents a meal. I think it would be better for us to eat with the Japanese and to have the same food, but we aren't allowed to go to their mess even if we prefer, and we can't bring Japanese guests to ours.

The food served in the internment camps was the worst during the early days of the experiment. Internees complained about hour-long waits for bland, inadequate meals consisting largely of starches, occasional canned fruit and vegetables, and either processed or organ meat. Government officials initially boasted about feeding internees at an average cost of thirty-eight cents a day, twelve cents less than was spent on the daily ration of a U.S. soldier. The emphasis on cutting costs meant that portions were small, and no attempts were made to offer special diets to those with different caloric requirements or medical needs. Internees recall watching relatives die in diabetic comas, and others reported ailments that were related to malnutrition. The prisoners were fed with such lackluster care that incidents of food poisoning were common in the camps.

Over time conditions improved, in large part due to the organizational efforts of detainees. Some went on strike from the jobs they were assigned in protest over the inadequacy and poor quality of the food. Others rioted over food shortages and collectively bargained with administrators for the right to have more control over their own food supply. Jane Dusselier argues that "foods became critical artifacts in the camps, representing a site of agency and identify formation." By protesting their mistreatment, Japanese Americans asserted their own humanity and highlighted the inhumanity of those who held them in captivity. For them, food did not serve as a symbol of patriotism as it did for many other Americans during the war years. Instead it was a sign of citizenship denied. However, the Japanese did not take their dispossession lightly and managed to win concessions that made their imprisonment more bearable. They gained the right to grow gardens at the camps, to bring in food from the outside world and cook it in their individual quarters, and to serve prominent roles in cooking and distributing camp rations.

No other military conflict in the twentieth century required Americans to think as carefully about the implications of what appeared on their dinner tables as World War I and World War II. However, the idea that food decisions and patriotism are linked did not disappear. American kitchens became a flashpoint for conflict during the Cold War in 1959, when Vice President Richard Nixon visited Moscow and sparred with Nikita Khrushchev in what has become known as the "kitchen debate." The setting for their discussion was the American National Exhibition in Moscow, which was designed to give viewers some insights into what life was like in the United States in the hope of creating more cross-cultural understanding.

The centerpiece of the exhibit was a six-room ranch-style house equipped with all of the latest appliances. Nixon proudly claimed that a blue-collar worker could afford the monthly payments on such a home, which cost about $14,000. Stephen Bates argues that although that is perhaps narrowly true, the worker who was stretched to his limit to make those payments would not have been able to purchase the $5,000 furnishings as well. For Nixon, however, the fine points of American family budgets were not what was at stake that day but rather the abundance of goods available to American consumers. He was not alone. The show kitchen was so popular that it had already drawn larger crowds than even the satellite *Sputnik* when both were displayed in Milan, Italy.

Nixon proudly proclaimed that housewives had a choice of various appliances made by different manufacturers and that all of these devices were designed to make the housewife's life easier. He asked his rival, "Would it not be better to compete in the relative merits of washing machines than in the strength of rockets?" Unimpressed, Khrushchev replied that "The Soviets do not share this capitalist attitude toward women." He depicted women as workers and economic partners rather than, as Nixon had done, essentially another piece of kitchen equipment perfectly placed inside the idealized American home.

Although Americans felt entitled to material abundance, in this case the latest advances in kitchen technology, Khrushchev stubbornly refused to be impressed. He denounced the lemon squeezer on display as a "silly thing," remarking that tea required only a couple of drops of lemon juice. Refusing to be dazzled by Nixon's celebration of American culinary technology, he sardonically asked, "Don't you have a machine that puts food in the mouth and pushes it down?" Nixon could not win the war over American superiority in domestic arrangements because Khrushchev refused to legitimate Nixon's unquestioning assumption that material abundance and having choices among consumer goods was a marker of cultural superiority. However, Nixon's faith was shared by many in the United States who were relieved that the war years had passed and that they were no longer required to demonstrate their love of country by forgoing favorite foods and other pleasures.

Both those who fell sway to Graham's message that denying oneself certain foods was good for both the body and the soul and those who had to grapple with the U.S. government's calls for austerity during wartime had to fight against overwhelming cultural assumptions that to be an American meant to have plenty. Even for many of the omnipresent poor, the American dream of a potentially better future and a chicken in every pot proved to be compelling. Those who experimented with vegetarianism or with substituting coveted foods for those regarded as less savory in an attempt to demonstrate either piety or patriotism showed that food choices are an important way to publicly demonstrate a belief system. American food habits reveal a variety of deeply held ideas, including attitudes about the issue of racial identity, a complicated issue in an increasingly multicultural environment.

7

⚜

Food Habits and Racial Thinking

Historically, many complicated and contradictory American ideas about racial difference have been reflected in the nation's attitude toward food. Throughout time, American eaters with strong English culinary cultural ties have been both attracted and repelled by the food practices of other groups. This ambivalence has led to the embrace, modification, or incorporation of foreign foods as well as to the rejection of what was unfamiliar. However, even when the dominant culture proved willing to adopt the foodways of minority groups, this did not always equate with a similar willingness to embrace the people who created the food traditions. Generally, both the food and the people from white ethnic groups were adopted more readily than those of people of color.

Among white immigrants, Italians were often singled out and initially criticized for their use of expensive imported ingredients and fondness for garlic, which was deemed too pungent by those used to blander cooking styles. However, these culinary prejudices were relatively short lived. Within decades of their arrival to the United States in large numbers, the Italian American cuisine they had created became one of the nation's most popular. Not only did Italian American–owned eateries soon become destinations for special occasions, but beginning in the 1920s, many Americans from other backgrounds began to experiment with making Italian American–inspired food in their own homes. Spaghetti went very quickly from being viewed as an exotic novelty to becoming a staple of the diet of Americans, enjoyed and prepared by individuals from a variety of backgrounds.

Other new European arrivals were not precluded from similar culinary xenophobia. For example, many Americans initially regarded German sausage-making traditions with some suspicion, joking about the provenance of the meat used to make those unfamiliar treats. Suspicion of the German-speaking immigrants and the food traditions that accompanied them were translated into doggerels—often chanted or sung—that asked questions such as "how could you be so mean to grind up all those doggies in your hot dog machine?" However, despite these early suspicions—"hot dogs" so named for their association with the sausage-shaped German dachshund—later became an iconic American food. A uniquely American hybrid of Viennese sausages and frankfurters, hot dogs were made and devoured in mass quantities as a widely accepted American treat by the late nineteenth century.

However, for Americans of color—some of whom were conquered, imported, or incorporated against their will—their relationship to mainstream food culture was more tenuous and changeable. Chinese immigrants, most of whom came to the United States willingly, were greeted as a misunderstood and often despised group of foreigners. Their unique food traditions were viewed with both curiosity and suspicion. Mexican Americans, whose food soon became wildly popular, saw their foodways appropriated and financially exploited by outsiders. No other group has played a more central and contradictory role in the American culinary imagination than African Americans, whose food habits have been imagined and reimagined as both appalling and appealing in popular culture.

AMBIVALENT ATTITUDES ABOUT CHINESE FOOD

Chinese immigrants began arriving in the United States in significant numbers after gold was discovered in California in 1848. Between 1849 and 1852 more than twenty-five thousand Chinese people, nearly all men, traveled to the United States to seek their fortune. Although some financed their own journey, many came as contracted employees who were obligated to work in order to pay for the cost of their passage to the United States. Initially, the newcomers were regarded with curiosity and interest, but as their numbers swelled and as many early mines became depleted of gold, hostility toward nonwhites, who were considered economic competitors, grew. Organized groups formed for the purpose of terrorizing the Chinese and others who were regarded as alien and compelling them to leave the area. The state of California bolstered these efforts by imposing a monthly three-dollar tax on "foreign miners." The tax could consume up to half of a Chinese miner's monthly income, and this punishing fee led many Chinese immigrants to abandon the profession.

Although faced with resentment and discrimination, the immigrants continually strove to find new avenues of supporting themselves in order to make their long journey to the United States profitable for themselves as well as for the families that many had left behind. They not only worked as miners but comprised a significant part of the labor force that built the transatlantic railroad as well. They were hired because railroad developers hoped that the eager immigrants would be more tractable than the largely Irish workforce, whom many employers accused of being drunk and difficult to manage. The Chinese workers gained a reputation for being willing and able workers. Railroad magnate Leland Stanford deemed them "quiet, peaceable, patient, industrious, and economical." More than ten thousand Chinese immigrants found employment working for the railroads, but their success earned them the continued ire of laborers from other ethnic groups who resented the competition for jobs.

The antipathy they faced caused many Chinese men to seek opportunities for self-employment, and Chinese laundry workers became ubiquitous in West Coast cities such as San Francisco, which had a large population of immigrants. Others began working as fishermen or as farmers and merchants. However, each new occupational endeavor was met with much hostility from the white working classes. Although consumers enjoyed having the arduous task of laundry done economically and efficiently by someone else, many worried about the allegedly unsanitary conditions in Chinese-owned businesses. Fishermen in the San Francisco Bay complained that their Chinese competitors were so effective that they were depleting the ocean of sea life, and one white Californian disdainfully proclaimed that the "Chinese mode of cultivation" is "filthy and disgusting."

Racism and resentment toward the Chinese grew in proportion to the Chinese population. Initially the overwhelming majority of migrants to the United States had been male; many planned to return to their families after earning some money. Tradition bound Chinese women to their homes, and the expense of the journey to the United States further precluded many from coming. However, some women eventually made the journey to join their husbands, creating families in what had once been a series of small colonies of Chinese bachelors. As the Chinese began to have children born in the United States and as their presence began to seem more permanent than transient, hostility grew still further. In what was ostensibly a measure to prevent prostitutes from coming to the country, Congress responded to the increasing antagonism by banning all Chinese women from immigrating to the country in 1875. Unable to satisfy the reigning xenophobia with this measure, in 1882, when the Chinese American population was 105,000, Congress voted to bar any further Chinese immigration. This was the first time that race had been used to justify banning an entire group of people from entering the country. Nonetheless, the measure was exceedingly popular, and Congress decided to make the ban permanent in 1902.

These measures had the enthusiastic support of the American Federation of Labor. Testifying before Congress, AFL leader Samuel Gompers proclaimed, "American labor should not be exposed to the destructive competitions of aliens who do not, will not, and cannot take up the burdens of American citizenship, whose presence is an economic blight and a patriotic danger." Interestingly, the title of Gompers's remarks used Chinese food habits as a way to identify and differentiate them from "American" laborers: *Some Reasons for Chinese Exclusion: Meat v. Rice, American Manhood against Asiatic Coolieism, Which Shall Survive?* Secretary of state James G. Blaine concurred that Chinese competition was unfair to American workers, observing, "You cannot work a man who must have beef and bread alongside of a man who could live on rice."

In was in the midst of this intensely racist atmosphere that Americans from other backgrounds first encountered Chinese food, and these interactions were inevitably shaped by the prevailing attitudes. Initially culinary contact between white Americans and Chinese immigrants took place in San Francisco's Chinatown in the 1850s. At the time, the area was a virtually all-male enclave, and a number of restaurants soon sprang up to provide inexpensive meals for the single men in the area. Some establishments also actively sought out white working-class trade and had hybrid menus containing standard, inexpensive American fare like baked beans and some Chinese fusion dishes like egg foo yung, an omelet infused with Chinese flavors. More adventuresome white eaters began seeking out more authentic Chinese food early on, but these thrill seekers looking for an exotic experience were generally either youthful Bohemians out to prove their daring and open-mindedness or ultrawealthy city dwellers who had the leisure time for such experiments and the social standing needed to flout convention. Middle-class eaters were far less likely to venture into the new culinary realm, associating, as they did, Chinatown with vice such as opium dens and prostitution.

Early food adventurers were often appalled by the foods they discovered. Samuel Bowles, a newspaper reporter who attended an elaborate Chinese feast in San Francisco in 1865 found the experience thoroughly unappetizing, commenting that "the one universal odor and flavor soon destroyed all appetite." He was "rescued" from the experience by a friend who summoned him away, and the two went to an American restaurant where they happily devoured a "square meal" of mutton, squab, and potatoes washed down by a bottle of champagne. Benjamin Taylor was similarly unimpressed with his 1878 meal, which he described as consisting of "Pale cakes with a waxen look. . . . They are sausages in disguise. . . . Then giblets of you-never-know-what, maybe gizzards, possibly livers, perhaps toes." When the writer Mark Twain first encountered Chinese food in 1863 or 1864, he refused the "small, neat sausages" he was offered because "we suspected that each link contained the corpse of a mouse." Indeed, the overwhelming reason outsiders gave for not daring to venture to Chinatown for dinner was the belief that local cooks were poised to feed unsuspecting non-Chinese guests animals such as rats, cats, and dogs, which American taboos forbade them from eating.

For all of the detractors, Chinese food slowly built up a base of European American fans. Politician Schuyler Colfax attended the same feast that Bowles escaped from, and after trying forty different dishes, he left the experience with a far different impression, exclaiming, "Hereafter, upon every invitation, I shall sup with the Celestials, and say grace with all my heart." In 1851, a white miner enthusiastically proclaimed, "The best eating houses in San Francisco are those kept by Celestials and conducted Chinese fashion." Decade by decade, mainstream American eaters became more and more open to the adventure offered by Chinese food. Some came to enjoy the thrill of

Chinese Grocery Store in Chinatown, New York, 1942. Many Chinese American immigrants have made their living in the food industry, catering not only to members of their own community but to other Americans who began to sample the cuisine beginning in the late nineteenth century. *Source*: Library of Congress, Prints & Photographs Division, Farm Security Administration—Office of War Information Photograph Collection, LC-USW3-007297-E.

journeying into Chinatown, an experience that many considered to be deliciously dangerous both because of the "vice" that they might uncover and because a perpetual mystery lingered over what proteins were used in various dishes. However, armed with the names of dishes that other white eaters had deemed "safe," the European American presence in Chinatown restaurants continued to increase. Restaurant owners learned how to cater to this set of customers and soon learned to modify traditional foods to meet their taste expectations. They also imported inexpensive decorations like lanterns and drawings of beautiful women from China to sate diners who wanted to sample an experience that not only tasted but also looked exotic.

As Chinese workers made their way east from California to work on the railroad, they brought their foodways with them, exposing many Americans outside San Francisco to their style of cooking. New York's Chinatown was attracting visitors by the late nineteenth century. However, many isolated areas of the Midwest could not boast Chinese restaurants until the 1930s or even later. Once the expectations were set for how Chinese food for white consumers should taste and how the restaurants should appear, seemingly identical Chinese restaurants began to spring up throughout the country. Unwilling to change a formula that apparently worked, Chinese entrepreneurs pragmatically created environments and tastes that satisfied mainstream desires.

Ironically, the appetite for Chinese food increased at the same time that calls for Chinese exclusion were at the strongest. Historian Samantha Barbas notes, "Though their encounters with Chinese Americans may have done relatively little to change deeply-held racial prejudices, they did alter middle-class eating preferences." Diners found it possible to simultaneously enjoy the food and disdain the people whose cultural creation it was. This may have been possible because after Chinese immigration was cut off, their domestic enemies could feel less threatened by those already living in the United States due to the fact that limits were now being imposed on their population growth. Barbas also speculates that whites could temporarily sublimate their prejudices and venture into Chinatown for an evening's adventure because they were not threatened when they encountered Chinese people in the subservient roles of cooks and waiters. While the Chinese as direct competitors for jobs and business seem to pose a danger to some white Americans, the idea of Chinese servants was far more acceptable.

Indeed, in the late nineteenth century, many wealthy residents of San Francisco preferred hiring Chinese servants to Irish ones. Chinese employees would work for less money, and they did not have to bear the stereotypical baggage of being considered poor cooks as Irish servants did. The Irish who came to the United States seeking material advantages had come from a food-poor society where they had subsisted primarily on potatoes. In contrast, the Chinese brought with them a complicated set of ideas about cuisine. The Chinese maintained ideas about proper eating habits that strongly resembled medieval European ideas about eating in order to balance the humors. The Chinese saw food as medicine and thus took great care with the way in which it was preserved and prepared. This attitude was reflected in the care with which Chinese servants were known for preparing the American-style meals mandated by their white employers. One employer raved about the culinary skills of his trusted servant Hop Sing, whom he regarded as a good cook but whom he never allowed to make any of his native specialties. He suspected that after leaving his employ, Sing would return to China and live out his days eating "lizard pies and rat catsup." Ostensibly that was fine with him as long as those ingredients did not find their way into his kitchen.

Lisa Heldke's concept of "culinary imperialism" might also offer an explanation for why white Americans increasingly found Chinese people threatening and undesirable and Chinese food alluring. Americans not only ate Chinese food, but they also altered it as restaurant owners changed their offerings to please the American palate. In adopting and changing Chinese food habits, American eaters were asserting their cultural dominance. One iconic Chinese American menu item that demonstrates the role that American tastes played on Chinese cooking techniques in this country is the dish of chop suey.

No one knows precisely when or where the dish of chop suey emerged, but it is definitely a creation of the American West. One origination story claims that a group of unruly miners went to a Chinese restaurant at closing time and demanded that the proprietor feed them even though he was nearly out of food and was closing for the day. To help diffuse the racially charged interaction, the Chinese cook allegedly assembled a dish of leftovers and garbage, which he served to the hungry diners, who were delighted by his improvisation and ignorant of the fact they were eating scraps and refuse. Whoever served the dish the first time likely labeled it "shap sui" in Cantonese, a phrase that refers to small bits being blended together.

Early versions of the dish may have been robust in flavor. Early consumers recall eating a diverse array of ingredients, including various tidbits of offal, mushrooms and other vegetables, and whatever seasonings were available in the kitchen. Later, as Chinese cooks sought to reach broader and less adventuresome mainstream customers, the dish was standardized and made blander in appearance and in taste. Stephen Coe mourns the fact that the dish "lost all of its earthy and mysterious ingredients and became a bland stew of some readily identifiable meat or seafood with a mélange of bean sprouts, bamboo shoots, onions, and water chestnuts, all cooked to exhaustion." As chop suey expanded in popularity, it began to be served in cafeterias and lunchrooms throughout the nation as an alternative to soup or sandwiches for lunch. Some white cooks often used their race as a selling point, urging customers to eat chop suey at white-owned establishments, where it was purportedly prepared in more sanitary conditions than in Chinese restaurants. The ultimate form of culinary imperialism over Chinese food may be the chow mein sandwich, a culinary hybrid that became popular in Rhode Island in the 1920s. The unlikely concoction consisted of Chinese noodles with chop suey ingredients and flavorings served on a hamburger bun.

Food studies scholar Sherrie Inness argues that hybrid Chinese American foods like chop suey can be interpreted as more than an outgrowth of American cultural dominance over a numerically smaller group. After all, Chinese American, rather than white American, cooks created the initial versions of most of these fusion foods, and they did so for a variety of reasons, including the inability to procure the necessary ingredients to create more authentically Chinese recipes. They also did so deliberately, exhibiting pragmatism and agency in order to lure less adventuresome eaters into Chinese restaurants. White customers were an economic necessity in areas with only a small concentration of Chinese inhabitants, and independent Chinese businesses were often the only means of support available in a climate where Chinese workers were widely discriminated against. Furthermore, Chinese-inspired menus that drew on more familiar American tastes and styles of eating could also be used as arguments for assimilation into American culture. Anti-Chinese racism in the United States was historically so entrenched that members of the group were viewed by many as permanent aliens, regardless of personal aspirations about citizenship or a desire to remain in the country. Inness argues that in this context, "Some tame recipes were subversive, suggesting that Chinese foods (and Chinese people) should be accepted as contributions to U.S. culture."

One of the peculiarities of the introduction of Chinese food to the United States comes from the fact that many restaurateurs initially entered their profession less out of an interest in becoming food professionals than because it offered a way to make a living in a society that had closed off many other avenues of economic advancement to members of this despised group. Few nineteenth-century Chinese immigrants were trained cooks, and they were overwhelmingly men who had had little previous experience with home cooking as a result of their previous adherence to proscribed gender roles. Furthermore, most initial Chinese immigrants to the United States were from the southern part of China, from Guangdong Province, also known as Canton. Thus the cooks who introduced Chinese food to the United States were not trained professionals, and furthermore, they had exposure to the food practices of only one region of the vast country of China.

Early restaurant owners also willingly modified their traditional dishes to please American palates. In addition to the invention of menu items like chop suey, they adapted the Cantonese tradition of stir-frying to contain a far different meat-to-vegetable ratio than was common in China. In accordance with the carnivorous tastes of Americans, they created stir-fried dishes with large quantities of meat and relatively fewer vegetables. Because of these reasons, the Chinese food that first bewildered and intrigued American eaters reflected very little of the vast culinary imagination of China.

Over time, American exposure to Chinese food expanded. The Chinese Exclusion Act was finally repealed in 1943, and a general loosening of immigration restrictions after 1965 made further Chinese migration possible. This new group of arrivals came from various regions of China, bringing a larger cross-section of food culture with them. These new immigrants introduced the nation to the tastes of northern China, including the spicier flavors of Szechuan cooking. American fascination with Chinese food increased throughout the second half of the twentieth century, reaching its zenith in 1972 when Richard Nixon visited the country. Nixon's visit led to the re-opening of diplomatic relations with China, ending decades of icy relations caused by Cold War hysteria about communism. American spectators became fascinated by pictures of the president seated in front of elaborate Chinese banquet spreads, and the improved diplomatic relations led to a new openness toward the country's food and a desire on the part of savvy eaters to sample more authentic dishes. Although most Chinese American restaurants continued to sell inexpensive, familiar Cantonese-inspired dishes, a growing number sprang up to serve more authentic specialties from various regions of China. This development was accompanied by an increasing number of high-end Chinese restaurants catering to individuals with a desire to understand the rich food culture of the country rather than just to fill their stomachs with cheap, Americanized dishes like chop suey.

The new fascination with Chinese food was also accompanied by a post–civil rights movement softening of outward racism. However, rumors about Chinese cooks serving rodents or kidnapped family pets to unsuspecting diners of the same kind that originated in the 1850s have persisted into the modern era. Now rumors are disseminated via e-mails spreading false information about restaurants being closed after rodent carcasses were found inside, or through rants and parodies posted on YouTube such as a play on Harry Chapin's folk song, "Cat's in the Cradle," titled "Cats in the Kettle." The singer warns potential patrons, "There's a cat in the kettle at the Peking room," claiming that the dish the diner ordered "ain't pork or chicken but a fat Siamese." In the lyrics to "My Birthday," the rapper Lil Wayne expresses a similar sentiment, declaring, "I kill dogs like I'm making Chinese food."

Far from benign, these rumors and malicious jokes point to an ongoing American ambivalence about Chinese food, which many still find both delicious and dangerous. Although dogs and cats are consumed as food in some regions of China, there is no evidence substantiating the various contemporary claims about Chinese restaurants in the United States following that practice. However, the persistent rumors and insinuations on the subject point to an ongoing racist anxiety about the food practices of a group that was once considered so foreign and incapable of assimilation that they were banned from immigrating to the United States. For some eaters, no matter how much it is modified to please American palates and regardless of whether or not the Chinese American cook was born in the United States, Chinese food will always bear the taint of being marginal, suspect, and somewhat outside the mainstream. This is in spite of the paradoxical fact that it is the nation's second–most popular ethnic cuisine after Italian food.

THE APPROPRIATION OF MEXICAN FOODS

In a similar fashion, mainstream American eaters have been far more willing to embrace the foodways of Mexican Americans than to welcome Mexican Americans as U.S. citizens. Vicki Ruiz has noted the painful irony of the fact that "one can eat at a Mexican restaurant in Orange County and overhear other diners complaining about 'illegal aliens.'" As with Chinese food, the history of America's relationship to Mexican food has been a contradictory one of rejection and appropriation. This history is made even more intriguing by the fact that Mexican food is itself a hybrid, a creation of the Americas, which draws on key agricultural items indigenous to the hemisphere, primarily beans, tomatoes, and corn. These food items, though prepared differently in various regions, were ultimately adopted to some extent by all European arrivals to the Americas. In Mexican cooking these staples were augmented by European imports such as domesticated animals and, in some areas, the introduction of wheat. According to Jeffrey Pilcher, "For Mexican Americans, fusion cuisine is not a trendy new discovery but a historical process reaching back for centuries." Mexican foodways are foundationally a mestizo blending of Native American and Spanish cooking traditions.

Beliefs in the racial inferiority of Mexican American people have sometimes been translated into criticisms of the food habits of people of Mexican descent. In the early twentieth century, Progressive Era reformers urged Mexican Americans to modify their food habits in order to elevate themselves culturally and better assimilate into mainstream society. According to historian George Sanchez, "Within the rubric of Americanization efforts, food and diet management became yet another tool in a system of social control intended to construct a well-behaved, productive citizenry." In a 1929 booklet by Pearl Idelia Ellis of the Department of Americanization and Homemaking of the Covina City Schools titled *Americanization through Homemaking*, Ellis argues that assimilation of Mexican Americans needed to begin in the home. Ellis was attempting to adopt a tolerant attitude, and she hoped to help her students improve their lives and minimize the racism they were subjected to by adopting mainstream food tastes. However, she had a complete lack of respect or understanding for their cultural heritage, expecting them to discard their customs wholesale. She confidently generalized, "Mexican families are mal-nourished." Although she acknowledged the economically disadvantaged status of many of her pupils elsewhere in her assimilationist manifesto, she did not judge their diet to be lacking in sufficient quantity but declared that they suffered "from not having the right varieties of foods."

Ellis warned that Mexican American children who did not eat proper foods would become lazy and poor students. As adults, she believed that alleged nutritional deficiencies would lead them to lives of crime. To stave off this possibility, she advocated teaching cooking skills to Mexican American girls, who should learn how to make bland dishes drawn from the nation's English culinary heritage. Her pupils were taught to replace flavorful salsa and mole with a dull white sauce made of flour, milk, and fat. Traditional dishes such as the rich beef tripe stew of *menudo* were to be replaced by oyster, potato, or celery soups. School lunches should consist of lettuce or cheese sandwiches made on bread and not tortillas. To Ellis and others like her, full citizenship—if it were ever to be offered—must be accompanied by a wholesale abandonment of traditional eating habits. In her imagination, Mexican foods were not only unhealthful but criminal, making those who consumed them permanent social pariahs.

Despite the revulsion they felt toward Mexican American foods, reformers were unsuccessful at permanently changing the habits of this group of eaters. Furthermore, they were not even able to convince other white Americans about the undesirability of the Mexican recipes they scorned as unhealthful and crime producing. Despite racism and growing segregation, Mexican Americans and European Americans had extensive interpersonal contact that led to much cross-cultural fertilization, especially in the kitchen.

One of the sites of extensive culinary interactions between Mexicans who were incorporated into the United States and their American conquerors was in Texas, where a cuisine that eventually became known as "Tex-Mex" emerged. The basis for this fusion was the *norteño* cuisine of northern Mexico, which was characterized by its use of flour rather than corn tortillas and the utilization of large quantities of beef. These two characteristics were the result of European influence as both wheat and cattle were Spanish introductions. These ingredients were prepared with culinary techniques and other ingredients—most notably the chili—drawn from indigenous traditions and local agricultural resources. After conquest by the United States, the food traditions of this region continued to change as Mexican cooks adapted their recipes to fit the tastes of Anglo consumers who demanded a less spicy flavor profile, plates brimming with food rather than individual smaller courses, large portions of choice cuts of meat, and eventually ingredients, like cheddar cheese, not used in traditional Mexican cooking.

One of the most iconic dishes of Tex-Mex cooking is chili con carne. The dish probably originated as a simple mole, made with the common locally available ingredients of oregano, red chili, and cumin, which were cooked with chunks of meat, most commonly beef, to create a spicy stew. The dish was invented in the Southwest, likely in the early nineteenth century. Legends say that early cooks of chili con carne were camp followers of either the Spanish colonial army or of the Mexican army, and they improvised the dish using the supplies they had on hand. Another similar but more elaborate origination story claims that the stew was made by washerwomen who worked for the American army. They allegedly used the large pots that they washed clothes in by day to make chili con carne in the evenings.

Written references to the dish do not appear until the later part of the century. In 1874, traveler Edward King described dining on Tex-Mex chili, writing that a "fat, swarthy Mexican mater-familias will place before you various savory compounds, swimming in fiery pepper, which biteth like a serpent; and the tortilla, a smoking hot cake, thin as a shaving, and about as eatable, is the substitute for bread." Although King sarcastically labeled eating southwestern food to be "an event in your gastronomic experience," other culinary adventurers had more positive impressions.

Many European Americans encountered the dish as tourists in San Antonio beginning in the 1880s after the region became accessible by train, and indeed a visit to the area would not be complete without sampling the regional specialty, which was far spicier than most dishes in the figurative American cookbook of the day. Capitalizing on this influx of visitors to the region, a group of local Mexican American women, who quickly became dubbed the "chili queens," began selling chili and other food items to both locals and tourists in the city's outside plazas. For more than half a century, the chili queens were a beloved addition to the urban landscape. Lifelong San Antonian Felix Almaraz remembers watching them conducting business as a young boy in the 1930s:

> On Saturdays my family would bring my brother and me to the marketplace. The plaza was buzzing with life, with people yelling greetings to each other. The chili queens would bring their pots and their fires and set up shop for the night. Their makeshift tables were decorated with ribbons, papier-mâché, and red-and-white oilcloths. There were handcrafted lanterns on the tables, little *farolitos*. For a dime, you could get chili con carne, tamales, beans, coffee. The chili queens were entrepreneurs. They were business ladies. And they made enough money to take care of their families.

Existing photographs of the chili queens at work in the plazas reveal a diverse group of customers—both in racial and in socioeconomic terms. The various members of the scene gathered there out of different motivations—to earn a living, to grab an inexpensive meal, to support interethnic businesses, to sample "local color," and to indulge in sexual fantasies. Many white men were drawn to the chili queens because of racist associations of women of

Mexican descent as equally willing sexual objects and as servants. Watching the carefully attired women both cook and serve simultaneously fed both fantasies. In 1894, the local *Daily Express* played into the dream of the chili queen seductress with its description of "Sadie, the acknowledged 'queen' of all 'queens,' on account of her beauty, her vivacity, and aptitude at repartee." For their part, the chili queens may have savvy enough to delicately exploit the racist and sexist daydreams of some members of their clientele in order to attract the trade necessary to earn money to support their families. The writer Stephen Crane was thrilled when one of the queens took a rose out of a corsage she was wearing and pinned it to his lapel. It seems reasonable to speculate that he may have rewarded this playfully seductive gesture by ordering another bowl of chili.

This quaint scene, which was fraught with such a wide range of meanings, quickly became a major tourist attraction. Unfortunately, it also became a concern to reformers in the early twentieth century who wanted to make San Antonio into an orderly, modern city. In their minds, the eclectic and interracial gatherings that sprang up over bowls of chili did not meet this criterion. They began—citing health concerns as a justification—a crusade to remove the chili queens from the plazas. They also began transforming the public spaces by filling them with shrubs and trees. This created public green spaces but also inevitably transformed the way the plazas were utilized. Initially, the chili queens were able to relocate their businesses to less interracial spaces in public areas near Mexican American communities. By 1936, they were required to move their outdoor kitchens into enclosed, screened tents, which satisfied health inspectors and reformers intent on reducing urban chaos but took away much of the charm and easy fraternization made possible in the outdoor cooking scenes. Cumbersome bureaucratic procedures designed to appease health inspectors reduced the queens' margin of profit, causing many to abandon the occupation. Others were lured to abandon the trade by the possibility of lucrative wartime employment as the nation mobilized for World War II. By 1943, the chili queens had disappeared, but they left behind a lingering nostalgia for the rich cultural contribution they had made to the city.

Ironically, chili, which was popularized in large part by these female entrepreneurs who had descended from those who originally created the dish, has since been transformed into what Jeffrey M. Pilcher calls a "symbol of the dominant masculine culture." Indeed, contemporary chili cook-offs are often male-dominated spaces. Amy Bentley observes that many aspects of Tex-Mex cuisine, such as grilled meats and barbecue as well as hot chili peppers, have been appropriated and redesigned as machismo foods, things that men can prepare without absorbing the perceived cultural taint of domesticity and femininity. Cooking outside and consuming potentially foreboding ingredients has been culturally reframed as "manly." Viewed through this lens, the gradual displacement of the chili queens takes on both a racist and a sexist tint. In the family lore of Gracelia I. Sanchez, the tale of the chili queens is told simply in those terms:

> Abuelita Teresita, my great-grandmother, was one of the Chili Queens who worked downtown in the market area, selling food to the men who worked in *el mercado* until the businessmen complained and kicked them out. Today, the Chili Queens are a fond memory, and the businessmen who ran *estas mujeres* out of business have a yearly celebration each spring to honor these *mujeres*. But hey, let's forget our racist history because we need to market our Mexican people and culture to the tourists.

No doubt her family's analysis accurately describes one dimension of a multiperspectival story. Jeffrey M. Pilcher points to others, observing that many middle-class Mexican Americans were ambivalent about the outdoor kitchens of chili queens and the aura of sexuality that surrounded them. Their public presence did not, after all, mesh with notions of middle-class respectability, where women played a private, domestic role in family affairs. These groups were likely supportive of attempts to displace the chili queens. Furthermore, gourmets and Mexican food purists—many of whom had arrived in San Antonio as refugees during the Mexican Revolution—were scornful of the hybrid cuisine they found there and were thus all too happy to see the chili queens delegitimized. Articulating the culinary sensibilities of this group, Francisco J. Santamaria disdainfully described chili con carne as a "detestable food with false Mexican title."

The controversies surrounding the chili queens reveal how contested the meanings assigned to one food item can be and the fact that far larger issues than merely nourishing human bodies are involved with decisions about what to eat. Although disputes about the meanings of various food traditions may have, as in the case of the chili queens, been waged both in and outside ethnic communities, in the history of Mexican American food the primary conversation has been among the heirs of the cuisine and culturally disconnected entrepreneurs who have had a tremendous influence in how Mexican American food is currently marketed and sold.

In analyzing the now ubiquitous Taco Bell restaurant chain, whose carefully designed stores have "architecture reminiscent of the Alamo," Suzanne Bost observes that "U.S. consumption of Mexican food" is often associated "with the historical framework of colonialism." In the case of Mexican American food, as with Chinese food, culinary imperialism has often been manifested by the variously articulated consumer demand that foods be modified to satisfy blander mainstream tastes of the kind offered at Taco Bell. This kind of appropriation certainly took place with chili con carne, which made its national debut in 1893 at the World's Columbian Exposition in Chicago.

After being sold at the fair, it became widely popular and was soon served in variations in regions throughout the country. Many—like chili served with beans or the Cincinnati custom of serving chili on top of spaghetti—bear little resemblance to the original. Although the state of Texas declared it the "state dish" in 1977, many chili eaters, and those who participate in chili cook-offs in places as far flung from the Southwest as Boston, seem often to have forgotten its origins.

Perhaps the most obvious example of the culinary colonialism of Mexican American foods comes from the widely successful sale and marketing of the foods by people from outside the ethnic group. Taco Bell, whose cheap renditions of Tex-Mex favorites make food purists cringe, was owned first by PepsiCo and later by the spinoff Yum! Brands, Inc., a gigantic entity that owns Kentucky Fried Chicken, Pizza Hut, and Long John Silver's among other chains. Old El Paso, a brand that makes salsa and other components of Tex-Mex cuisine, is owned by the iconic American food corporation Pillsbury, Inc. The largest producer of Mexican-inspired foods in the country, Old El Paso, has executives who are not concerned with authenticity to a particular food tradition but with pleasing "mainstream America." In internal company memos, one executive admitted, "We always put the word Mexican in quotes."

A seemingly endless number of entrepreneurs not of Mexican descent have found ways to capitalize on Tex-Mex food traditions in particular. For example, in 1932 Anglo San Antonio resident Elmer Doolin began marketing fried masa meal chips he called "fritos," which were made with a recipe he purchased from a Mexican café owner. In 1959, his company merged with a potato chip manufacturing company owned by Herman W. Lay, and Frito-Lay went on to eventually become one of the largest snack food producers in the world. Perhaps the most overtly sinister appropriation of Mexican food products is Minuteman Salsa, created by Houston businessman and anti-immigrant activist Ryan Lambert, who argues that salsa made by Mexicans or with Mexican ingredients is "at odds with our values." In addition to marketing a variation of a Mexican heritage food to make a profit, Lambert donates a portion of his profits to the Minuteman Project, a group of civilians who have organized themselves to patrol the nation's southern border to prevent undocumented Mexicans from crossing it.

Not only have corporations made tremendous profits marketing inauthentic variations of Mexican foods, but ironically, many European American chefs have made names for themselves by introducing Americans to more authentic Mexican foods, particularly those from regions beyond the borderlands and upscale versions of Tex-Mex favorites. Food writer Leslie Brenner has noted that white chefs Mary Sue Milliken, Susan Feniger, Bobby Flay, and Rick Bayless have become celebrities by expanding American understandings of Mexican food beyond the template established at bland chain restaurants such as Chili's. However, she notes that "in general it has not been

Women Making Tortillas in San Antonio, Texas, 1939. Many entrepreneurs who are not of Mexican descent have learned culinary techniques from Mexican Americans such as the women shown here and made large financial profits from their knowledge. *Source*: Library of Congress, Prints & Photographs Division, Farm Security Administration—Office of War Information Photograph Collection, LC-USF33-012057-M2.

Mexican-Americans who have made a name cooking Mexican or Mexican-inspired food in the United States." Although there are some exceptions to this rule such as Aarón Sanchez, owner and executive chef of Centrico in New York City, who has become a regular face on television, generally—as Brenner observes—"the food press tends not to take Latinos seriously."

Amy Bentley points to the overwhelming paradox that Americans "seem easily to sever the people from the food." During the contemporary cultural moment, Americans eat vast quantities of Mexican-inspired food—much of it produced by white-owned corporate entities—while anti-immigration sentiment aimed primarily at Mexican people grows year by year. U.S. citizens of Mexican descent—even those who have resided in what is now U.S. territory for generations—are not immune from this enmity. Laws and proposed laws allowing racial profiling by the police in an attempt to expel undocumented immigrants have left many citizens of Mexican descent feeling vulnerable and stigmatized. People of Mexican descent are underrepresented in boardrooms and halls of governance and even on television, where their presence is either ignored or they are portrayed as criminals, as undocumented immigrants, or as otherwise somehow not fully American. The failure of Congress to pass even timid immigration reform such as the Dream Act, which would provide undocumented high-school graduates who were brought to the United States as children a chance to earn their citizenship, is indicative of the current mood on the subject. Young people eligible to participate in the proposed program have been raised in the United States, and most consider themselves culturally "American." They would have to pass a background check and essentially earn their citizenship by receiving a college degree or joining the military. The fact that this legislation has not been adopted demonstrates that a wide embrace of Mexican American foods has not necessarily translated into greater empathy for or understanding of the particular problems of people of Mexican descent living in the United States, even the most vulnerable.

Chinese and Mexican foods were not encountered by mainstream American eaters until the nineteenth century, when ideas about what the new nation's food consisted of had already been established. However, from the colonial period on, race has been a factor in American decisions about what to eat and what eating particular foods signified. The first interracial exchanges of information about food were, of course, between Europeans and Native Americans. The next followed quickly, after the forced importation of African laborers beginning in the seventeenth century. The new African arrivals quickly found themselves enslaved for life, and some were given the task of preparing food. Thus, this group played a particularly influential, hands-on role in the establishment of American food traditions.

AFRICAN AMERICAN EATERS AND FOOD STEREOTYPES

Because of the peculiarities of American racism, the African American influence in the creation of United States food culture has not always been acknowledged or has sometimes only been partially recognized. At the same time that American eaters were trying to decide how to balance contemporary racist attitudes toward Chinese and Mexican people with a desire to sample the products of those cultures, they were still grappling with their relationship to the foundational American food influence provided by African American people. Because Native American, European, and African American foodways became intertwined beginning in the seventeenth century to create a unique American style of eating, Americans of later centuries had often lost sight of the multicultural origins of their food, regarding it simply as "southern" or more broadly as "American." So in contrast to encounters with Chinese or Mexican American food, white American eaters were not generally discovering unfamiliar foods when they ate items prepared by or derived from the traditions of black people. However, even easily recognizable foods were still fraught with frequent anxieties about racial differences.

In the popular imagination of the nineteenth and twentieth centuries, African American cooks and eaters were regarded in ambivalent terms. Black people were simultaneously depicted as potential culinary contaminators and also as innately talented cooks. They were described sometimes as hardworking, loyal servants and at other times as carefree loafers who dined on stolen foods. Whatever the stereotype, black people were imagined as fundamentally different in terms of their sense of taste from whites, and these beliefs were used to justify ongoing racism.

Despite the highly visible role that black women historically played in white kitchens, they have not always been given full credit for their culinary contributions. As with Chinese and Mexican Americans, their food knowledge has sometimes been appropriated and marketed by members of the dominant culture. In the decades following the emancipation of the enslaved people, many white, predominantly female, food writers attempted to document the foods of their childhoods, which had often been prepared by enslaved African Americans or later by black domestic servants. Emma and William McKinney's 1922 book, *Aunt Caroline's Dixieland Recipes: A Rare Collection of Choice Southern Dishes*, is one of the books of this genre. In their introduction, the authors gushingly proclaim, "In the art of cooking the 'Old Southern Mammy' has few equals and recognizes no peers." They claim that the recipes that follow have "been drawn from the treasured memories of Aunt Caroline Picket, a famous old Virginia cook, the 'pinch of this' and 'just a smacker of that' so wonderfully and mysteriously combined by the culinary masters of the Southland have been carefully and scientifically analyzed and recorded in this volume." In what is a common convention in the cookbooks of the time period, they purport to elevate a black cook's allegedly instinctual ability to prepare food by describing it with a scientific precision they associate with white people. However, tellingly, their beloved "Aunt Caroline" is not listed as an author of the book, though she is credited in the title of specific recipes such as "Aunt Caroline's Corn Bread" and potentially in "Mammy's Graham Muffins." Even if the recipes are allegedly hers, it seems unlikely that their titles are her invention. Given the historical and racist implications of names for dishes such as "Johnny Reb Cake," "Jeff Davis Muffins," and "Pickaninny Cookies," it seems unlikely "Aunt Caroline" would have named them that way.

In an even more overt attempt to profit from the culinary skills of African American cooks, a number of white women writers wrote columns or cookbooks using the voice and persona of fictional black cooks. Perhaps most famous in this genre is the work of Eleanor Purcell, a columnist for the *Baltimore Sun*, who wrote a food column in the voice of "Aunt Priscilla," who gave advice rendered in dialect. In a 1929 cookbook written in the voice of the fictional "Aunt Priscilla," Purcell gives this intriguingly cross-cultural recipe for "Chili Con Carne":

CHILI CON CARNE

Take 2 young chickens
1 medium sized onion
1 teaspoon of salt
3 level tablespoons of flour
8 or 9 red peppers
1 clove of garlic
About ¼ pound of butter
A dash of cayenne

Cut up de chicken as for fryin', an' sprinkle each piece wid salt an' pepper. Melt a piece of butter de size of an egg in yo' skillet, lay in de chicken, lettin' each piece get a delicate brown, but shakin' de pan often so's not to let it burn.

Take out de sees an' de inside seams of de pepper, cover 'em wid boilin' water an' cook till soft. Den rub 'em through yo' sieve. Scrape de onion an' mince de garlic real fine. Den add onion, garlic an' salt to de pepper. Put de' chicken into a big saucepan, dump in de pepper sauce an' add enough boilin' water to cover. Let cook till de chicken am nice an' tender. Den take out de chicken an' lay on yo' hot dish. Rub together a piece of butter de size of an egg an' de flour, thin down wid a little piece of de sauce from de chicken, an' stir into de rest of de sauce for thickenin'. Let cook till all flavor of de flour has cooked away, add a dash of cayenne, pour over de chicken an' serve.

A wall of nice cooked rice round de edge of yo' dish, wid de chicken an' sauce in de middle am mighty fine.

This variation of a recipe for a food that was originally created by Mexican American women and written by a white woman in what she regards as black dialect reveals a great deal of the complexity of the relationship between American ideas about food and American ideas about race. Purcell manifests an interest in and appreciation of both Mexican and African American food customs, but she also feels free to distort and manipulate these traditions for her own benefit.

Another white cookbook author who adopted black dialect as a marketing ploy and hoped to capitalize on the reputation black women had for being excellent cooks was Emma Speed Sampson, whose 1931 *Miss Minerva's Cookbook: De Way to a Man's Heart* features drawings of caricatured African American figures—with dark skin and exaggerated features—throughout. Not only does Sampson deliver recipes in the fictional voice of "Miss Minerva," she also creates an imaginary commentary to accompany the meals. In the recipe for "Baked Fish," "Miss Minerva" observes that "Cull'd folks an' cats are alike in they yearnin' fer fush." Sampson also imagines "Miss

Minerva" indulging in antebellum nostalgia as she remembers "Ol' Marster" eating cherry pie and singing "his little cherry pie song." She fantasizes that "all the chillims would j'ine in an' sometime I'd make so bold as ter rumble away a little myself." Thus not only was a fictional black character useful as a vehicle for delivering recipes, she could also be used to rewrite a brutal history of misery during the era of slavery as she remembers race relations during the era in terms of an interracial sing-along enjoyed over slices of pie.

Although racism was hardly only a Southern phenomenon, many interactions between blacks and whites around the issue of food took place in the South where the institution of slavery had been the most entrenched and where the black population was the largest. White southerners were often afraid of being somehow contaminated by the African Americans that they came into proximity with. Social anthropologists Allison Davis, Burleigh Gardner, and Mary Gardner spent nearly two years as participant observers studying the inhabitants of Natchez, Mississippi, beginning in 1933. They noted a general white belief in the "organic inferiority of the Negro," noting that local whites were loath to eat or drink from the same plates used by black people. Although African Americans frequently worked in white homes and cooked in white kitchens, it was a common practice to provide separate dishes for their use. Contradictory behavior and attitudes of this kind were common. As a child, white southerner Melton McLaurin drank from the same cup as black children and frequently ate food prepared and no doubt tasted by black cooks. Nonetheless, he was struck with horror after he thoughtlessly placed his mouth on the same needle his black friend Bobo had similarly used while trying to fill a basketball with air. He was terrified that he might contract a nameless tropical disease, which he assumed commonly afflicted African Americans.

One of the reasons that whites were able to overcome their irrational fear that they could be potentially contaminated by black people and to eat food prepared by a black cook was the widespread belief that blacks were natural cooks. Writing in *Harper's* in 1887, Charles Gayarré likely expressed the sentiments of many when he remarked:

> The negroes are born cooks, as other less favored beings are born poets. The African brute, guided by the superior intelligence of his Caucasian master, in the days of slavery . . . gradually evolved into an artist of the highest degree of excellence, and had from natural impulses and affinities, without any conscious analysis of principles, created an art of cooking for which he should deserve to be immortalized.

This passage leaves no doubt as to Gayarré's belief in inherent black inferiority, but although black people lack in intelligence in his estimation, by their very nature, each African American is uniquely gifted in the culinary arts. Having embraced this assertion, many thought it would be wasteful and indeed even against nature not to take advantage of this unique skill given to a group of otherwise inferior people.

This train of thought can help explain the pervasiveness of symbols like Aunt Jemima, a fictional creation who began as a character in a minstrel show and later became an iconic figure in American advertising as the trademark for Aunt Jemima pancakes and related products made by the Quaker Oats Company. Aunt Jemima has become one of the most tenacious and successful images in American advertising. Originally adopted in 1890, she endures today. Despite extensive protests spearheaded by the National Association for the Advancement of Colored People (NAACP) among others, Quaker Oats refused to retire Aunt Jemima, agreeing only to some modernizing of her image. Due to the incredible marketing effectiveness of the character, the company ultimately felt that it could not afford to dispense with her.

What, then, is it about Aunt Jemima that white American consumers continue to find so appetizing? For over one hundred years the consumers of Aunt Jemima pancakes have been purchasing a fantasy, what M. M. Manring has called "the idea of a slave, in a box." By buying this instant pancake mix, consumers were invited to also buy a dose of Southern nostalgia, a plantation fantasy where whites enjoyed lives of leisure as they were served by unfailingly cheerful figures like Aunt Jemima who liked nothing more than to use their innate cooking skills to serve white folks. Aunt Jemima and other Southern advertising themes featuring black servants were so compelling that Manring has suggested they helped pave the way for regional reconciliation after the Civil War. Both northerners and southerners could find comfort in depictions of black servility and in the idea that the kitchen or dining room was the proper place for an African American, not the halls of government.

Black foodways were also a source of amusement to whites. In the hundred or so years following the Civil War, popular culture was rife with stereotyped depictions displayed on objects ranging from postcards to folk art to menus of blacks engaged in various acts of eating or of food play. One aspect of popular culture where these ideas were particularly prominent was in the realm of popular entertainment, in the form of so-called coon songs. Popular at around the turn of the twentieth century, these tunes, which were performed generally, though not always, by white musicians, typified African Americans as incompetent, lazy, violent, lascivious, and foolish and as having voracious appetites. The racial slur "coon," which became almost immediately identified with these songs, became widespread in the American vernacular by around 1880. This term may have originated as a shortened form of "barracoon," a temporary structure that housed slaves before they were sold. However, "coon" is also a diminutive of the word "raccoon," an animal associated with poor southerners who got much of their protein from raccoons and other animals deemed unworthy for middle-class consumption. James M. Dorman thus suggests African Americans may have been derisively labeled "coons" due to their supposed preference for eating the animal.

These "coon songs" were performed widely in music halls throughout the country, and over six hundred were published in sheet music form. Fred Fisher's song "If the Man in the Moon Were a Coon" sold over three million copies. In many of these songs, black people are depicted as enthusiastic consumers of foodstuffs ranging from watermelons to pork chops, to opossums, to chicken. Sheet music for an 1898 song, "A Coon's Trademark," contains a number of black stereotypes, featuring drawings of a razor, a chicken, and a watermelon alongside a caricatured black image.

Watermelons and chicken are the two most common foodstuffs portrayed in these songs and accompanying images, leading to ongoing cultural sensitivity among many in the black community concerning these foods. Common images of black people enjoying fruits, like watermelon, have implied a linkage of fruit to tropical environments and contributed to the idea of African Americans as carefree, lazy, exotic, and outside of the American mainstream. Associations of African Americans and chickens have historically been so pervasive that Psyche Williams-Forson labels the "historical relationship between chicken and black people . . . [as] one of the many linchpins of white racist

African American Boys Eating Watermelon, 1902. Historically, African Americans have often been negatively stereotyped as being unusually fond of eating watermelon, a sentiment that is captured in this staged photograph. *Source*: Library of Congress, Prints & Photographs Division, Miscellaneous Items in High Demand Collection, LC-USZ62-69641.

propaganda that claimed black inferiority." This is peculiar partially because traditionally impoverished African Americans actually ate very little chicken, an expensive food. Most poor southerners, white and black, got most of their animal protein from cheap cuts of pork.

The pervasive, lighthearted cultural images mocking black people as chicken thieves are particularly harsh if one realizes that blacks who stole chicken did so out of hunger and necessity, not greed or laziness. If white society perceived African Americans as people who delighted in consuming chicken, it was because they structured society to make sure that such treats, which middle-class whites could take for granted, were exceedingly rare for the poorer classes. Any white guilt over black hunger could be easily laid to rest by another culinary stereotype of African Americans, the idea that black people had a much coarser sense of taste than whites and that they actually required less food.

The writer Richard Wright encountered this belief firsthand as a young man while working for a white family performing household chores before and after school. Breakfast and dinner were to be included in his wages. The first meal provided by his employer was stale bread and moldy molasses. Seeing the food, he thought to himself, "Goddamn . . . I can't eat this. . . . The food was not even clean." The woman of the household was, however, appalled at Wright's fussiness and refused to offer him sustenance of a higher quality, saying, "I don't know what's happening to you niggers nowadays." She promised to save the molasses for Wright's dinner. The idea that African American eaters did not require or deserve the same quality or quantity of food as whites dates back to the era of slavery, when masters fed their human property as cheaply as possible in spite of the fact that African Americans were responsible for producing much of the food supply. This sad irony was not lost on African Americans, who captured these inequalities in a work song, transcribed below in dialect:

> We raise de wheat,
> Dey gib us de corn;
> We bake de bread,
> Dey gib us de crust;
> We sif de meal,
> Dey gib us de huss;
> We peel de meat,
> Dey gib us de skin;
> And dat's de way
> Dey take us in;
> We skim de pot,
> De gib us de liquor,
> And say dat's good enough for a nigger.

The idea that black people happily consumed things that would seem loathsome to the more refined tastes of middle-class whites was of course also manifested in the association of African Americans with widely considered trash animals like opossums and raccoons and with chitterlings, a food widely considered to be "dirty." These associations were partially accurate due to the fact that rural blacks did consume these foods; however, so did their poor white neighbors. Conventional wisdom, however, insisted on racial differences and stated that blacks could physically survive on less food than whites could. This myth was used to justify the perpetuation of dramatic inequalities. During the lean years of the Great Depression, the state of Arkansas paid white families who were eligible for state-funded welfare an average of twelve dollars a month while black families typically received half that amount.

These pervasive stereotypes of African American eating habits as being somehow different from those of other Americans, humorous, or dirty have not disappeared in the twenty-first century. Before his election to office, racist critics of President Barack Obama circulated e-mailed images of the annual White House Easter egg hunt being transformed into a search for tiny egg-shaped watermelons. In their 1992 film, *To Grandmother's House We Go*, the beloved child actors the Olsen twins are portrayed as rewarding an African American street performer by throwing two chicken legs into his open saxophone case instead of coins. The musician looks at the little girls, quizzically asking, "Hey, did you just drop a chicken bone in my case?" One of the twins replies, "There's still some meat on there." Apparently mollified, he responds, "Oh, okay." This scene is not so different from those sung about in "coon songs" in the previous century.

For some, stereotypes about black racial difference when it comes to eating habits are so entrenched that it is a surprise when these expectations are not fulfilled. Conservative talk show host Bill O'Reilly was, for example, shocked when his visit to the famous Harlem soul food restaurant, Sylvia's, did not live up to his racist stereotypes about black behavior. Without feeling compelled to suppress the nature of his expectations, he publicly admitted that "there wasn't one person in Sylvia's who was screaming, 'M-Fer, I want more iced tea.'"

Thus throughout history, Americans have developed an increasingly voracious and multicultural appetite. However, interest in a wide variety of food traditions has not always been accompanied by a respect for or interest in the people who created those foods. Some early twentieth-century American reformers hoped that this nation of immigrants could be transformed into a "melting pot," one society with a shared common culture. Theoretically, ethnic divisions would blur and combine to form one shared American culture. The theory always seemed more applicable for members of white ethnic groups than for people of color, who were the brunt of far more severe forms of discrimination than white immigrants, who were more successful at casting off the taint of otherness. Ironically enough, while limited in its application or, many argue, in its desirability, the metaphor of the melting pot applies fairly well to United States culinary history. Although English foodways were a predominant influence in the overall food culture, Americans as a whole have been remarkably willing to integrate the tastes and techniques from people from a wide variety of cultural backgrounds into their routine diets. This same level of acceptance has not always, despite conscious efforts on the part of many to rectify past wrongs and to battle racism, been transferred into the society at large. Because attitudes about food are linked to so many important societal issues, food choices continue to be linked with political issues in the twenty-first century.

8

❧

The Politics of Food

In the twentieth century, the majority of Americans consumed what has been labeled the "Standard American Diet," a set of eating habits that cookbook author and food writer Mark Bittman despairingly claims is appropriately named because "it's SAD." Although most nutrition experts recommend a diet high in fruits, vegetables, and whole grains and low in fat, meat, and sugar, the SAD diet is high in meat, fat, and sugar and contains few fruits and vegetables. Most of the grains that are consumed are eaten in their refined and least nutritious form. This modern diet is closely related to the one that Sylvester Graham railed against in the nineteenth century, but it is generally deemed even less healthful because of the abundance of factory-farmed meats and industrial food it contains.

Although health experts have convincingly argued that unprecedented levels of obesity and health problems like type 2 diabetes are linked directly to the food choices of Americans, these habits, which have long historical antecedents, have proved to be nearly impossible for many to break. From the beginning of European colonization, settlers wished to eat more abundantly and to eat more animal protein than generations before them, a goal that was achieved. In the twenty-first century, an average American eats more than two hundred pounds of meat a year. This sense of culinary entitlement has been a defining feature of American food culture as each generation has measured its well-being by the large quantities, particularly of meat, that it could consume. Eating recommendations from doctors and nutritionists have been able to make only relatively small inroads in the face of habit and history. Furthermore, American corporations and even the federal government have made it cheap and easy for Americans to eat unhealthful meals.

Many critics of American eating habits have questioned not only the food choices Americans have made but also the ethics of how food is currently produced and the safety of the food supply. Detractors of the SAD have isolated issues of concern in addition to the impact the diet has on human health. Many have expressed distress about how animals are treated as vast quantities are raised and slaughtered to satisfy the national craving for animal protein. Others have augmented the unease about animal welfare with concerns about how intensive agriculture, both to produce meat and to grow the staple crops utilized in industrial food products, impact the natural environment.

CRITIQUES OF AGRIBUSINESS PRACTICES

By the late twentieth century, the vast majority of the meat that Americans consumed came from intensive farming operations, agribusinesses, rather than from the cheerful family farms that are often depicted in food advertisements. The trend continues in the twenty-first century. Today, nearly all of the chickens and turkeys, 95 percent of the pigs, and 78 percent of cattle that Americans eat are produced by large-scale agricultural enterprises. The Environmental Protection Agency labels these facilities straightforwardly as "Concentrated Animal Feeding Operations." CAFOs can house thousands or even tens of thousands of animals in confined areas away from natural vegetation. Most animals are held in small spaces with little room to move beyond that needed to eat, urinate, and defecate.

Animal welfare advocates argue that animals raised in factory farms are unable to act according to their natural instincts. For example, hogs, generally social creatures, are unable to freely socialize because they are kept in stalls with little room to move. Furthermore, there is no possibility for them to root or to nest in their concrete environments. Distressed hogs frequently exhibit neurotic behavior such as gnawing on the tails of those confined in proximity to them. This action has become so common in factory farms that piglets now routinely have their tails docked in a process done without anesthesia. Other animals, such as chickens, have been so genetically modified through selective breeding that they cannot behave as chickens once did because their bodies do not allow it. Because of the American consumer's growing demand for breast meat, chickens have been bred to have enormous breasts and are fed growth hormones that reduce the amount of time from birth to market. Their bones cannot keep up with the rapid growth of their muscles, and at least 90 percent develop chronic leg problems. Many spend their last days of life in such pain that they refuse to move. According to a University of Arkansas study, if humans grew at the same rate as factory farm–produced chickens, an average person would weigh 349 pounds by his or her second birthday.

Contemporary critics of factory farms are the political descendants of those who advocated for the Pure Food and Drug Act at the turn of the twentieth century as they try to raise public consciousness and ask for more government oversight of meat production. CAFOs have proved to be reluctant to allow journalists, activists, and others from outside the industry to visit their operations. Because of this, some investigators have gone to great lengths to covertly document conditions in these facilities. Some, like Upton Sinclair before them, have taken jobs in the various stages of meat-processing operations to gain insights into their methods. Others have snuck into these facilities by cover of night to secretly photograph the conditions they find.

Despite these efforts, no federal laws regulate the welfare of farm animals. Such weak state anticruelty laws as they exist are negated by the concept of "common farming practices" that make any custom legal as long as it is performed widely. Therefore, castrating young animals without anesthesia or confining calves to veal crates where they do not have the room to stretch their limbs or to turn around are legal practices. Even though they cause animal suffering, these methods are legal simply because they are standard operating procedure on factory farms.

Not only has the treatment of animals living on CAFOs been criticized, but the method of their slaughter has become increasingly a subject of scrutiny as well. Because of the scale of these operations, slaughtering animals is an immense task that requires precision and coordination. When the system fails, animal rights advocates argue, animals suffer. Although federal law does not mandate standards for the treatment of animals on the farm, it does dictate that mammals must be stunned before they are slaughtered. However, even the most effective slaughterhouses can stun cattle on the first try only 95 percent of the time, which means that sometimes cows make it to the next phase of the slaughter assembly line, where they are skinned and dismembered while still conscious. Chickens, too, are often processed while still aware of their surroundings when rushed workers fail to make sure their throats are cut before their bodies are thrown in scalding water. According to one worker in the killing room, those who are still alive when boiled "flop, scream, kick, and their eyeballs pop out of their head in pain."

In addition to the charge that they are guilty of causing excessive animal suffering, the CAFOs that fulfill Americans' desire for inexpensive, abundant meat are frequently criticized for the pollution they create. In fact, the world's livestock produces more greenhouse gasses than all combined forms of transportation. CAFOs produce millions of pounds of manure each year, 130 times the amount of waste produced by humans. This excrement is not processed by a sewage system but is allowed to accumulate into pools, known euphemistically as "lagoons," which can be twenty-five feet across and eighteen feet deep. These pollute water and spread disease. People who live near CAFOs report a far wider set of health complaints than the general population, with conditions ranging from gastrointestinal disorders to respiratory problems. Many also report psychological symptoms to the strain of living with the constant stench of unprocessed feces. Unsurprisingly, animals raised in these filthy environments are as prone to illness as the humans who live near these operations.

To ensure the relative health and marketability of their meat, CAFO operators feed their animals a steady supply of antibiotics to stave off illness. In the United States animals are given at least 17.8 million pounds of antibiotics each year, while humans consume a much smaller 3 million pounds. The overuse of antibiotics has led to the creation of pathogens that can resist these medications, a development that could potentially compromise the health of both animals and humans.

Antibiotics are not the only pharmaceuticals that are fed to factory-farmed animals. Many are also given growth hormones, which are excreted with the animal's waste and find their way into the water supply, where they can cause health problems for both animals and people. Studies have also linked some of these hormones, which are present in the meat and milk of the animals who ingest them, with certain kinds of cancer. Some have also argued that young girls who consume dairy and meat containing growth hormones might go through puberty earlier as a result of the intervention of these chemicals. Citing concerns for its impact on human health, the European Union has outlawed the use of bovine somatogave (BST), a hormone still frequently given to cows in the United States to increase their milk production.

In the case of both pollution and antibiotic use, the federal government has been reluctant to pass stringent guidelines, generally deferring to the will of the powerful corporations that depend on intensive agriculture to make a profit. For example, in deference to agribusiness, the United States Department of Agriculture has made the decision not to directly tell consumers to avoid certain kinds of foods that are not good for them. Because the meat industry wields such enormous political and financial power and many in the government are beholden to those interests, the USDA has refused to make the recommendation that Americans eat less meat even though current knowledge about nutrition supports that advice. Instead, Americans are told much more vaguely to eat "less fat" and left to draw their own conclusions about what that means. For their part, meat suppliers can work to negate this timid and vague recommendation through advertising campaigns that portray meat as a nutritious food that Americans are entitled to see large quantities of on their dinner plates.

Although the fact that powerful food industries wield enormous influence over even segments of the federal government that are charged with guarding the health of its citizens is an open secret and one that many scholars and journalists have found ways to document, it is an issue that many with ties to either the government or industry approach with trepidation. When Marion

Nestle, chair of the Department of Food Studies at New York University, who has worked as an advisor about nutrition to several government agencies, set out to write a book on the subject, she discovered, "I could not find *anyone* who would speak to me 'on the record.'" Nonetheless, she finds substantial evidence from "off the record" sources, government documents, the work of investigative journalists, and other sources to substantiate her claim that

> [T]he food industry uses lobbying, lawsuits, financial contributions, public relations, advertising, partnerships and alliances, philanthropy, threats, and biased information to convince Congress, federal agencies, nutrition and health professionals, and the public that the science relating diet to health is so confusing that they need not worry about diets: When it comes to diets, anything goes.

For Americans, who have historically relished the freedom of dietary choice and who associate prosperity with an abundant rather than a quality food source, industry's propaganda campaign has been an easy sell. Many critics of the SAD, however, have argued that government's role in perpetuating a diet that nutritional science deems harmful goes far beyond giving industry control of the message about proper foods or failing to more aggressively regulate the conditions of factory farms. The federal government has played a tremendous role in subsidizing the key agricultural products that feed animals raised in CAFOs and that are used in industrial foods rather than giving incentives to producers of more diverse crops.

In 2006 in his bestselling book *The Omnivore's Dilemma*, journalist Michael Pollan painstakingly documented the relationship between agribusiness, government, and the processed-food industry in the promotion of the highly subsidized crop of corn. He reveals that corn, an agricultural product that once formed the backbone of the diet of many Native Americans and that sustained the early European colonists despite their initial reluctance to eat it, plays an equally large role in the contemporary American diet. However, its presence is largely hidden. He claims, "There are some forty-five thousand items in the average American supermarket and more than a quarter of them contain corn." Only a small minority of these foods utilize corn in an easily recognizable form: as a kernel or transformed into cornmeal. Other times its presence is disguised behind multisyllabic chemical names, such as "polydextrose," a soluble fiber made from corn. It is also present in the increasingly ubiquitous "high fructose corn syrup," which is used to sweeten a wide array of industrial food products such as soda and even some ostensibly "healthful" products, such as commercially produced whole wheat bread.

Corn's prominent role in the American diet is a reflection in part of the versatility of the grain; however, it is also the result of government intervention. Currently, the price corn can be sold for is below the cost of production.

In 2005, it sold for approximately a dollar less a bushel than it cost to grow. Farming corn is an economically viable undertaking only because of large government subsidies paid to farmers. The federal government spends about five billion dollars a year on corn subsidies. However, farmers, many of whom manage to eke out only a modest living, are not the primary beneficiaries of this largesse. The federal government is primarily benefiting the industrial food producers, who purchase the grain at artificially cheap prices.

Economic pressures have forced farmers to plant more and more corn and to stop growing a diverse assortment of crops on their lands. In an attempt to make their fields more productive, they use large quantities of synthetic nitrogen fertilizer, which requires an enormous amount of fossil fuel to produce. Pollan estimates that every bushel of corn grown in this fashion requires up to a third of a gallon of oil to grow, which means each acre of corn represents about fifty gallons of oil. Not only is intensive corn production responsible for contributing to the depletion of and dependency on fossil fuels, nitrogen fertilizers have other detrimental environmental repercussions as well. They seep into the water supply, harming human, animal, and other plant life.

Besides finding its way into a surprising number of processed foods in the supermarket, subsidized corn is also fed to animals housed in CAFOs, which means that the federal government is indirectly providing a subsidy to those meat producers who purchase vast quantities of the grain. A pioneering critic of the food system, Frances Moore Lappé has calculated that it takes twenty-one pounds of grain to produce one pound of beef, making meat production a staggeringly inefficient way to utilize food resources. In addition to concerns about waste, opponents of factory farming have also been critical of the practice of feeding corn to cattle, which are not biologically designed to digest the grain and would consume grass in a more natural environment than that of the concrete CAFO facilities. A corn diet can give cows potentially deadly gas, bloating, and acidosis, which can lead to a variety of other health concerns. To prevent these conditions, animals that would have been healthy if raised in a natural environment are fed a steady stream of antibiotics. A veterinarian employed by a CAFO who administers these drugs admitted to Pollan, "Hell, if you gave them lots of grass and space, I wouldn't have a job."

Given the complicated and, to the uninitiated, bewildering world of agribusiness, it is unsurprising that food has become a far more important political issue than ever before in the United States. Americans have new opportunities to see their dining decisions as political ones. The majority may not yet link the food they pile on their plates with their political identities, but there is a general trend in the direction of making more conscious food decisions. Michael Pollan has defined the twenty-first century "food movement" as being bound together by a shared "recognition that industrial food production is in need of reform because its social/environmental/public health/animal welfare/gastronomic costs are too high." The luxury of worrying about the ethical options involved in eating is, however, not one enjoyed by those who have to worry about finding enough food to eat. On the other hand, the more fortunate have created a number of identity categories related to food choices, ranging from locavores, flexitarians, and conscientious omnivores, to vegetarians and vegans, to those who support the ascendency of industrial foods, to those who refuse to make a political issue out of eating, to those who think America's obsession with her collective stomach has gone too far.

HUNGER IN A LAND OF ABUNDANCE

The USDA reports that in 2010, 14.5 percent of households in the United States were food insecure, and 5.4 percent had very low food security. For some in this group, food insecurity means having few food choices, little variety, and the availability of only undesirable food to eat. For people in this category, hunger may not necessarily be an issue, but malnutrition and the health concerns that go along with unhealthful eating may be. For those with very low food security, food shortages and hunger are present. Very-low-income Americans are eligible for the Supplemental Nutrition Assistance Program (SNAP) that provides government funds to buy food. In 2011, 44,708,726 individuals received SNAP, but benefits are fairly meager, averaging $133.85 per individual each month, a figure that gives SNAP recipients relatively few culinary choices.

Other low-income U.S. residents report difficulty in accessing food, particularly fresh fruit and vegetables, because they live in what have become known as "food deserts." Food deserts are low-income areas that do not have a grocery store. In urban areas, to qualify as a food desert, residents must need to travel more than a mile to a grocery store, and in rural areas they must have to travel more than ten miles. Because many of the residents in these areas live in poverty, they may lack access to transportation, making it difficult to travel great distances to purchase food. In 2009, the USDA estimated that 11.5 million people, 4.1 percent of the total U.S. population, lived in food deserts. In some areas, the situation is particularly acute. A Tulane University study found that almost 60 percent of low-income residents of New Orleans live more than three miles from a grocery store, and of this number only 58 percent own vehicles.

For these Americans, having enough food to eat is a more pressing issue than choosing or rejecting foods on the basis of political beliefs. However, these hungry Americans are frequently the source of political discussions as they are stigmatized by some for their poverty and used by politicians to secure votes. In 2012 in a racially tinged comment designed to appeal to a segment of the electorate, Rick Santorum, a candidate for the Republican nomination for U.S. president, indirectly criticized the recipients of food assistance. He proclaimed that he did not want to "make black people's lives better by giving them somebody else's money. I want to give them the opportunity to go out and earn the money." His statement should be examined in the context of a political discourse that depicts the recipients of food stamps as lazy and as predominantly members of minority groups despite that fact that 49 percent of SNAP recipients are white. Echoing a similar sentiment, Newt Gingrich, another candidate for the presidency, proclaimed that if invited to address a National Association for the Advancement of Colored People meeting, he would tell the attendees "why the African American community should demand paychecks and not be satisfied with food stamps." Gingrich's comments, too, give the erroneous impression that the numerical majority of those who face food insecurity in the United States are African American. He also wrongly implies that members of this group are content with their status.

At other times, struggling Americans have been promised help by more beneficent politicians like New Orleans mayor Mitch Landrieu, who pledged fourteen million dollars in loans to build grocery stores in needy neighborhoods. Some community activists have tried to fight both hunger and the health impact of the SAD by planting gardens in inner cities to give residents ready access to healthful foods. In 2012 Hantz Farms is in the process of buying vacant land in the blighted city of Detroit to create the world's largest urban garden. The Greater Boston Food Bank's Mobile Pantry brings fresh ingredients to residents who live in a food desert in the Germantown neighborhood of Quincy, Massachusetts. Residents live on average eight miles away from the nearest grocery store, and their neighborhood food options consist primarily of a doughnut shop, a pizzeria, and a convenience store. Efforts like these are attempting to chip away at hunger in a country that has always prided itself on having an abundance of food.

FOOD PRACTICES AS POLITICAL BEHAVIOR

For more fortunate Americans, the existence of a wide variety of food choices has provided them with dilemmas about what they should eat and what their choices mean. Some have responded to the ethical problems posed by factory farming by identifying as conscientious omnivores, locavores, or flexitarians. Journalist Michael Pollan is perhaps the best-known example of a conscientious omnivore. In his book *The Omnivore's Dilemma* he not only exposes many of the abuses of factory farming, but he also points out some of the pitfalls for those who wish to eat responsibly. He observes, for example, that consumers who wish to buy organic produce to support more environmentally aware agricultural practices often purchase food that was shipped great distances. To explain why this is problematic, he cites the research of Cornell University scientist David Pimentel, who estimates that producing and shipping a box of organic salad from the West Coast to the East Coast takes fifty-seven calories of fossil fuel for each food calorie. Thus for Pollan there are no easy or universally applicable answers to what it means to eat ethically. For him, being a conscientious eater means that he must be mindful about his food decisions and constantly grapple with the fine points of eating behind his overarching food philosophy of "Eat food. Not too much. Mostly plants."

He also contemplates the issue of meat eating and gives serious thought to the problem of animal suffering. He concludes that "What's wrong with eating animals is the practice, not the principle." It would be wrong, in Pollan's estimation, to eat animals raised in a CAFO, where they invariably suffered, but not those who were allowed to live good lives and act upon their animal instincts, with plenty of space and food on their way to a painless death. However, given the ubiquity of factory-farmed animals, Pollan's ethical position is one that is hard to maintain and nearly impossible to live up to outside of areas with the critical mass of consumers necessary to support small-scale, free-range meat production. Finding ethical sources of meat was, in fact, so problematic for novelist Barbara Kingsolver that she ate an almost exclusively vegetarian diet until she moved to a farm where she could raise and slaughter her own animals or buy humanely raised meat from her farmer neighbors.

Kingsolver publicized the growing locavore movement with her best-selling 2007 book *Animal, Vegetable, Miracle: A Year of Food Life*, where she documents her family's experiences with eating predominantly foods that they could produce or acquire near their home in rural Appalachia. Although the family allowed themselves a few modest indulgences in things like coffee, chocolate, and spices that were not produced locally, the vast majority of their diet for that year was what they could produce themselves on their farm, subsidized by trips to their local farmer's market.

Kingsolver's experiment was motivated not only by her rejection of the environmentally unfriendly practices of intensive agriculture, which produces food that is routinely shipped long distances from producer to consumer, but also by her general disdain for American food culture. She claims, "[F]ood remains at the center of every culture. Ours now runs on empty calories." She is a champion not only of producing her own food but also of preparing it, claiming, "Cooking is the great divide between good eating and bad."

For Kingsolver and her family, rejecting the SAD and environmentally detrimental farming practices was a crucial aspect of their identity. Kingsolver and her husband, Steven L. Hopp, carefully explained to their teenage daughter's friend why buying bananas that had traveled a great distance to the supermarket was an inferior choice to eating locally and organically produced fruits. Kingsolver described in great detail what it took for the family to maintain their ideals. They planted an enormous garden, which required such intensive care that the family was reluctant to travel and left the farm under a cloud of anxiety that something might go wrong with their food supply without their constant care. They raised, slaughtered, and bred poultry. They canned and dried produce, stockpiled local meat, baked bread, foraged for mushrooms, and made cheese. In her description of that year, most of her energy and her waking hours were spent producing, cooking, or eating food.

Many Americans who admire Kingsolver's passion for food and her conscientious approach to eating, who lack the time, resources, skills, or inclination to make eating locally the center of their lives, have still borrowed some lessons from the locavore movement. Even large retailers like Walmart have begun to stock more locally grown produce in response to consumer demands for food that has not traveled great distances to reach them. This group of eaters has begun to recognize its power as consumers and has seen that collective food choices can have real world impact. However, most in this group remain unwilling or unable to devote the time and energy it would take to, like the Kingsolver family, abandon most mainstream sources of food supplies.

A new group of eaters often identified as "flexitarians" exhibits a spirit of compromise. This group has not sworn off meat eating but has reduced its meat consumption due to environmental and health concerns. The "Meatless Monday" movement has successfully convinced many Americans to abstain from eating meat on Mondays "for your health and the health of the planet." People in this group can use their food choices as a way to label themselves as environmentally or health conscious without having to reject completely the SAD, a choice made by a growing number of vegetarians and vegans.

In 2008 *Vegetarian Times* magazine conducted a study that found that 7.3 million people, or 3.2 percent of the United States population, are vegetarians. Of this number, one million are vegans who, unlike vegetarians, who consume dairy products and eggs, will not eat any animal products at all. They also found that 10 percent of American adults could possibly be defined as "flexitarians" who eat a "vegetarian-inclined" diet. Although those who have reduced their meat consumption or who do not eat animal protein are still a minority of the population, their numbers are growing, and their impact is beginning to be felt by meat producers. The USDA predicts that Americans will consume 12.2 percent less meat in 2012 than was eaten in 2007.

Writer Jonathan Safran Foer surprised fans of his literary novels when in 2009 he published his own vegetarian manifesto, *Eating Animals*. Foer's vegetarian identity is at root an instinctive one, based primarily on his disgust at animal suffering, which he documents in great detail. This core sense was bolstered by environmental concerns as he did more research on the subject. Despite his misgivings, as a young adult he ate meat because maintaining the SAD diet was an easy default position. Meat "tasted good." However, he described his abandonment of his vegetarian identity as the product of a "willful forgetting" of the reality of the slaughterhouse. His found it more imperative to live up to his vegetarian ideals after he became a father and knew he would have to explain his food choices to his son. He ultimately realized:

Whether I sit at the global table, with my family or with my conscience, the factory farm, for me, doesn't merely appear unreasonable. To accept the factory farm feels inhuman. To accept the factory farm—to feed the food it produces to my family, to support it with my money—would make me less myself, less my grandmother's grandson, less my son's father.

Foer's food politics do not have space for the compromises of flexitarians, and he rails against the idea that omnivores who blithely attend dinner parties cheerfully proclaiming that they will "eat anything" are more "socially sensitive" than vegetarians. The uncomfortable relationship between being a vegetarian guest in the home of an omnivorous host was, in fact, one of the reasons that Michael Pollan abandoned his own flirtation with vegetarianism. Although he felt "[h]ealthy and virtuous" in some ways, he could not escape the sense that his dietary restrictions were read as poor manners, a concern that Foer ultimately labeled trivial in the face of the larger issue of animal cruelty.

The stance taken by vegetarians and vegans is often the source of backlash, which sometimes comes in the form of jokes or mild ribbing at the dinner table. When Foer was still working out his ethical position about food consumption, his father would sardonically ask, "Any dietary restrictions I need to know about tonight?" Other times it is more serious. The owner of a short-lived vegetarian restaurant in Omaha, Nebraska, told a reporter for the *New York Times* that someone threw several pounds of ground beef at the doors of the restaurant in what was likely an accusation that meat-free food somehow hurt the state's cattle industry. Celebrity chef Gordon Ramsay has gained notoriety for his many critiques of vegetarianism, including his hyperbolic claim that "my biggest nightmare would be if the kids ever came up to me and said, 'Dad, I'm a vegetarian.' Then I would sit them on the fence and electrocute them."

However, other less radical political positions about food have also been the subject of criticism. First Lady Michelle Obama has planted an organic garden at the White House. She has also targeted childhood obesity through her Let's Move campaign, which promotes exercise and healthful eating habits. However, even these seemingly uncontroversial initiatives have earned her criticism. Republican congressman Jim Sensenbrenner was overheard complaining that Obama "lectures" the country about eating right while she has a "big butt." Conservative radio talk show host Rush Limbaugh made similarly snide remarks about the famously physically fit First Lady's physique, saying, "Leaders are supposed to be leaders. If we are supposed to eat roots, berries and tree bark, show us how." Congresswoman Michele Bachmann claimed that Obama's dietary recommendations are an attempt to create a "nanny state." In July 2011, Obama received widespread criticism for "hypocrisy" when she was spotted eating a hamburger and French fries and drinking a shake at a Washington, DC, hamburger joint.

Unsurprisingly perhaps, Obama's loudest critics all come from members of the opposing political party. However, class antagonisms as well as political ones often come into play in discussions of food and politics in what Hank Steuver of the *Washington Post* has referred to as the "arugula divide." The higher cost of organic foods as opposed to conventional ones has led many to criticize advocates of healthful eating as culinary elitists who do not understand the food options of the less well-off. *New York Times* columnist Frank Bruni has noted that "class tensions in the food world . . . sadly mirror those in society at large." He imagines the acid-tongued celebrity chef Anthony Bourdain as a "blue-state paternalist" pitted against southern home-style cook Paula Deen, "a red-state populist [arguing] over correct living versus liberty in all its artery-clogging, self-destructive glory." Echoing these antagonisms, Missouri farmer Blake Hurst claims that critics of the quality of America's food supply do not respect farmers. Hurst resents the portrayal of farmers in much of the expanding literature about factory farming. He writes that farmers are often "painted as either naïve tools of corporate greed, or economic nullities forced into their present circumstances by the unrelenting forces of the twin grindstones of corporate greed and unfeeling markets." He believes that the authors of these texts generally do not respect his years of accumulated wisdom, his ability to make complicated ethical decisions, and his business acumen.

The Center for Consumer Freedom was founded in 1996 with money provided by the Phillip Morris tobacco company to combat various critics of the SAD, whom they describe as a "growing cabal of activists . . . [who] include self-anointed 'food police,' health campaigners, trial lawyers, personal-finance do-gooders, animal-rights misanthropes, and meddling bureaucrats." Many of the supporters of the Center for Consumer Freedom have financial ties to the food industry and thus direct financial incentives to fight demands for greater government oversight of food production and stricter requirements for animal welfare, environmental protection, and food safety. However, their message also resonates with many average consumers who value what they regard as their culinary freedom of choice.

Many appreciate the affordability of meat raised in CAFOs, and they do not have qualms about the potential health hazards that go along with consuming large quantities of processed food. In the pages of the *Wall Street Journal*, historian Peter Coclanis writes in favor of the "much maligned 'industrial' food system," implying that greater regulations are not necessary because of what he sees as the impressive "safety of our food supply." In *Time* magazine, Josh Ozersky defends industrial food against critics like food writer Mark Bittman, an advocate for home cooking, claiming, "Whatever the future holds, it isn't going to be 300 million Americans feeding themselves with handmade tagliatelle from pristine Vermont CSAs." He argues that Americans are busy, that some industrial food tastes good, and that average consumers enjoy eating it. He does not share Pollan's dismay about the role government-subsidized corn plays in the creation of many of these foods, arguing, "There are now 300 million Americans or so, and less space. If the barons of agriculture hadn't engineered the monstrous phalanxes of corn that everyone is so aghast at, food would be more expensive, and a lot of poor people would be dying from starvation instead of courting diabetes."

While Coclanis and Ozersky overtly defend aspects of America's industrialized food system, most Americans defend it only implicitly by participating in the system without critically analyzing it. Food producers, after all, operate to make a profit and would not manufacture the cake mixes, sodas, and boxed macaroni and cheese that line the notorious "middle aisles" of the supermarket, which Bittman and others urge conscientious eaters to avoid, if there were not an ample number of consumers buying those products. For these Americans, habit and convenience trump political concerns.

FOOD AS ENTERTAINMENT

For yet another segment of American eaters, food is primarily a form of entertainment rather than a political issue. Many of those who regard food primarily as entertainment find an outlet for their fascination with cooking and eating by watching television shows on cable television's Food Network. The station was founded in 1993 after investors noted that since everyone is engaged in some fashion in American food culture, the potential viewing audience was virtually limitless. When the network was launched, it had access to a cable audience of 6.8 million viewers. By 2004, it reached 86.3 million homes. Viewers can tune into a wide variety of programming ranging from instructional cooking shows, to travel shows that prominently feature local restaurants, to programs that document cooking and baking competitions. This programming has elevated chefs like Bobby Flay, Mario Batali, and Aarón Sanchez from well-respected practitioners of their craft with a dedicated local base of restaurant customers to nationally known celebrities.

Some of the fans of the Food Network no doubt plan to hone their cooking skills while watching television, but others view the network as something to do simply to heighten their cultural awareness, perhaps while eating convenience foods or restaurant food prepared by someone else. Food writer Andrew Smith argues, "These viewers wish to become more knowledgeable about food so they can order properly at a restaurant or hold their own in culinary conversations with their peers." In a food-obsessed culture, knowledge about cooking techniques, celebrity chefs, and the latest restaurants has become a sign of sophistication and trendiness among a certain segment of the population.

However, although some programs educate viewers about innovative cuisine and elevated culinary techniques, others reinforce traditional American eating habits. Guy Fieri's "Diners, Drive-Ins, and Dives" shows the animated host touring the country and eating casual restaurant fare, which generally fits within the SAD paradigm of meat-, fat-, and carbohydrate-heavy meals. In addition to watching Fieri gobble overstuffed sandwiches and gooey desserts, viewers can watch Paula Deen, a spokesperson for factory-produced hams, cook southern-style foods that rely heavily on butter and processed ingredients. Despite numerous criticisms for her partnership with Smithfield Foods, Deen has insisted that it is a good company, one that "share[s] my family values and traditions." Some members of the food movement felt vindication of their belief system in 2012 when Deen admitted to having been diagnosed with type 2 diabetes, a condition closely tied to the SAD diet. Nonetheless, regardless of their culinary perspective, for the smiling celebrities on the Food Network, food is not a political issue.

Book sales reflect the growing fascination with both cuisine that stays within the traditional boundaries of the SAD as well as more expansive culinary ideas. Cookbooks have proved to be a recession-proof item, objects that apparently bring Americans comfort during times of uncertainty. While total book sales decreased 4.5 percent due to the economic downturn between 2009 and 2010, cookbook sales increased 4 percent during that same period. Those with the financial means to do so can further fuel their culinary fascination by indulging in the explosion of cooking tours, cooking classes, and the specialty cooking and food stores that have arisen to feed the insatiable appetite many Americans have for food both as nourishment and as entertainment.

For *Atlantic* contributing editor B. R. Myers this obsession with food is off-putting. He argues that although most celebrity chefs and members of the food intelligentsia outwardly denounce factory-farmed animals and processed foods, he is unimpressed by their piety, which he believes merely serves to justify gluttony. He points out that many critics of factory farming eat other ethically suspect foods like endangered animals or meats of unknown provenance in the name of being polite. Corn-fed beef also appears on the menus of many chefs who would describe themselves as conscientious food buyers. Myers is horrified by food critic Jeffrey Steingarten's description of a pig who died an excruciating death as a "filthy beast deserving its fate" and unconvinced by attempts to justify copious meat eating such as Pollan's claim that "meat-eating has shaped our *souls*." For foodies of a certain bent, he claims, the "single-mindedness" of those who put the pleasure of eating above all ethical concerns reveals a "littleness of soul."

Myers's critique would be welcomed by philosopher and animal rights advocate Peter Singer, who has expressed consternation at the fact "that we don't usually think of what we eat as a matter of ethics." For some Americans, Singer's critique is true, but as the twenty-first century unfolds, more Americans than ever are attaching enormous ethical and political significance to their eating decisions. Indeed, many Americans throughout history have understood that food is much more significant than a means to gain nourishment. Choices about cooking and eating can be used not only to demonstrate political identifications but as a means for exhibiting ideas of nationality and patriotism, gender, race and ethnicity, and technology and change. The study of food habits is one of the most exciting tools scholars have for studying how Americans have historically identified themselves, and the subject continues to yield endless clues about identity issues we face in the present day.

A Note on Sources

ARCHIVAL SOURCES

While formulating the ideas that went into this book, I consulted a wide variety of archival and other primary materials at a number of libraries, including the following: the Jazz Archive at Tulane University (food-related sheet music); the Louisiana Research Collection at Tulane University (food-related ephemera, cookbooks, Cross Keys Plantation Papers, Lemann Family Papers, Natalie Vivian Scott Papers); the David Walker Lupton African American Cookbook Collection at the W. S. Hoole Special Collections Library at the University of Alabama; the New York Public Library (cookbooks and recipe manuscripts, Colles Family Papers, Peoples Institute Records, Frederick August Bartholdi Papers, the Menu Collection); the Library of Congress (cookbooks, America Eats Collection, a wide variety of food-related photographs); National Agricultural Library; the Schlesinger Library at the Radcliffe Institute for Advanced Study (cookbooks, food-related ephemera, Women's Educational and Industrial Trade Union Papers); and Archives Center of the National Museum for American History (food-related sheet music, Estelle Ellis Collection, Charlotte Cramer Sachs Papers, Frances Baker Product Cookbooks, Products Cookbook Collection).

GENERAL SOURCES

Readers looking for a broad introduction to the general topic of U.S. food history would do well to consult the following books: *The Oxford Companion to American Food and Drink* (Oxford: Oxford University Press, 2007), edited by Andrew F. Smith; Andrew F. Smith, *Eating History: 30 Turning Points in the Making of American Cuisine* (New York: Columbia University Press, 2009); *The New Encyclopedia of Southern Culture: Foodways* (Chapel Hill: University of North Carolina Press, 2007), edited by John T. Edge; Richard Pillsbury, *No Foreign Food: The American Diet in Time and Place* (Boulder, CO: Westview, 1998); Reay Tannahill, *Food in History* (New York: Three Rivers, 1988); Waverly Root and Richard de Rochemont, *Eating in America: A History* (New York: William & Morrow, 1976); Sandra L. Oliver, *Food in Colonial and Federal America* (Westport, CT: Greenwood, 2005); Susan Williams, *Food in the United States: 1820s–1890* (Westport, CT: Greenwood, 2006); Megan J. Elias, *Food in the United States, 1890–1945* (Santa Barbara, CA: ABC Clio, 2009); Linda Murray Berzok's important synthesis *American Indian Food* (Westport, CT: Greenwood, 2005); John F. Mariani, *The Dictionary of American Food and Drink* (New Haven, CT: Ticknor and Fields, 1983); and Alan Davidson, *The Oxford Companion to Food* (Oxford: Oxford University Press, 2006). I utilized all of these sources generously while writing this book.

INTRODUCTION

John L. Hess and Karen Hess's unabashedly opinionated *The Taste of America* (1972; Champaign: University of Illinois Press, 2000) provides readers a great deal of information about U.S. food history along with the authors' assessment of more contemporary eating practices. Felipe Fernández-Armesto's lively *Near a Thousand Tables: A History of Food* (New York: Free Press, 2002) provides a sweeping overview of world food history from the "invention of cooking" through the modern day. For definitions of the interdisciplinary field of "food studies" as well as an introduction to research methods in the field, see Warren Belasco, *Food: The Key Concepts* (Oxford: Berg, 2008); and Jeff Miller and Jonathan Deutsch, *Food Studies: An Introduction to Research Methods* (Oxford: Berg, 2009). My thinking about issues of food history and identity construction were strengthened by reading the following: Hasia R. Diner, *Hungering for America: Italian, Irish, and Jewish Foodways in the Age of Migration* (Cambridge, MA: Harvard University Press, 2002); Ron Scapp and Brian Seitz, eds., *Eating Culture* (Albany: State University of New York Press, 1998); and Debra Lupton, "Food and Emotion," in *The Taste Culture Reader: Experiencing Food and Drink*, edited by Carolyn Korsmeyer (Oxford: Berg, 2005).

CHAPTER 1: THE CUISINE OF CONTACT

Food in Colonial and Federal America, by Sandra L. Oliver, provides a straightforward and reader-friendly overview of foodways during the time period discussed in this chapter. James McWilliams's masterful *A Revolution in Eating:*

How the Quest for Food Shaped America (New York: Columbia University Press, 2005) is an essential read.

Nathaniel Philbrook's engaging *Mayflower: A Story of Courage, Community, and War* (New York: Viking, 2006) offers a comprehensive account of the Pilgrims' early days in Massachusetts, as does Nick Bunker's *Making Haste from Babylon: The Mayflower Pilgrims and Their World* (New York: Vintage Books, 2010). William Cronon's pioneering study *Changes in the Land: Indians, Colonists, and the Ecology of New England* (New York: Hill and Wang, 1983) provides invaluable information about how both the colonists and the native peoples used the land to feed themselves. Laura Thatcher Ulrich's important study *Good Wives: Image and Reality in Northern New England* (New York: Vintage 1991) gives insights into the important role women played in colonial households. Gary Nash's classic study *Red, White, and Black: The Peoples of Early North America*, 3rd edition (Englewood Cliffs, NJ: Prentice Hall, 1992) aided me in constructing the historical framework for this chapter, as did Karen Ordhal Kupperman's *The Jamestown Project* (Cambridge, MA: Harvard University Press, 2007) and Karen Ordahl Kupperman, "Apathy and Death in Early Jamestown," *Journal of American History* 66.1 (1979): 24–40. For an intriguing reading of the sources about cannibalism in Jamestown, see Rachel B. Herrmann, "The 'tragicall historie': Cannibalism and Abundance in Colonial Jamestown," *William & Mary Quarterly* 68.1 (2011): 47–74. A good study of colonial drinking habits is Sarah Hand Meacham, *Every Home a Distillery: Alcohol, Gender, and Technology in the Colonial Chesapeake* (Baltimore: Johns Hopkins University Press, 2009).

Primary sources documenting early colonial food habits can be found in Camplin Burrage, "The Earliest Minor Accounts of Plymouth Plantation," *Harvard Theological Review* 13.2 (1920): 315–344 and Edward Winslow's *Mourt's Relation: A Journal of the Pilgrims at Plymouth*, edited by Dwight B. Heath (Bedford, MA: Applewood Books, 1963). I also benefited tremendously from the ready availability of electronic versions of classic early American primary texts. I consulted William Bradford's *Of Plymouth Plantation*, which can be accessed courtesy of the Early America's Digital Archive at http://www.mith2.umd.edu/eada/html/display.php?docs=bradford_history .xml; and History Matters: The U.S. Survey Course on the Web provided me with an electronic copy of "A Letter Home from Massachusetts Bay in 1631," http://historymatters.gmu.edu/d/5787.

Information about the first Thanksgiving and the controversy surrounding its modern observance can be found in Kenneth C. Davis, "A French Connection," *New York Times*, November 25, 2008; Robert Jensen, "No Thanks to Thanksgiving," *Alternet*, November 23, 2005, available at http://www.alternet.org/story/28584; Kathleen Curtin and Sandra L. Oliver, *Giving Thanks: Thanksgiving Recipes and History, from Pilgrims to Pumpkin Pie* (New York: Clarkson Potter, 2005); Nathaniel Philbrick, "Thanksgiving without the Myths," *Martha's Vineyard Times*, November 22, 2006; James McWilliams, "They Held Their Noses and Ate," *New York Times*, November 24, 2005; Megan Gambino, "Ask an Expert: What Was the Menu at the First Thanksgiving?" Smithsonian.com, November 21, 2011, available at http://www.smithsonianmag.com/history-archaeology/Ask-an-Expert-What-was-on-the-menu-at-the-first-Thanksgiving.html; and "Thanksgiving at Plimoth Plantation: Kathleen Curtin," *Archeology*, November 21, 2006, available at http://www.archaeology.org/online/interviews/curtin.html.

Trudy Eden's important study *The Early American Table: Food and Society in the New World* (Dekalb: Northern Illinois University Press, 2008) offers a fascinating overview of early modern medical knowledge, which she carefully applies to a detailed history of early American foodways. Another important book for understanding how the early colonists understood nutrition is Ken Alba's *Eating Right in the Renaissance* (Berkeley: University of California Press, 2002). In *Food and Drink in Britain: From the Stone Age to Modern Times* (New York: Harper and Row, 1974), C. Anne Wilson gives an excellent overview of the English ideas about food that shaped the aspirations of early American diners. I also gained useful insights from P. W. Hammond, *Food & Feast in Medieval England* (Phoenix Mill: Sutton Publishing, 1993); Clarissa Dickson Wright's *A History of English Food* (New York: Random House, 2011); and two articles that appear in *Food: The History of Taste* (Berkeley: University of California, 2007), edited by Paul Freedman: "Feasting and Fasting: Food and Taste in Europe in the Middle Ages," by C. M.Woolgar, and "New Worlds, New Tastes: Food Fashions after the Renaissance," by Brian Cowan.

For more information about Native American foodways and European attitudes toward native foods, readers can turn to Linda Murray Berzok's important synthesis *American Indian Food*; Susan Sleeper-Smith's "Agrarian Dynamics of the Columbian Exchange," in *Transatlantic Rebels: Agrarian Radicalism in Comparative Perspective*, edited by Thomas Summerhill and James C. Scott (East Lansing: Michigan State University Press, 2004): 1–20; Thomas Wessel, "Agriculture, Indians, and American History," *Agricultural History* 50.1 (1976): 9–20; and Helen C. Rountree, "Powhatan Indian Women: The People Captain John Smith Barely Saw," *American Society for Ethnohistory* 45.1 (1998): 1–29.

Readers interested in learning more about maize can turn to Nicholas P. Hardeman's impressive study, *Shucks, Shocks, and Hominy Blocks: Corn as a Way of Life in Pioneer America* (Baton Rouge: Louisiana State University Press, 1981); Paul Weatherwax, *Indian Corn in Old America* (New York: Macmillan, 1954); Betty Fussell, *The Story of Corn* (New York: North Point Press, 1992); and Theresa Mendez's "Corn," in *Rooted in America: Foodlore of Popular Fruits and Vegetables*, edited by David Scofield Wilson and Angus Kress Gillespie (Knoxville: University of Tennessee Press, 1999).

Insights about Puritan ideas about food can be found in Martha L. Finch's "Pinched with Hunger, Partaking of Plenty: Fasts and Thanksgivings in Early New England," in *Eating in Eden: Food and American Utopias,* edited by Etta M. Madden and Martha L. Finch (Lincoln: University of Nebraska Press, 2006), 35–53; and in Frederick Kaufman's playful *A Short History of the American Stomach* (Orlando: Harcourt, 2008). Katherine A. Grandjean's "New World Tempests: Environment, Scarcity, and the Coming of the Pequot War," *William and Mary Quarterly* 68.1 (2011): 75–100 intriguingly inserts the issue of food scarcity into her analysis of the cause of the Pequot War. The most comprehensive overview of the subject of Puritan food can be found in Keith Stavely and Kathleen Fitzgerald's *America's Founding Food: The Story of New England Cooking* (Chapel Hill: University of North Carolina Press, 2004). Nineteenth-century New England food habits are well documented in *Saltwater Foodways: New Englanders and Their Food at Sea and Ashore in the Nineteenth Century* (Mystic, CT: Mystic Seaport Museum, 1970).

CHAPTER 2: FOOD AND THE FOUNDING

Readers desiring to contemplate further the contradiction between slavery and freedom in the United States may wish to examine Edmund S. Morgan's classic study, *American Slavery, American Freedom: The Ordeal of Colonial Virginia* (New York: Norton, 1975).

Those interested in African American contributions to the American diet can begin their investigation by looking at two classic books about slavery in the United States: Eugene Genovese's *Roll, Jordan, Roll: The World the Slaves Made* (New York: Vintage, 1976) and Charles Joyner's *Down by the Riverside: A South Carolina Slave Community* (Urbana: University of Illinois Press, 1984). More detailed studies of the subject include: Jessica B. Harris, "Three Is a Magic Number," *Southern Quarterly* 44.2 (2007): 9–15; Jessica Harris, *High on the Hog: A Culinary Journey from Africa to America* (New York: Bloomsbury, 2011); Frederick Douglass Opie, *Hog and Hominy: Soul Food from Africa to America* (New York: Columbia University Press, 2008); Sam Bowers Hilliard, *Hog Meat and Hoecake: Food Supply in the Old South, 1840–1860* (Carbondale: University of Illinois Press, 1972); and Herbert C. Covey and Dwight Eisnach, *What the Slaves Ate: Recollections of African American Foods and Foodways from Slave Narratives* (Santa Barbara, CA: ABC-CLIO, 2009). Information about the transference of African foodways to the Americas during the transatlantic slave trade is available from Marcus Rediker's *The Slave Ship: A Human History* (New York: Viking, 2007); Robert L. Hall's "Africa and the American South: Culinary Connections," *Southern Quarterly* 44.2 (2007): 19–52; and in the groundbreaking study by Judith A. Carney and Richard Nicholas Rosomoff, *In the Shadow of Slavery: Africa's*

Botanical Legacy in the Atlantic World (Berkeley: University of California Press, 2009). Judith Carney's *Black Rice: The African Origins of Rice Cultivation in the Americas* (Cambridge, MA: Harvard University Press, 2001) and Karen Hess's *The Carolina Rice Kitchen: The African Connection* (Columbia: University of South Carolina Press, 1992) detail the African origins of rice cultivation in the United States.

I gained important insights about ideas about food and eating during the era of the American Revolution from Caleb Train's "Tea and Antipathy," *New Yorker*, December 20 and 27, 2010: 132–128; Trudy Eden's "'This Fatal Cake': The Ideals and Realities of Republican Virtue in Eighteenth-Century America," in *Eating in Eden: Food and American Utopias*, edited by Etta M. Madden and Martha L. Finch (Lincoln: University of Nebraska Press, 2006), 187–202; and Mark McWilliams's "Distant Tables: Food and the Novel in Early America," *Early American Literature* 38.3 (2003): 365–393. James McWilliams's masterful *A Revolution in Eating: How the Quest for Food Shaped America* is a must-read for anyone interested in this subject. I owe McWilliams a tremendous intellectual debt for shaping my thinking about a number of aspects of the food habits of this era, especially for the concept of "republican" food.

There is a vast amount of information available about the food preferences of Thomas Jefferson. These three books offer valuable introductions to the subject: Dave DeWitt's *The Founding Foodies: How Washington, Jefferson, and Franklin Revolutionized American Cuisine* (Naperville, IL: Sourcebooks, 2010); Jack McLaughlin's *Jefferson and Monticello: The Biography of a Builder* (New York: Henry Holt, 1988); and John Hailman's *Thomas Jefferson on Wine* (Jackson: University Press of Mississippi, 2006). For more information about James Hemings, Thomas Jefferson's enslaved French-trained chef, see Annette Gordon-Reed, *The Hemings of Monticello* (New York: Norton, 2008).

In addition to the secondary works listed above, this chapter benefited from the consultation of a number of firsthand accounts, including Frederick Douglass's *Narrative of the Life of Frederick Douglass* in *The Classic Slave Narratives*, edited by Henry Louis Gates, Jr. (New York: Signet Classic, 2002). Frederick Bartholdi's diary kept while on his 1871 trip to the United States is held at the New York Public Library. I utilized a number of electronic versions of primary texts, including: Mary Rowlandson, *Narrative of the Captivity and Restoration of Mrs. Mary Rowlandson* (1682), available at http://onlinebooks.library.upenn.edu/webbin/gutbook/lookup?num=851; Alexander Falconbridge, "The African Slave Trade" (1788, http://www.gilderlehrman.org/historynow/12_2004/pdf/MS2A.pdf; History Matters: The U.S. Survey Course on the Web provided me with electronic copies of the following documents: Elizabeth Sprigs, "'We Unfortunate English People Suffer Here': An English Servant Writes Home," http://historymatters.gmu.edu/d/5796 and "'Our Plantation Is Very Weak': The Experiences of an Indentured Servant in Virginia, 1923," http://historymatters.gmu.edu/d/6475. James Revel's "The

Poor Unhappy Transported Felon's Sorrowful Account of His Fourteen Years Transportation, at Virginia, in America," can be read here: http://docsouth .unc.edu/southlit/revel/menu.html. Excerpts from Benjamin Franklin, *Poor Richard's Almanack*, which was published annually from 1732 to 1758, can be viewed here: http://www.archive.org/stream/poorrichardsalm01frangoog/ poorrichardsalm01frangoog_djvu.txt. Thomas Jefferson's quote about "the quantity of animal food eaten by the English" can be found in a 1785 letter to Abigail Adams, the full text of which is available here: http://etext.virginia .edu/etcbin/toccernew2?id=JefLett.sgm&images=images/modeng&data=/ texts/english/modeng/parsed&tag=public&part=37&division=div1.

While writing this chapter, I examined a number of significant historical cookbooks, including Sarah Josepha Hale's *Mrs. Hale's New Cook Book* (Philadelphia: T. B. Peterson, 1857); Mary Randolph's *The Virginia Housewife* (Baltimore: Plaskitt, Fite, 1838); Lydia Maria Child's *The American Frugal Housewife* (New York: SS & W. Wood, 1841); Amelia Simmons's *American Cookery* (Albany, NY: George R. and George Webster, 1796); and Hannah Glasse's *The Art of Cookery, Made Plain and Easy* (London: L. Wanford, 1781). These are all available in full-text versions online and in hard copy at the Schlesinger Library at the Radcliffe Institute for Advanced Study, Harvard University.

CHAPTER 3: FOODWAYS IN THE ERA OF EXPANSION AND IMMIGRATION

For information about European influences other than English ones on colonial foodways, see Adam F. Smith, "The Food and Drink of New York from 1624 to 1898," in *Gastropolis: Food & New York City*, edited by Annie Hauck-Lawson and Jonathon Deutsch (New York: Columbia University Press, 2009); Oliver, *Food in Colonial and Federal America*; Craig Clairbone, Q & A (about scrapple), *New York Times*, November 18, 1981; and Dr. Alexander Hamilton's *Itinerarium: Being a Narrative of a Journey from Annapolis, Maryland, through Delaware, Pennsylvania, New York, New Jersey, Connecticut, Rhode Island, Massachusetts and New Hampshire, from May to September, 1744*, edited by Albert Bushnell Hart (Saint Louis, MO: W. K. Bixby, 1907). For changing New England attitudes about the clam and other shellfish, see Stavely and Fitzgerald, *America's Founding Food*.

The most sophisticated treatment of the creation of Louisiana foodways during the colonial area can be found in Shannon Lee Dawdy, "'A Wild Taste': Food and Colonialism in Eighteenth Century Louisiana," *Ethnohistory* 57.3 (2010): 388–414. Further information about Cajun and Creole foodways can be found in Lafcadio Hearn, *Gombo Zhèbes: Little Dictionary of Creole Proverbs* (New York: Will H. Coleman, 1885); Bethany Ewald Bultman, "A True and Delectable History of Creole Cooking," *American*

Heritage, December 1986: 66–73; Daniel H. Usner, *Indians, Settlers, and Slaves in a Frontier Exchange Economy* (Chapel Hill: University of North Carolina Press, 1992); Richard Campenella, *Bienville's Dilemma: The Historical Geography of New Orleans* (Lafayette: Center for Louisiana Studies, 2008); Marcelle Bienvenu, Carl A. Brasseaux, and Ryan A. Brasseaux, *Stir the Pot: The History of Cajun Cuisine* (New York: Hippocrene Books, 2005); Christopher Morris, "Impenetrable but Easy: The French Transformation of the Lower Mississippi Valley and the Founding of New Orleans," in *Transforming New Orleans and Its Environs*, edited by Craig E. Colton (Pittsburgh: University of Pittsburgh Press, 2000); Ira Berlin, *Many Thousands Gone: The First Two Centuries of Slavery in North America* (Cambridge, MA: Harvard University Press, 2000); Ernest Gueynard, "Louisiana's Creole-Acadian Cuisine," *Revue de Louisiane/Louisiana Review* 1 (1973): 8–19; Lyle Saxon, *Old Louisiana* (New Orleans: R. L. Crager, 1950); Julia Reed, "In Creole Kitchens, Chefs Mix Cultures and Stir Well," *New York Times*, February 20, 2005; and "New Orleans Foodways," "Cajun Foodways," "Gumbo," and "Restaurants, New Orleans," in Edge, *The New Encyclopedia of Southern Culture: Foodways*. Cookbooks I consulted include Howard Mitchuam, *Creole Gumbo and All That Jazz: A New Orleans Seafood Cookbook* (Reading, MA: Addison-Wesley, 1978); *The Picayune Creole Cook Book* (New Orleans: The Picayune, 1901); and Lafcadio Hearn, *La Cuisine Creole: A Collection of Culinary Recipes from Leading Chefs and Creole House Wives, Who Have Made New Orleans Famous for Its Cuisine* (New Orleans: F. F. Hansell, 1895).

A history of the development of American restaurant culture can be found in John Mariani's *America Eats Out: An Illustrated History of Restaurants, Taverns, Coffee Shops, Speakeasies, and Other Establishments That Have Fed Us for 350 Years* (New York: William Morrow, 1991) and in "Delmonico's," in Andrew F. Smith's *Eating History: 30 Turning Points in the Making of American Cuisine*. Charles Dickens's impression of the dining scene in America can be read in *American Notes* (1842), available here: http://www.gutenberg.org/cache/epub/675/pg675.html. For a contemporary favorable English perspective on the food scene in New Orleans, see "French Market," *All the Year Round: A Weekly Journal*, December 26, 1874.

Feast or Famine: Food and Drink in American Westward Expansion, by Reginald Horsman (Columbia: University of Missouri Press, 2008), and *Wagon Wheels Kitchens: Food on the Oregon Trail*, by Jacqueline Williams (Lawrence: University Press of Kansas, 1993), offer detailed accounts of securing and preparing food during the era of westward expansion. Additional information can be found in Linda Civitello, *Cuisine and Culture: A History of Food and People* (Hoboken, NJ: Wiley, 2004); Michael Wise, "Colonial Beef and Blackfeet Reservation Slaughterhouse, 1879–1895," *Radical History Review* 110 (2011): 59–82; and Lillian Schlissel, ed., *Women's Diaries of the Westward Journey* (New York: Schocken Books, 1982). Southwestern foodways of the era are written about in Carmella Padilla, *The Chile Chronicles:*

Tales of a New Mexico Harvest (Sante Fe: Museum of New Mexico Press, 1997); Zilkia Janer, *Latino Food Culture* (Westport, CT: Greenwood, 2008); Jeffrey M. Pilcher, *Food in World History* (New York: Routledge, 2006); Donna R. Gabaccia, *We Are What We Eat: Ethnic Food and the Making of Americans* (Cambridge, MA: Harvard University Press, 1998); Meredith E. Abarca, *Voices in the Kitchen: Views of Food and the World from Working-Class Mexican and Mexican American Women* (College Station: Texas A&M University Press, 2006); Brett Williams, "Why Migrant Women Feed Their Husbands Tamales: Foodways as a Basis for a Revisionist View of Tejano Family Life," in *Ethnic and Regional Foodways in the United States: The Performance of Group Identity*, edited by Linda Keller Brown and Kay Mussell (Knoxville: University of Tennessee Press, 1984); and most notably in Jeffrey M. Pilcher's landmark study *¡Que vivan los tamales! Food and the Making of Mexican Identity* (Albuquerque: University of New Mexico Press, 1998).

Hasia R. Diner's seminal *Hungering for America: Italian, Irish, and Jewish Foodways in the Age of Migration* is the richest treatment of foodways during the era of immigration and should be required reading for anyone interested in the subject. Jane Ziegelman's readable *97 Orchard: An Edible History of Five Immigrant Families in One New York Tenement* (New York: Harper Collins, 2010) offers an engaging look at the food habits of Lower East Side residents in the late nineteenth and early twentieth centuries. Other sources that deal with the subject of immigrant foodways include Donna R. Gabbacia, *We Are What We Eat: Ethnic Food and the Making of Americans*; John F. Mariani, "Everybody Likes Italian Food," *American Heritage Magazine* 80.8 (1989); Megan J. Elias, *Food in the United States, 1890–1945*; Harvey Levenstein, *Revolution at the Table: The Transformation of the American Diet* (Berkeley: University of California Press, 2003); Gaye Tuchman and Harry Gene Levine, "New York Jews and Chinese Food: The Social Construction of an Ethnic Pattern," in *The Taste of American Place: A Reader on Regional and Ethnic Foods*, edited by Barbara G. Shortridge and James R. Shortridge (Lanham, MD: Rowman & Littlefield, 1998), 163–186; Don Siegel, *From Lokshen to Lo Mein: The Jewish Affair with Chinese Food* (Jerusalem: Gefen Publishing, 2005); Cara De Silva, "Fusion City: From Mt. Olympus Bagels to Puerto Rican Lasagna and Beyond" and "From the Big Bagel to the Big Roti? The Evolution of New York City's Jewish Food Icons," in *Gastropolis: Food & New York City*, edited by Annie Hauck-Lawson and Jonathon Deutsch; Patricia Volk, "Deli," *American Heritage* 53.1 (2002); and NPR Books, Ari Shapiro, Host, "A Fine Day for Chinese Food," December 25, 2007, available at http://www.npr.org/templates/story/story.php?storyId=17599785. Ronald Takaki's *A Different Mirror: A History of Multicultural America* (Boston: Back Bay Books, 1993) provides an excellent historical context for appreciating the history of the ethnic groups discussed in this chapter. Contemporary attitudes about immigrant foodways can be found in a series of articles in *The*

Cook: A Weekly Handbook of Domestic Culinary Art for All Housekeepers: "An Overwhelming Recipe," 32.2 (1885): 5; "Jewish Dietary Laws," 16.1 (1885): 9; "Jewish Cookery," 38.3 (1885): 7; and "Jewish Cookery," 35.2 (1885):7. Representative contemporary recipes can be found in Mrs. Simon Kander's *The Settlement Cook Book* (Milwaukee: Settlement Cook Book Co., 1901).

CHAPTER 4: TECHNOLOGY AND TASTE

Each of these more general studies offers useful insight into the subject of the impact of the Second Industrial Revolution on the American food supply and on attitudes about food practices: Susan Williams, *Food in the United States: 1820s–1890*; Richard Pillsbury, *No Foreign Food: The American Diet in Time and Place* (Boulder, CO: Westview, 1998); Reay Tannahill, *Food in History*; Audrey H. Ensminger et al., *Foods and Nutrition Encyclopedia* (Boca Raton: CRC Press, 1994); and Waverly Root and Richard de Rochemont, *Eating in America: A History*.

For more detailed descriptions of some of the technological advances written about in the chapter, see the following: Andrew F. Smith, "Oliver Evans's Automated Mill," in *Eating History: 30 Turning Points in the Making of American Cuisine*; Donald C. Jackson, "Turnpikes in Southeastern Pennsylvania," in *Early American Technology: Making and Doing Things from the Colonial Era to 1850*, edited by Judith A. McGaw (Chapel Hill: University of North Carolina Press, 1994); Albro Martin, *Railroads Triumphant: The Growth, Rejection, and Rebirth of a Vital American Force* (New York: Oxford University Press, 1992); Oscar Edward Anderson, *Refrigeration in America: A History of a New Technology and Its Impact* (Princeton, NJ: Princeton University Press, 1953); and Seymour Dunbar, *A History of Travel in America* (Indianapolis: Bobbs-Merrill, 1915). More information about the Erie Canal can be found in Carol Sheriff, *The Artificial River: The Erie Canal and the Paradox of Progress, 1817–1862* (New York: Hill and Wang, 1996); Edwin G. Burrows, "Little Short of Madness," *American Heritage* 59.4 (2009); and at the website of the New York State Canal System: http://www.canals.ny.gov/cculture/history/finch/index.html.

The discussion of the banana as a food associated with the period of industrialization was drawn largely from Joe Gray Taylor, *Eating, Drinking, and Visiting in the South: An Informal History* (Baton Rouge: Louisiana State University Press, 1982); Virginia S. Jenkins, "Bananas," in *Rooted in America: Foodlore of Popular Fruits and Vegetables*, edited by David Scofield Wilson and Angus Kress Gillespie (Knoxville: University of Tennessee Press, 1999); Susan Williams, *Savory Suppers and Fashionable Feasts: Dining in Victorian America*, and "Banana Pudding," in *The New Encyclopedia of Southern Culture: Foodways*, edited by Edge.

The period cookbooks I consulted while writing this chapter included: Fannie Merrit Farmer, *The Boston Cooking-School Cook Book*, rev. ed. (Boston: Little, Brown, 1916); Estelle Woods Wilcox, *The Dixie Cook-book* (Atlanta, GA: L. A. Clarkson,1885); *Atlanta Woman's Club Cook Book* (Atlanta, GA: Johnson Dallis, 1921); *Miss Leslie's Complete Cookery: Directions for Cookery, in Its Various Branches* (Philadelphia: Henry Carey Baird, 1851); Sarah Tyson Heston Rorer, *Canning and Preserving* (Philadelphia: Arnold, 1887); and *Helps for the Hostess* (Camden, NJ: Campbell Soup Company, 1916).

America's infatuation with meat can be traced in Roger Horowitz's *Putting Meat on the American Table* (Baltimore: Johns Hopkins University Press, 2006) and Betram B. Fowler, *Men, Meat, and Miracles* (New York: Julian Messner, 1952). Problems with the meat supply and attempts to reform the system are discussed in Jason Pickavance, "Gastronomic Realism: Upton Sinclair's *The Jungle*, the Fight for Pure Food, and the Magic of Mastication," *Food & Foodways* 11 (2003): 87–112; "The Week," *The Nation*, Thursday, March 1, 1906: 167; Walter Goodman, "Starving the Pure Food Act. After Fifty Years-Neglect," *The Nation*, June 16, 1956; and Upton Sinclair, *The Jungle* (1906), which is available online in various places, including here: http://sunsite.berkeley.edu/Literature/Sinclair/TheJungle. For more information about the embalmed beef scandal during the Spanish-American War, see "The Army Meat Scandal," *New York Times*, February 1, 1899; R. A. Alger, "The Food of the Army during the Spanish War," *North American Review* 172.530 (1901): 39–58; Ben Proctor, *William Randolph Hurst: The Early Years, 1863–1910* (New York: Oxford University Press, 1998); and Spencer C. Tucker, ed., *The Encyclopedia of the Spanish American and Philippine American Wars* (Santa Barbara, CA: ABC-CLIO, 2009).

The enormous influence that safe canned goods had on the American food supply is explained in Sue Shepard's *Pickled, Potted, and Canned: How the Art and Science of Food Preserving Changed the World* (New York: Simon & Schuster, 2000); A. W. Bitting, *Appertizing: The Art of Canning; Its History and Development* (San Francisco: Trade Press Room, 1937); C. Hampe, Jr., and Merle Wittenberg, *The Lifeline of America: Development of the Food Industry* (New York: McGraw-Hill, 1964); and Dorothy Deneen and James M. Volvo, *Daily Life in Civil War America* (Santa Barbara, CA: Greenwood, 2009). More information about military rations during the Civil War can be found in Barbara Haber, *From Hardtack to Home Fries: An Uncommon History of American Cooks and Meals* (New York: Penguin, 2002).

CHAPTER 5: GENDER AND THE AMERICAN APPETITE

Ruth Schwartz Cowan's *More Work for Mother: The Ironies of Household Technology from the Open Hearth to the Microwave* (New York: Basic Books,

1983); Susan Strasser's *Never Done: A History of American Housework* (1982; reprint, New York: Henry Holt, 2000); and Mary Drake McFeely, *Can She Bake a Cherry Pie: American Women and the Kitchen in the Twentieth Century* (Amherst: University of Massachusetts Press, 2000) are excellent studies of women and their historical relationship to domestic responsibilities, which I drew upon heavily in the first part of the chapter. The literature on the changing economic roles of men and women and on nineteenth-century ideas about "proper" female behavior is vast and expanding. For an overview of historical writing about the idea of the "separate sphere" for women, including a discussion of how this model is not as applicable for women of color, see Kim Warren, "Separate Spheres: Analytical Persistence in United States Women History," *History Compass* 4 (2006): 1–16.

For more information about Melusina Peirce's ideas about cooperative housekeeping, see her *Co-operative Housekeeping: How Not to Do It and How to Do It* (Boston: James Osgood, 1884). Readers interested in learning more about Charlotte Perkins Gilman's life story could begin with her essay, "Why I Wrote the Yellow Wallpaper," available online at www.charlotteperkinsgilman.com. More extended analysis of her ideas about women and domestic life and about her class attitudes can be found in Ann Mattis, "'Vulgar Strangers in the Home': Charlotte Perkins Gilman and Modern Servitude," *Women's Studies* 39 (2010): 283–303, and in Dolores Hayden, "Charlotte Perkins Gilman and the Kitchenless House," *Radical History Review* 21 (1979): 225–247.

Rebecca Sharpless's *Cooking in Other Women's Kitchens* (Chapel Hill: University of North Carolina Press, 2010) offers a sophisticated interpretation of the life experiences of African American cooks in the American South. Laura Shapiro's masterful *Perfection Salad: Women and Cooking at the Turn of the Twentieth Century* (Berkeley: University of California Press, 1986) and Megan Elias's excellent study *Stir It Up: Home Economics in American Culture* (Philadelphia: University of Pennsylvania Press, 2008) give insight into how women tried to achieve professional respect for performing domestic tasks with scientific precision. Additional insights about the domestic science movement can be found in Levenstein, *Revolution at the Table: The Transformation of the American Diet*, which contains a detailed account of the work of the New England Kitchen.

Relevant books written by domestic reformers include Ellen Richards, *The Chemistry of Cooking and Cleaning: A Manual for Housekeepers* (Boston: Estes and Lauriat, 1882); Mary Hinman Abel, *Practical Sanitary and Economic Cooking Adapted for Persons of Moderate and Small Means* (Rochester, NY: E. R. Andrews, 1889); and Fannie Farmer, *The Boston Cooking-School Cook Book* (1896; reprint, Boston: Little, Brown, 1918). See also "Bad Diet Makes Drunkards," *The Cook: A Weekly Handbook of Domestic Culinary Art for All Housekeepers*, 38.2 (1885), 8. The Women's Educational and Industrial Trade Union papers, which yield unending insights into how Progressive

Era reformers thought improved food practices could cure a variety of social ills, are housed at the Schlesinger Library at the Radcliffe Institution for Advanced Study, Harvard University. The papers of Charlotte Cramer Sachs, who invented the Joy cake mix, are held by the Archives National Museum of American History. The Colles Family Papers at the New York Public Library contain the letters from Juliet Corson quoted in this chapter.

Janet Theopano's *Eat My Words: Reading Women's Lives through the Cookbooks They Wrote* (New York: Palgrave, 2002); Laura Schenone's *A Thousand Years over a Hot Stove* (New York: Norton, 2003); Sherrie Inness, *Secret Ingredients: Race, Gender, and Class at the Dinner Table* (New York: Palgrave Macmillan, 2006); and Williams, *Food in the United States: 1820s–1890* all provided me with valuable context while composing this chapter.

Further reading about the association of certain foods with men or women can be found in Jane Dusselier's "Bonbons, Lemon Drops, And Oh Henry! Bars: Candy, Consumer Culture, and the Construction of Gender, 1895–1920," in *Kitchen Culture in America: Popular Representatives of Food, Gender, and Race*, edited by Sherrie A. Inness (Philadelphia: University of Pennsylvania Press, 2001), 13–49; Tim Miller's "The Birth of the Patio Daddy-O: Outdoor Grilling in Postwar America," *Journal of American Culture* 33:1 (2010): 5–11; and Carol J. Adams's influential study, *The Sexual Politics of Meat: A Feminist-Vegetarian Critical Theory* (New York: Continuum, 1990).

Harvey Levenstein, *Paradox of Plenty: A Social History of Eating in Modern America* (New York: Oxford University Press, 1993) and Laura Shapiro, *Something from the Oven: Reinventing Dinner in 1950s America* (New York: Viking, 2004) both offer excellent overviews of 1950s food practices. For some recipes from the era, see Peg Bracken, *The I Hate to Cook Book* (New York: Harcourt, Brace, and World, 1960). More extensive biographical information about Julia Child can be found in Laura Shapiro, *Julia Child* (New York: Viking, 2007), and great details about female professional chefs are available in Ann Cooper, *A Woman's Place Is in the Kitchen: The Evolution of Women Chefs* (New York: Van Nostrand Reinhold, 1998).

CHAPTER 6: THE PIOUS OR PATRIOTIC STOMACH

There are a number of excellent studies about Sylvester Graham's dietary philosophies. See Jayme A. Sokolow, *Eros and Modernization: Sylvester Graham, Health Reform, and the Origins of Victorian Sexuality in America* (Rutherford: Fairleigh Dickinson University Press, 1983); Stephen Nissenbaum, *Sex, Diet, and Debility in Jacksonian America: Sylvester Graham and Health Reform* (Westport, CT: Greenwood Press, 1980); Richard H. Shyrock, "Sylvester Graham and the Popular Health Movement, 1830–1870," *Mississippi Valley*

Historical Review 18.2 (September 1931); and Williams, *Food in the United States: 1820s–1890.*

General information about the Shakers can be found in Amy Stechler Burns, *The Shakers: Hands to Work, Hearts to God* (New York: Aperture Foundation, 1987). Stephen J. Stein offers a more scholarly approach in *The Shaker Experience in America: A History of the United States Believers* (New Haven, CT: Yale University Press, 1992). My account of the food practices of the Shakers is drawn from Priscilla J. Brewer's intruiging study *Shaker Communities, Shaker Lives* (Hanover: University Press of New England, 1986).

For firsthand accounts of the Fruitlands experiment, see Clara Endicott Sears, ed., *Bronson Alcott's "Fruitlands" with "Transcendental Wild Oats" by Louisa M. Alcott* (Boston: Houghton Mifflin, 1915). Good secondary accounts include Frederick C. Dahlstrand, *Amos Bronson Alcott: An Intellectual Biography* (Rutherford: Fairleigh Dickinson University Press, 1982); Richard Francis, "Circumstances and Salvation: The Ideology of the Fruitlands Utopia," *American Quarterly* 25.2 (May 1973): 202–234; David P. Edgell, "Charles Lane at Fruitlands," *New England Quarterly* 33.3 (September 1960): 374–377; F. B. Sanborn, *Bronson Alcott at Alcott House, England and Fruitlands New England (1842–1844)* (Cedar Rapids, IA: Torch Press, 1908); and Joseph J. Thorndike, Jr., "Fruitlands," *American Heritage* 37.2 (1986).

More extensive summaries of John Harvey Kellogg's life and work can be found in Richard W. Schwarz, "Dr. John Harvey Kellogg as a Social Gospel Practitioner," *Journal of the Illinois State Historical Society* 57 (March 1964): 5–22; Scott Bruce and Bill Crawford, *Cerealizing America: The Unsweetened Story of American Breakfast Cereal* (Boston: Faber and Faber, 1995); Smith, "The Kelloggs' Cornflakes," in *Eating History: 30 Turning Points in the Making of American Cuisine*; and Roger L. Rosentreter, "Cereal City," *Michigan History Magazine* 83.4 (July/August 1999): 8–13.

While writing this chapter, I utilized a wide variety of government documents housed at the National Agricultural Library pertaining to food conservation and rationing efforts during World War I and World War II. Additional material about food conservation during the war years can be found in Alice D. Kamps, *What's Cooking, Uncle Sam? The Government's Effect on the American Diet* (Washington, DC: The Foundation for the National Archives, 2011); Alfred E. Cornbise, *War as Advertised: The Four Minute Men and America's Crusade, 1917–1918* (Philadelphia: American Philosophical Society, 1984); Levenstein, *Revolution at the Table*; Marsha Gordon, "Onward Kitchen Soldiers: Mobilizing the Domestic during World War I," *Canadian Review of American Studies* 29.2 (1999): 61–87; Helen Zoe Veit, "'We Were a Soft People': Asceticism, Self-Discipline and American Food Conservation in the First World War," *Food, Culture, and Society* 10.2 (Summer 2002): 168–189; Frank M. Surface and Raymond L. Bland, *American Food in the World War and Reconstruction Period: Operations under the Organization of Herbert*

Hoover 1914 to 1924 (Palo Alto, CA: Stanford University Press, 1931); Amy Bentley, *Eating for Victory: Food Rationing and the Politics of Domesticity* (Chicago: University of Illinois Press, 1998); Emily Yellin, *Our Mother's War: American Women at Home and at the Front during World War II* (New York: Free Press, 2004); Mark Weiner, "Democracy, Consumer Culture, and Political Community: The Story of Coca Cola during World War II," *Food & Foodways* 6.2 (1996): 109–129; and Jane Dusselier, "Does Food Make Place? Food Protests in Japanese American Concentration Camps," *Food & Foodways* 10 (2002): 137–165.

Insights into attitudes about food rationing during World War II can be gleaned from Pauline E. Parker, ed., *Women of the Homefront: World War II Recollections of 55 Americans* (Jefferson, NC: McFarland, 2002) and Judy Barret Litoff and David C. Smith, eds., *Since You Went Away: World War II Letters from American Women on the Home Front* (New York: Oxford University Press, 1991). Representative World War I–era cookbooks that emphasize substituting abundant for scarcer incredients include Florence Powdermaker, *Food Guide for War Service at Home*, prepared under the direction of the United States Food Service Administration, 1918, and C. Houston Goudiss and Alberta M. Goudiss, *Foods That Will Win the War and How to Cook Them* (New York: Forecast Publishing, 1918).

Elaine Tyler May, *Homeward Bound: American Families in the Cold War Era* (New York: Basic, 2008); Stephen Bates, "Cold War, Hot Kitchen," *Wilson Quarterly* 33.3 (Summer 2009): 12–13; and Michelle Hill, "My Kitchen's Better Than Yours," *Michigan History Magazine* 83.4 (July/August 1999): 50–53 offer analyses of the "kitchen debate."

CHAPTER 7: FOOD HABITS AND RACIAL THINKING

The following sources inspired my thinking in this chapter: Linda Keller Brown and Kay Mussell, *Ethnic and Regional Foodways in the United States: The Performance of Group Identity*; Gabaccia, *We Are What We Eat: Ethnic Food and the Making of Americans*; Vicki L. Ruiz, "Citizen Restaurant: American Imaginaries, American Communities," *American Quarterly* 60.1 (March 2008): 1–21; "Let's Cook Thai: Recipes for Colonialism," in *Pilaf, Pozole, and Pad Thai: American Women and Ethnic Food*, edited by Sherrie Inness (Amherst: University of Massachusetts Press, 2000); Leslie Brenner, *American Appetite: The Coming of Age of a National Cuisine* (New York: Perennial, 1997); Richard Wright, *Black Boy* (1945; reprint, restored ed., New York: HarperPerennial, 2006); and Michael B. Dougan, *Arkansas Odyssey* (Little Rock, AR: Rose, 1994).

Further reading about Chinese American foodways and American attitudes about Chinese food can be found in Andrew Coe, *Chop Suey: A Cultural*

History of Chinese Food in the United States (Oxford: Oxford University Press, 2009); Bryan R. Johnson, "Let's Eat Chinese Tonight," *American Heritage* 38.8 (1987); "'Unnatural, Unclean, and Filthy': Chinese American Cooking Literature Confronting Racism in the 1950s," in Inness, *Secret Ingredients: Race, Gender, and Class at the Dinner Table*; American Federation of Labor, *Some Reasons for Chinese Exclusion: Meat v. Rice, American Manhood against Asiatic Coolieism, Which Shall Survive?* (Washington, DC: Government Printing Office, 1902); and Frank H. Wu, "The Best 'Chink' Food: Dog Eating and the Dilemma of Diversity," in *The Gastronomica Reader*, edited by Darra Goldstein (Berkeley: University of California Press, 2010), 218–233.

I drew on Daniel D. Arreola, *Tejano South Texas: A Mexican American Cultural Province* (Austin: University of Texas Press, 2002) and George Sanchez, *Becoming Mexican American: Ethnicity, Culture, and Identity in Chicano Los Angeles, 1900–1945* (New York: Oxford University Press, 1995) for some historical context in this chapter. The literature about Mexican and Mexican American foodways is expanding and includes Amy Bentley, "From Culinary Other to Mainstream America: Meanings and Uses of Southwestern Cuisine," in *Culinary Tourism*, edited by Lucy M. Long (Lexington: University of Kentucky Press, 2004); Jeffrey M. Pilcher, "From Montezuma's Revenge to 'Mexican Truffles,'" in *Culinary Tourism*, edited by Lucy M. Long; Nikki Silva and Davia Nelson, "The Chili Queens of San Antonio," in *Hidden Kitchens: Stories, Recipes, and More from NPR's the Kitchen Sisters* (New York: Rodale, 2005); Donna R. Gabaccia and Jeffrey M. Pilcher, "'Chili Queens' and Checkered Tablecloths: Public Dining Cultures of Italians in New York City and Mexicans in San Antonio, Texas, 1870s–1940s," *Radical History Review* 110 (Spring 2010): 109–126; Gracelia I. Sanchez, "La Cultura, la Comunidad, la Familia, y la Libertad," *Frontiers: A Journal of Women Studies* 24. 2 (2003): 75–86; Suzanne Bost, "Women and Chile at the Alamo: Feeding U.S. Colonial Mythology," *Nepantla: Views from South* 4.3 (2003):493–522; and Jeffrey Pilcher, "Who Chased Out the 'Chili Queens'? Gender, Race, and Urban Reform in San Antonio, Texas, 1880–1943," *Food and Foodways* 16.3 (2008): 173–200. For attempts to use foodways to assimilate Mexican Americans, see Pearl Idelia Ellis, *Americanization through Homemaking* (Los Angeles: Wetzel, 1929).

Cookbooks written by white authors adopting caricatured African American personas include Emma McKinney and William McKinney, *Aunt Caroline's Dixieland Recipes: A Rare Collection of Choice Southern Dishes* (Chicago: Laird & Lee, 1922); Eleanor Purcell, *Aunt Priscilla in the Kitchen: A Collection of Winter-Time Recipes, Seasonable Menus and Suggestions of Afternoon Teas and Special Holiday Parties* (Baltimore: Aunt Priscilla Publishing Co., 1929); and Emma Speed Sampson, *Miss Minerva's Cookbook: De Way to a Man's Heart* (Chicago: Reilly & Lee Co., 1931).

For more information about white attitudes about African American cooking and eating, see Allison Davis, Burleigh B. Gardner, and Mary R. Gardner, *Deep South: A Social Anthropological Study of Caste and Class* (Chicago: University of Chicago Press, 1941); Charles Gayarré, "A Louisiana Sugar Plantation of the Old Régime," *Harper's* (March 1887): 606–621; and Media Matters for America, "Reilly Surprised That There Was 'No Difference' between Harlem Restaurant and Other New York Restaurants," September 21, 2007, http://mediamatters.org/items/200709210007.

Details about the advertising icon Aunt Jemima can be found on the Quaker Oats Company website, "Aunt Jemima—Our Historical Timeline," available at http://www.auntjemima.com/aj%5Fhistory, and in M. M. Manring, *A Slave in a Box: The Strange Career of Aunt Jemima* (Charlottesville: University of Virginia Press, 1997). Karen L. Cox's *Dreaming of Dixie: How the South Was Created in American Popular Culture* (Chapel Hill: University of North Carolina Press, 2011) also contains a valuable discussion about how images of African American cooks have been used to market consumer products.

I examined sheet music at the Jazz Archive at Tulane University and at the Archives of the National Museum of American History at the Smithsonian. An excellent overview of the genre of the "coon song" can be found in James M. Dorman, "Shaping the Popular Image of Post-Reconstruction American Blacks: The 'Coon Song' Phenomenon of the Gilded Age," *American Quarterly* 40 (1988): 450–471. Other sources related to African American foodways of interest to readers include Psyche Williams-Forson, "Chickens and Chains: Using African American Foodways to Understand Black Identities," in *African American Foodways: Explorations of History and Culture*, edited by Ann L. Bower (Urbana: University of Illinois Press, 2007), 127–128; Doris Witt, "From Fiction to Foodways: Working at Intersections of African American Literary and Cultural Studies," in *African American Foodways: Explorations of History and Culture*, edited by Ann L. Bower (Urbana: University of Chicago Press, 2007); and Psyche Williams-Forson, *Building Houses out of Chicken Legs: Black Women, Food, and Power* (Chapel Hill: University of North Carolina Press, 2006).

CHAPTER 8: THE POLITICS OF FOOD

In the twenty-first century, writing about food and politics is proliferating rapidly. The topics surveyed in this chapter and the sources consulted here constitute only a small fraction of what is available. Readers should use these suggestions as only a starting point for further investigations of these complex issues.

Food activist, cookbook author, and journalist Mark Bittman's writings touch on many pressing contemporary issues related to the food supply. I drew on many insights gleaned from his columns while writing this chapter, including: "Bad Food? Tax It, and Subsidize Vegetables," *New York Times*, July 23, 2011, and "We're Eating Less Meat. Why?" *New York Times*, January 10, 2012.

Michael Pollan has emerged as one of the most well-known figures in what he has labeled the "food movement." I summarize many of his conclusions made in *The Omnivore's Dilemma: A Natural History of Four Meals* (New York: Penguin, 2006) here. I also draw upon his *In Defense of Food: An Eater's Manifesto* (New York: Penguin Books, 2008) and his article "The Food Movement Rising," *New York Review of Books*, June 10, 2010. Other significant contemporary books that deal with a variety of issues related to food ethics, which are discussed in this chapter, are Peter Singer and Jim Mason, *The Ethics of What We Eat: Why Our Food Choices Matter* (New York: Rodale, 2006); Jonathon Safran Foer, *Eating Animals* (New York: Little, Brown, 2009); James McWilliams, *Just Food: Where Locavores Get It Wrong and How We Can Truly Eat Responsibly* (New York: Little, Brown, 2009); Marion Nestle, *Food Politics: How the Food Industry Influences Nutrition and Health* (Berkeley: University of California Press, 2002); Erick Schlosser, *Fast Food Nation: The Dark Side of the All-American Meal* (New York: Harper Perennial, 2005); and Barbara Kingsolver, *Animal, Vegetable, Miracle: A Year of Food Life* (New York: Harper Perennial, 2007). See also Frances Moore Lappé's *Diet for a Small Planet* (New York: Ballatine, 1971), one of the pioneering texts of this genre and the first extended analysis of the practice of eating grain-fed beef. For thoughts on how academics can use their skills to engage with the "food movement," see Rebecca O'Neill, "'You Say Tomato, I Say Tomahto': Applying the Tools of Food History to the Food Movement Dialogue," *Radical History Review* 110 (2011): 161–166.

For the historical antecedents of the "food movement," see Warren Belasco, *Appetite for Change: How the Counterculture Took on the Food Industry* (Ithaca, NY: Cornell University Press, 2006). For world histories of vegetarianism, see Tristram Stuart, *The Bloodless Revolution: A Cultural History of Vegetarianism from 1600 to Modern Times* (New York: Norton, 2006) and Colin Spencer, *Vegetarianism* (New York: Four Walls Eight Windows, 1993). I drew on these sources to discern modern attitudes toward vegetarianism in the United States: "Are You a Flexitarian? Meat Eating Vegetarians Transform the Movement," March 16, 2004, available at http://www.msnbc.msn.com/id/4541605/ns/health-fitness/t/are-you-flexitarian; "Meatless Mondays," available at http://www.meatlessmonday.com; A. G. Sulzberger, "Meatless in the Midwest: A Tale of Survival," *New York Times*, January 10, 2012; "Vegetarianism in America," *Vegetarian Times*, available at http://www.vegetariantimes.com/features/archive_of_editorial/667; "Macca Slams 'Stupid' Gordon Ramsay for Anti-vegetarian Rant," *Daily Mail Reporter*, August 29, 2008, available at http://www.dailymail.co.uk/tvshowbiz/

article-1050349/Macca-slams-stupid-TV-chef-Gordon-Ramsay-anti-vegetar
ian-rant.html#ixzz1jNX2mc2Z.

While writing about modern issues of food insecurity, I utilized information from the U.S. Department of Agriculture, available here: http://www.ers .usda.gov/Briefing/FoodSecurity. Interested readers will be able to find a great deal of statistical information about some of the issues briefly touched on, such as food deserts, at the USDA website. See also John Pope, "Loans Offered to Lure Groceries," *New Orleans Times-Picayune*, March 16, 2011; Mary Clare Jalonick, "GOP Candidates Wade into Food Stamp Debate," Associated Press, January 9, available at http://abcnews.go.com/Politics/wireStory/ gop-candidates-wade-food-stamp-debate-15319171; "Gingrich: African-Americans Should Demand Paychecks, Not Food Stamps," Associated Press, January 5, 2012, available at http://www.wjla.com/articles/2012/01/gingrich -african-americans-should-demand-paychecks-not-food-stamps-71106.html; and John Hanc, "A Mobile Oasis in a Food Desert," *New York Times*, November 1, 2011. For information about one attempt to remedy urban food scarcity, see the Hantz Farms Detroit website: www.hantzfarmsdetroit.com/ introduction.html.

For more information about criticism against Michelle Obama's campaign against childhood obesity, see "Jim Sensenbrenner Sorry for Saying Michelle Obama Has 'Big Butt,'" *Los Angeles Times*, December 22, 2011, available at http://latimesblogs.latimes.com/nationnow/2011/12/lawmaker-to-apologize -for-saying-michelle-obama-has-a-big-butt.html; "Conservatives Heap Criticism on Michelle Obama's Campaign against Childhood Obesity," McClatchy Tribune Service, February 27, 2011, available at http://www.cleveland.com/ nation/index.ssf/2011/02/conservatives_heap_criticism_o.html; John Amis, Associated Press, "First Lady Michelle Obama Discusses Her 'Let's Move' Program at North Point Community Church in Alpharetta, GA," January 12, 2012, available at http://abcnews.go.com/Health/michelle-obama-shake; and Mikaela Conley, "Michelle Obama's Shake Shack Burger Indulgence Defended by Nutritionists," July 12, 2011, available at http://abcnews.go.com/Health/ michelle-obama-shake-shack-burger-indulgence-defended-nutritionists/ story?id=14049393.

For defenses of industrial food, see Blake Hurst, "The Omnivore's Delusion: Against the Agri-intellectuals," July 30, 2009, *The American*, available at http://www.american.com/archive/2009/july/the-omnivore2019s-delusion -against-the-agri-intellectuals; Peter A. Coclanis," Food Is Much Safer Than You Think," *Wall Street Journal*, June 14, 2011, A13; Josh Ozersky, "In Defense of Industrial Food," *Time*, August 26, 2011, available at http://ideas.time .com/2011/10/26/in-defense-of-industrial-food/#ixzz1jRrGbLnO; and on the website of the Center for Consumer Freedom, http://www.consumerfreedom .com.

For more information about television programming related to food and the issue of food as entertainment, see Rachel Slocum, Jerry Shannon, Kirsten Valentine Cadiuex, and Matthew Beckman, "'Properly, with Love, from Scratch': Jamie Oliver's Food Revolution," *Radical History Review* 110 (Spring 2010): 178–191; B. R. Myers, "Fed Up: Gluttony Dressed Up as Foodie-ism Is Still Gluttony," *Atlantic*, March 2011, 81–88; Andrew F. Smith, "TVFN," in *Eating History: 30 Turning Points in the Making of American Cuisine*; Kevin Downey, "Food Network Setting a Bigger Table," *Media Life Magazine*, March 15, 2005, available at http://www.medialifemagazine .com/news2005/mar05/mar14/2_tues/news4tuesday.html; Hank Stuever, "Jamie Oliver's Food Revolution Regurgitates the Worst of TV Reality Pap," *Washington Post*, March 20, 2010, available at http://www.washing tonpost.com/wp-dyn/content/article/2010/03/19/AR2010031901683.html; Anna Burger, "Paula Deen's Recipe for an Unhappy Family: Smithfield Pork," *Huffington Post*, April 19, 2007, available at http://www.huffington post.com/anna-burger/paula-deens-recipe-for-an_b_46303.html; Stacy Finz, "Cookbook Sales Flourish," *San Francisco Chronicle*, May 7, 2011, available at http://www.sfgate.com/cgi-bin/article.cgi?f=/c/a/2011/05/06/BU FL1JCVKT.DTL#ixzz1jSDjnZMg; and Frank Bruni, "Unsavory Culinary Elitism," *New York Times*, August 24, 2011.

Index

231

About the Author

Jennifer Jensen Wallach is an associate professor of history at the University of North Texas, where she teaches African American history. She is the author of *Closer to the Truth Than Any Fact: Memoir, Memory, and Jim Crow* (2008) and *Richard Wright: From Black Boy to World Citizen* (2010) and is the co-editor of *Arsnick: The Student Nonviolent Coordinating Committee in Arkansas* (2011). In 2010, History News Network named her a "Top Young Historian."